DESIGNING TESTS FOR

EVALUATING STUDENT ACHIEVEMENT

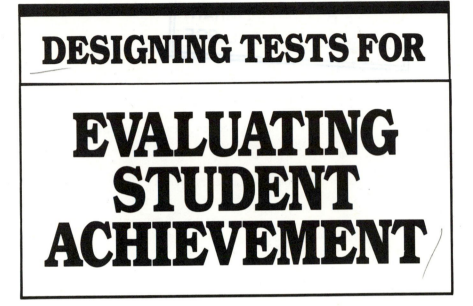

DESIGNING TESTS FOR
EVALUATING STUDENT ACHIEVEMENT

James S. Cangelosi
Utah State University

Longman
New York & London

Designing Tests for Evaluating Student Achievement

Longman, 95 Church Street, White Plains, N.Y. 10601
A division of Addison-Wesley Publishing Co., Inc.

Associated companies:
Longman Group Ltd., London
Longman Cheshire Pty., Melbourne
Longman Paul Pty., Auckland
Copp Clark Pitman, Toronto

Executive editor: Raymond T. O'Connell
Production editor: Ann P. Kearns
Text design: Jill Francis Wood
Cover design: Anne M. Pompeo
Text art: K & S Graphics, Susan J. Moore, and Martha Bradshaw
Production supervisor: Joanne Jay

Library of Congress Cataloging-in-Publication Data

Cangelosi, James S.
    Designing tests for evaluating student achievement / James S. Cangelosi.

    p. cm.
    Bibliography: p.
    Includes index.
    ISBN 0-8013-0263-3
    1. Examinations—Design and construction.   2. Educational tests
and measurements   I. Title.
LB3060.65.C36   1990
371.2'71—dc19
                                                          89-30279
                                                          CIP

ABCDEFGHIJ-ML-99 98 97 96 95 94 93 92 91 90

To Ruth Struyk

Contents

Preface

"What are they really learning from this lesson?" "Is Mavis ready to begin working with ratios?" "Should I pick up the pace or slow down this lesson?" "What things motivate these children to read?" "How well did my new strategy for introducing the differences between nouns and pronouns work?" "What grade did Norton earn in history?" "Caroline's father wants a progress report. What should I tell him?" "Should I reteach these sight words one more time?" "Did that last assignment change any attitudes about homework?" "Does Vincent have the psychomotor skills to write legibly?" "Can these students actually apply these principles or have they just memorized them?"

These are just some of the many questions teachers confront every working day. The number and variety of questions about which teachers must make judgments are unparalleled in other professions (Cangelosi, 1974; Clark & Peterson, 1986). To address these questions, teachers must evaluate their students' achievements (i.e., what students have learned or are learning). Thus teachers spend between 20 percent and 30 percent of their time directly involved in data- or information-gathering activities (Stiggins, 1988), including designing, synthesizing, selecting, administering, scoring, interpreting, and revising tests and other types of observations of students' performances and behaviors.

Tests and observations provide the information base for teachers' evaluations of student achievement. Unfortunately, studies examining the validities of tests commonly used in schools (both commercially prepared and teacher-prepared) and the evaluation methods of many teachers suggest that testing malpractice and inaccurate evaluations are widespread (Stiggins, Conklin, & Bridgeford, 1986).

Stiggins (1988, p. 365) points out one of the principal consequences of poorly designed tests:

Teacher-developed paper and pencil tests and many tests and quizzes provided by textbook publishers are currently dominated by questions that ask students to recall facts and information. Although instructional objectives and even instructional activities may seek to develop thinking skills, classroom assessments often fail to match these aspirations. Students who use tests to try to understand the teacher's expectations can see the priority placed on memorizing, and they respond accordingly. Thus poor quality assessments that fail to tap and reward higher-order thinking skills will inhibit the development of those skills.

There is a brighter side to this story. Many, but probably not most, teachers do manage to collect valid information that leads them to evaluate accurately their students' achievements. They evaluate not only what students have remembered but also how well they conceptualize, comprehend, apply, appreciate, are willing to try, and perform. In other words, teachers are able to evaluate how well students have achieved what is specified by the teachers' learning objectives.

Why do some teachers increase their effectiveness by accurately evaluating student achievement whereas others continue to follow the same outmoded evaluation practices of previous generations? It may be that most teachers have never been exposed to the latest methods for designing achievement tests in a way that is applicable to their needs.

Preservice and in-service teachers who read this book and complete its self-assessment exercises will learn practical ways of applying state-of-the-art strategies for evaluating student achievements. Based on inductive teaching principles for its concept-attainment objectives, deductive teaching principles for its application-level objectives, and expository teaching principles for its knowledge-level objectives, *Designing Tests for Evaluating Student Achievement* includes nine chapters:

1. "Student Achievement" is designed to (a) establish the role of teachers' formative and summative evaluations of student achievement within the overall teaching process, (b) provide a means for teachers to clarify what they mean by "student achievement" and define each learning goal with a set of objectives, and (c) provide a scheme for specifying the content and behavioral construct of each learning objective. As with all other chapters, each new idea or principle is illustrated with real-life, practical classroom examples.
2. "The Measurement of Student Achievement" introduces some ideas, principles, and terms fundamental to the design and selection of quality, cost-effective tests. Topics such as validity and reliability are presented for practical understanding, and esoteric terms and statistical formulas are avoided.
3. "Creating Cost-Effective Achievement Tests" introduces and illustrates a practical seven-step process for constructing valid and usable achievement tests and implementing an achievement-testing management system.
4. "Item Development Hints," the longest chapter, explains a five-step model for designing items and then gives suggestions for building

relevant, reliable, and usable tests with each of the following types of items: short answer, completion, multiple choice, true/false, multiple answer multiple choice, matching, weighted multiple choice, essay, oral discourse, product rating, performance observation, interview, and computer administered.

5. "Items for Cognitive Objectives" suggests how to measure achievement at each of the following cognitive levels: (a) simple knowledge, (b) knowledge of a process, (c) comprehension of a communication, (d) conceptualization, (e) application, and (f) beyond application.

6. "Items for Affective Objectives" suggests how to measure achievement at the following affective levels: (a) appreciation and (b) willingness to act.

7. "Items for Psychomotor Objectives" suggests how to measure achievement at the following psychomotor levels: (a) voluntary muscle capability and (b) ability to perform a specific skill.

8. "Interpreting Standardized Test Scores" illustrates some of the common uses and misuses of standardized tests in schools and explains how to interpret scores (e.g., stanines, percentiles, and grade equivalents) from standardized test reports.

9. "Grading and Reporting Student Achievement" (a) argues for professional behavior by teachers regarding communications of their evaluations of student achievement, (b) describes grade-reporting methods, (c) illustrates and critiques conventional techniques for converting test scores to grades, and (d) introduces and illustrates a new technique for converting scores to grades.

Designing Tests for Evaluating Student Achievement combines ideas from psychometric theory, learning theory, writing and communications models, and commonsense principles discovered through the experiences of classroom teachers.

I owe a debt of gratitude to the hundreds of classroom teachers and students whose ideas and examples influenced the writing of this text. I would like to acknowledge the work of the National Council on Measurement in Education (NCME) for its continuing contributions in the fight to improve the way student achievement is evaluated. NCME publications (e.g., *Journal of Educational Measurement* and *Educational Measurement: Issues and Practice*) emphasize the role teacher-produced tests play in the success of schools.

My dearest friend, Barb Rice, has my thanks for her editing, copyreading, and counsel.

Student Achievement

GOAL OF CHAPTER 1*

Chapter 1 illustrates (1) the vital role played by your evaluations of student achievement and (2) a method for clarifying what you mean by student achievement. More specifically, Chapter 1 will help you to

1. Distinguish between your formative and summative evaluations and clarify the role each plays as you meet your teaching responsibilities (*Cognitive: conceptualization*)
2. Define the learning goal for each unit you teach, using a set of objectives that clarify exactly what students are expected to achieve (*Cognitive: application*)
3. Specify the *content* (i.e., subject matter) of each objective you set for your students (*Cognitive: application*)
4. Specify the *behavioral construct* (i.e., how students are to deal with the content) as either (a) cognitive and simple knowledge, (b) cognitive and knowledge of a process, (c) cognitive and comprehension of a communication, (d) cognitive and conceptualization, (e) cognitive and application, (f) cognitive and beyond application, (g) affective and appreciation, (h) affective and willingness to act, (i) psychomotor and voluntary muscle capability, or (j) psychomotor and ability to perform a specific skill (*Cognitive: application*)
5. State the definition of the following: *formative evaluation, summative evaluation, learning goal, learning objective, content specified by a learning objective, behavioral construct specified by a learning objective, cogni-*

---

*The goals of this book are defined by objectives appearing at the beginning of each chapter. The terms in parentheses following each objective help clarify its meaning. These terms are defined and explained in Chapter 1 and used throughout the remainder of the book.

tive domain, affective domain, psychomotor domain, simple knowledge, knowledge of a process, comprehension of a communication, conceptualization, application, beyond application, appreciation, willingness to act, voluntary muscle capability, and *ability to perform a specific skill* (*Cognitive: simple knowledge*)

According to the classification scheme developed in this chapter, the intended behavioral construct for each of the previously stated objectives is indicated in the parentheses following the objective. You are not expected to understand why these objectives have been so classified until you have completed the chapter.

DIFFICULT DECISIONS

FORMATIVE EVALUATIONS

Consider the decisions confronting Ms. Curry as she conducts a math unit intended to teach her middle school students how to solve surface area problems.

Ms. Curry would like her sixth-graders to extend their understanding of the area of a rectangle to problems about surface areas of other figures, such as triangles. However, she feels that her students will be ready to learn about areas of triangles only after they know how to find rectangular areas and also understand *why* the area of a rectangle is the product of its length and width. Thus, her decision about *when* to teach the area of a triangle depends on her evaluations of how well students can (1) compute rectangular areas and (2) understand *why* a rectangular area equals the length times the width.

When Ms. Curry judges her students' proficiency with rectangular areas in order to decide if they're ready to move on to the next lesson, she is making a *formative evaluation. Formative evaluations are judgments about student achievement that influence a teacher's lesson plans.* As a teacher, your continuous evaluations guide what you do next. Should a lesson be extended or terminated? Is remediation needed? Is more advanced work appropriate? Is the pace of the lesson too fast or too slow? Should teaching strategies be altered? Answers to such questions are influenced by feedback from formative evaluations.

SUMMATIVE EVALUATIONS

Consider the decisions Ms. Curry makes at the conclusion of the math unit on surface area problems.

After spending two weeks teaching her sixth-graders how to solve surface area problems, Ms. Curry is responsible for reporting a level of achievement for each student. Students, parents, and supervisors expect Ms. Curry to report her judgments on student achievement in the form of letter grades (A, B, C, D, or F). To help her decide each student's grade, she develops and administers a test on surface area problems. Grades assigned for this unit affect the final math grades.

Ms. Curry's judgment regarding how well students learned how to do area problems is an example of a *summative evaluation*. *Summative evaluations are judgments that teachers use to report periodically on how well students have achieved.*

As a teacher, you will make far more formative than summative evaluations. Your formative evaluations will continually influence your teaching performance. However, because students and parents are so grade conscious, you are likely to find them keenly interested in your summative evaluations but barely aware of your ongoing formative evaluations.

A NEED FOR BETTER EVALUATION METHODS

To be an effective teacher, you must make accurate formative evaluations of student achievement. To fulfill the expectations of the students and parents you are hired to serve, you must make accurate summative evaluations of student achievement.

Unfortunately, many teachers inaccurately evaluate student achievement. They place their faith in poorly designed tests that often tax students' test-taking skills but don't reflect actual achievement of the teachers' goals and objectives (Stiggins, 1988). This unfortunate phenomenon is understandable when you consider the nature of the goals and objectives specified by school curricula. For example, Ms. Curry wants her students to understand why the area of a rectangle equals its length times its width. Learning theorists and curriculum experts agree that this is a vital goal for Ms. Curry's middle school students. However, mental activity, such as how well a student "understands why," is not directly observable in the way a student's physical height is directly observable. Consequently, you, Ms. Curry, and other teachers need to develop clever techniques for getting students to display what "goes on in their heads." Helping you develop such techniques is a primary goal of this book.

LEARNING GOALS

Sometimes accurate information about student achievement is unavailable because the question "Achievement of what?" has not been clearly answered.

One night, Mr. Little begins the task of developing a test he'll use in evaluating his fourth-graders' achievement during a two-week unit on the U.S. Constitution. Working with a word processor, he thinks to himself, "Let's see . . . I'll start with some completion items. What would be a good one for number 1? Anybody who listened in class would know about the seven articles. Okay, item 1 is. . . ."

He types, "1. There are _____ articles in the Constitution. 2. The fifth article deals with _____ ." "Good!" he thinks, "Now, I'm rolling. I need one that'll really tell me who studied." He types, "3. Write the first 15 words in the Preamble to the Constitution."

Mr. Little continues thinking: "Now what should I ask them next? . . . Ahhh . . . Oh, yeah!" He types, "4. How many delegates signed the Constitution? . . ."

Twenty-five minutes later, Mr. Little's unit test is ready to be printed.

Mr. Little wants to test his students' achievement of something that has to do with the U.S. Constitution. But what did he intend for them to gain from studying the Constitution in the first place? From the way he went about developing the test, he seems most interested in finding out who paid attention and who studied. The four test items in the example relate only to the recall of facts. Don't you think Mr. Little might have wanted his students to get more out of the unit on the Constitution than just some facts to be recalled (and soon forgotten)? If so, shouldn't his test contain some items that measure how well his students (1) comprehend the meaning of the document, (2) appreciate its importance, (3) understand why it was written, and (4) apply their understanding of the Constitution to current issues? Whether or not some of these or other types of learning should be reflected by Mr. Little's test depends on his purpose for teaching the unit. In other words, you, Mr. Little, or any other teacher can hardly develop or select meaningful tests in the absence of a clear understanding of what should be tested.

Teaching is helping students achieve specified *learning goals*. Formative and summative evaluations are concerned with how well students have achieved those learning goals. Thus, tests inform you about student achievement only if they relate to clearly defined learning goals.

A learning goal targeted by a unit of instruction is usually broadly stated. The following are examples of learning goals:

1. (For a kindergarten language arts unit) Associate the appropriate consonant sounds with the letters *b, d,* and *g.*
2. (For a second-grade citizenship unit) While in the classroom, display respect and consideration for the rights and feelings of others.
3. (For a fourth-grade social studies unit) Be aware of fundamental aspects of the U.S. Constitution, its history, and its influence today.
4. (For a sixth-grade math unit) Efficiently solve real-life problems that require finding sizes of surface areas.

5. (For a ninth-grade English unit) Critique essays written to sway readers' opinions.
6. (For a high school biology unit) Understand the fundamental elements and operations of food webs.
7. (For a high school physical education unit) Plan and follow a weight-lifting program for maintaining muscle strength.

Had Mr. Little kept a learning goal (e.g., the third in the list) in mind as he designed his test, it might be more meaningful than the one he haphazardly produced. However, learning goals, like those just listed, need to be further defined if they are to provide clear guidance for designing (1) lessons and (2) tests that help you make accurate formative and summative evaluations of student achievement.

Each of these seven goals indicates the purpose of the unit and what is meant by student achievement for that unit. However, if the teachers who formulated these goals would provide more details, student achievement could be pinpointed well enough for a meaningful test to be developed. For example,

1. Exactly what does the kindergarten teacher mean by "associate"? Is the goal for students to make the *b* sound when seeing the letter *b*? Or is it for the student to distinguish the *b* sound while listening to a variety of sounds? Chances are the teacher would like the unit to accomplish both goals, in addition to some other skills. A listing of these more specific skills would help clarify what appears to be a well-stated, appropriate learning goal.
2. The goal for the second-grade citizenship unit seems appropriate and provides some direction for the unit along with an idea on what is meant by student achievement. But definitions of *respect* and *consideration* vary. Once these terms are clarified, what would the teacher consider an appropriate "display" of respect and consideration for the rights and feelings of others?
3. Regarding the fourth-grade social studies goal, just how "aware" are the students expected to become? Just how much detail regarding "aspects," "history," and "influence" should the lessons and tests cover?
4. How complex should be the problems addressed by the sixth-grade unit? What geometric shapes should be included? What does the teacher mean by "real-life"? It may be that *real-life*, like *surface area*, is already understood by math teachers and, thus, needs no further clarification.
5. For what points and using what criteria should students critique the essays for the ninth-grade English unit? In what medium (e.g., written or oral discourse) should critiques be communicated? How sophisticated should the essays be? What range of topics will they cover?
6. For the high school biology goal, what cognitive or mental activity is targeted by the term *understand*? Does "fundamental elements and operations of food webs" clarify the content of the unit well enough in the mind of the biology teacher?

7. How advanced should be the plan developed in the physical education unit? Are the students to be evaluated on how well they develop a personalized plan for themselves or should the concern be only for general principles? How much of the goal involves being able to design strength programs (i.e., cognitive behavior)? How much emphasis is on the students' willingness to follow a program (i.e., affective behavior)? How much emphasis is on students' muscles responding to programs (i.e., psychomotor behavior)?

Well-stated learning goals provide a general idea about what a teaching unit is expected to accomplish and, thus, what is meant by student achievement. You clarify a learning goal by listing specific *learning objectives* that add up to or form the building blocks for that goal.

LEARNING OBJECTIVES

The math goal for sixth-grade students to "efficiently solve real-life problems that require finding sizes of surface areas" might be clarified by the following set of learning objectives:

1. Discriminates between the surface area of a figure and other quantitative characteristics of that figure (e.g., height and volume)
2. Explains why the area of a rectangle equals the product of its length and width
3. States the formula for the area of a rectangle
4. Given the dimensions of a rectangle, computes its area
5. Explains how the formula for the area of a right triangle can be derived from the formula for the area of a rectangle
6. Given the dimensions of a right triangle, computes its area
7. Explains how the formula for the area of a right cylinder can be derived from the formula for the area of a rectangle
8. Given the dimensions of a right cylinder, computes its surface area
9. When confronted with a real-life problem, determines whether or not computing the area of a surface will help solve that problem

These nine objectives add detail to the learning goal. The teacher's intended meaning of student achievement for this unit is clarified.

CONTENT SPECIFIED BY A LEARNING OBJECTIVE

Each objective should specify a *content*. *The content specified by an objective pinpoints the subject matter.* Surface area of figures is the general content area for the goal cited for the sixth-grade math unit. But each of the nine objectives that defines that goal specifies a more limited content:

OBJECTIVE	CONTENT
1	Surface areas
2	Formula for area of a rectangle
3	Formula for area of a rectangle
4	Formula for area of a rectangle
5	Formula for area of a right triangle
6	Formula for area of a right triangle
7	Formula for area of a right cylinder
8	Formula for area of a right cylinder
9	Real-life problems involving surface areas

BEHAVIORAL CONSTRUCT SPECIFIED BY A LEARNING OBJECTIVE

An objective, however, doesn't deal exclusively with content. An objective should also specify how students are expected to behave with, think about, or manipulate that content. In the sixth-grade math example, objectives 2, 3, and 4 specify the same content. However, they require students to deal quite differently with the formula for the area of a rectangle. Objective 2 requires students to explain why multiplying length and width yields the same result as counting out all the unit squares in a rectangular area. Objective 4 requires students to memorize the formula and compute with it. Testing how well students can explain why a formula is true (objective 2) is quite different from testing whether or not they can state the formula (objective 3) or can compute with it (objective 4). Although they specify the same content, objectives 2, 3, and 4, differ because they specify different *behavioral constructs*. An objective's behavioral construct refers to *the manner in which students are expected to deal with or behave toward the objective's content*.

Objectives 4, 6, and 8 in the surface area example specify different contents. However, all three require students to compute formulas; thus, they all specify the same behavioral construct.

BEHAVIORAL CONSTRUCT CLASSIFICATIONS

Familiarity with one of the published schemes for classifying behavioral constructs will help clarify the behavioral constructs of your own objectives. The scheme presented here is compiled from ideas stemming from a variety of sources (Bloom, 1984; Cangelosi, 1982; Guilford, 1959; Harrow, 1972; Krathwohl, Bloom, & Masia, 1964).

THREE DOMAINS

Behavioral constructs are conventionally classified into three domains: *cognitive, affective, and psychomotor*.

If the intent of an objective is for students to be able to do something mentally (e.g., remember a fact or deduce a method for solving a problem), the behavioral construct of the objective falls within the *cognitive domain*.

If the intent of an objective is for students to develop a particular attitude or feeling (e.g., a desire to read or willingness to work at something), the behavioral construct of the objective falls within the *affective domain*.

If the intent of an objective is for students to develop some physical attribute (e.g., muscle flexibility) or physical skill (e.g., manipulate a pencil to form letters), the objective falls within the *psychomotor domain*.

Most of what is taught in schools target student behaviors that fall within all three domains. For example,

---

Ms. Bohrer is helping Don, one of her kindergarten students, to print accurately uppercase *A*'s. She must teach him the cognitive skill of forming an *A*. Don will not learn to print *A*'s unless he is willing to try to form the letter correctly. But even if Don knows how to make *A*'s and wants to print *A*'s, he won't be able to do so if he lacks the necessary psychomotor skills to control a pencil.

Ms. Bohrer should make distinctions among the cognitive, affective, and psychomotor components of the skill she teaches because vast differences exist among how students manage to achieve each of the following objectives:

1. Recites the steps for printing an uppercase *A* (*Cognitive*)
2. Attempts to print an uppercase *A* as directed (*Affective*)
3. Manipulates a pencil well enough to follow the steps for printing an uppercase *A* (*Psychomotor*)

Because you use different methods for cognitive, affective, and psychomotor objectives, you must separately assess their achievement.

THE COGNITIVE DOMAIN

A behavioral construct within the cognitive domain is either *knowledge level* or *intellectual level*. An objective requiring students to *remember* some specified content (e.g., a name or principle) is a knowledge-level objective.

In the example of the nine objectives for the sixth-grade math unit, objectives 3, 4, 6, and 8 specify knowledge-level behavioral constructs. Objective 3 requires students only to memorize a formula. Objectives 4, 6, and 8 require students to recall a process for finding an answer.

An objective has an intellectual-level behavioral construct if it requires students to *use reasoning to make judgments* relative to the specified content. A student would hardly be able to explain *why* the area of a rectangle equals the product of its length and width (objective 2) simply by remembering that formula. Thus, objective 2, like 1, 5, 7, and 9, specifies an intellectual-level behavioral construct.

KNOWLEDGE-LEVEL COGNITION

Because of the differences between how achievement of two types of knowledge-level objectives are tested, a distinction is made between *simple-knowledge* and *knowledge-of-a-process* behavioral constructs.

Simple Knowledge The behavioral construct of a knowledge-level objective is considered *simple knowledge if the content for students to remember involves no more than a single response to a particular stimulus*. Each of the following is an example of a simple-knowledge objective:

1. (Kindergarten language arts) Identifies the appropriate letter by sight upon hearing the consonant sound for *b, d,* or *g*
2. (Fourth-grade social studies) States that the purpose of the Constitution is to provide a general plan for governing the United States
3. (Sixth-grade math) States the formula for the area of a rectangle
4. (High school biology) Lists the fundamental elements of a food web
5. (High school physical education) Upon hearing the name of a major muscle group, points to the location of that group on her or his own body

These objectives, like all simple-knowledge objectives, require students to remember correct responses to particular stimuli. The stimulus in the first example is one of three consonant sounds, and the response to be remembered is the letter that goes with that sound. The stimulus for the second is "purpose of the Constitution," and the desired response is "provide a general plan for governing the United States."

Knowledge of a Process The behavioral construct of a knowledge-level objective is considered *knowledge of a process if the content for students to remember is a sequence of steps in a procedure*. Each of the following is an example of a knowledge-of-a-process objective:

1. (Fourth-grade social studies) Describes the general process for amending the Constitution
2. (Sixth-grade math) Given the dimensions of a rectangle, computes its area
3. (High school biology) Given descriptions of interlinked food chains, sketches the resulting simplified food web
4. (High school physical education) Describes the steps for executing a flat bench press, military press, leg press, calf raise, tricep pull-down,

standing curl with curl bar, seated lat pull-down, and behind-the-neck press

Knowledge-of-a-process objectives require students to know how to execute procedures. Such objectives are concerned with methods for finding answers or accomplishing tasks, not with simply remembering answers. You simply remember that "11" is the answer to the question "What is $7 + 4$?" You know that answer because you achieved a simple-knowledge objective when you memorized the addition facts $1 + 1 = 2$ through $9 + 9 = 18$. However, unless you are quite unusual, you don't know the answer to the question "What is $137 + 86$?" But even though you don't have that sum memorized, you remember how to figure it out because you achieved a knowledge-of-a-process objective when you learned to add two-digit numbers to three-digit numbers.

You will find out from studying Chapter 5 that techniques for testing achievement of simple-knowledge objectives differ considerably from those for testing achievement of knowledge-of-a-process objectives.

INTELLECTUAL-LEVEL COGNITION

An intellectual-level cognitive objective can be classified as (1) comprehension of a communication, (2) conceptualization, (3) application, or (4) beyond application.

Comprehension of a Communication   A comprehension-of-a-communication objective requires students to *determine the explicit or implicit meaning of a message.* The substance of the message or the mode by which the message is communicated should be specified by the content of the objective.

The following are examples of comprehension-of-a-communication objectives that specify the substance of the messages to be understood by students:

1. (Fourth-grade social studies) Explains the general provisions in the Bill of Rights
2. (High school physics) Explains the meaning of Newton's Second Law

The following comprehension-of-a-communication objectives specify the mode by which messages are communicated:

1. (First-grade language arts) In his or her own words, retells a two- to four-minute story related by a classmate
2. (Fifth-grade science) From studying a weather map in a newspaper, describes temperature and precipitation in various locations
3. (Ninth-grade English) From reading an essay (with the sophistication level of a *Newsweek* or *Sports Illustrated* article), separately summarizes the author's conclusions and the evidence supporting those conclusions

Comprehension-of-a-communication objectives are concerned with students being able to interpret and translate ideas that have been expressed by others.

Conceptualization   A conceptualization objective requires students to *use inductive reasoning to either (1) distinguish examples of a particular concept (i.e., idea or abstraction) from nonexamples of that concept or (2) discover why a particular relationship exists.*

The following are examples of conceptualization objectives concerned with distinguishing examples of one concept from those of others:

1. (Third-grade language arts) Given a compound sentence, identifies the action verbs in that sentence
2. (Sixth-grade math) Discriminates between the surface area of a figure and other quantitative characteristics of that figure (e.g., height and volume)
3. (High school biology) Distinguishes examples of food webs from other mechanisms within an ecosystem

The content specified by each of these three objectives is a concept. *Action verb* is the concept of concern for objective 1; objectives 2 and 3, respectively, deal with *surface area* and *food web*.

The following are examples of conceptualization objectives concerned with discovering relationships:

1. (Kindergarten language arts) Explains the general relation between a word's letters and how the word "sounds"
2. (Sixth-grade math) Explains why the area of a rectangle equals the product of its length and width
3. (High school physical education) Explains the fundamental relationships among (a) weight work, (b) rest, and (c) nutrition

The content specified by each of these last three objectives is a relationship. Objective 1 requires kindergartners to realize that how a word sounds depends on the word's letters. Objective 2 requires students to understand why multiplying a rectangle's length and width gives the same results as counting the number of unit squares in the rectangle's interior. Students achieving objective 3 will understand how muscle strength is influenced by the interplay of weight work, rest, and nutrition.

Testing student achievement of conceptualization objectives is a difficult task you face as a teacher. How to assess successfully conceptualization and other types of cognitive achievement is the focus of Chapter 5.

Application   An application objective requires students to *use deductive reasoning to decide how to solve a specified type of problem.* Moreover, when confronted with a problem, students who achieve an application-level objective can determine whether or not a process, principle, fact, formula, law, or other relationship specified in the objective's content is relevant to the resolution of that problem.

The following are examples of application objectives:

1. (Fourth-grade social studies) Given a description of a well-publicized current issue, determines what, if any, bearing the Constitution has on the resolution of that issue
2. (Sixth-grade math) When confronted with a real-life problem, determines whether or not computing the area of a surface will help solve that problem
3. (High school biology) Given a description of an example of a food web, predicts the impact of each of a number of possible disruptions to that web
4. (High school physical education) Designs a personal weight-training program for maintaining overall, balanced muscle strength

Sometimes knowledge of a process is confused with application. Compare the second of the four previously stated application objectives to the following knowledge-of-a-process objective:

Given the dimensions of a rectangle, computes its area

Both objectives deal with computing area. But the application objective requires students to decide *when* to compute it, whereas the knowledge-of-a-process objective requires students to *remember how* to compute it. There's quite a difference between testing for application-level achievement and testing for knowledge-of-a-process achievement.

Cognition beyond Application   Some objectives require students to display cognitive behaviors that are more advanced than the application level. Bloom (1984) refers to three such behavioral constructs: (1) *analysis*, which requires students to break content into component parts; (2) *synthesis*, which requires students to produce content within a specified area; and (3) *evaluation*, which requires students to judge content according to criteria.

Objectives that require students to think creatively in order to examine, produce, or judge content go beyond application. Here are some examples:

1. (First-grade citizenship) Explains why or why not certain classroom rules of conduct are appropriate
2. (Fifth-grade math) Produces counter examples for false generalizations about multiplying and dividing fractions (e.g., "The product of two fractions is less than either one of the fractions")
3. (Ninth-grade English) Expresses and defends a personal value judgment about the validity of an argument presented in an essay
4. (High school business education) Based on a personal examination of an office management system, discriminates between features that contribute to overall office efficiency from those that detract from it

THE AFFECTIVE DOMAIN

Unlike cognitive and psychomotor objectives, affective objectives are not concerned with students' abilities to do anything. Affective objectives are concerned with their attitudes. How to assess student achievement of affective objectives is the focus of Chapter 6.

A behavioral construct within the affective domain is either *appreciation level* or *willingness-to-act level*.

Appreciation-Level Affective Behavior   An appreciation-level objective requires students to *believe that a content specified in the objective has value*. The following are examples:

1. (Second-grade citizenship) Wants classmates to succeed in their efforts to learn
2. (Fourth-grade social studies) Believes that the Constitution serves a valuable purpose
3. (Eighth-grade health) Would like to maintain a healthy diet
4. (High school chemistry) Admires systematic methods for testing hypotheses

Appreciation objectives require students to hold certain beliefs but do not require them to act on those beliefs.

Willingness-to-Act-Level Affective Behavior   Willingness-to-act objectives require students to *choose behaviors consistent with a specified belief*. By wanting to follow a healthy diet, an eighth-grader has achieved the third of the aforementioned appreciation-level objectives. However, to achieve at the willingness-to-act level, that eighth-grader would have to follow deliberately a diet he or she thinks is healthy (e.g., begin to eat more raw vegetables and less animal fats).

The following are examples of willingness-to-act objectives:

1. (Kindergarten language arts) Attempts to sound out the beginning sounds of words that start with either *b, d,* or *g.*
2. (Second-grade citizenship) Refrains from littering the classroom floor
3. (Seventh-grade science) Follows the "eight cardinal rules of safety" while in the science lab
4. (High school physical education) Follows a plan for maintaining overall, balanced muscle strength

THE PSYCHOMOTOR DOMAIN

Psychomotor objectives are categorized as either (1) *voluntary muscle capability* or (2) *ability to perform a specific skill*.

Voluntary Muscle Capability A voluntary-muscle-capability objective requires students to *use their bodies to perform physical work within certain specified parameters (e.g., time, weight, and distance)*. The content of voluntary-muscle-capability objectives should specify the muscle groups to be trained and the type of capabilities. General muscle capabilities can be classified as follows:

1. *Endurance,* which is the ability to continue an activity
2. *Strength,* which is the ability to oppose physical resistance
3. *Flexibility,* which is the range of motion in joints
4. *Agility,* which is the ability to respond to stimuli quickly and smoothly
5. *Speed,* which is the ability to reduce the amount of time it takes to move from one physical point to another

The following are examples of voluntary-muscle-capability objectives:

1. (Third-grade piano) Increases flexibility in both hands to maximize the distance between points that can be simultaneously reached by the thumb and the little finger of the same hand
2. (Seventh-grade physical education) Increases cardiovascular endurance so that a 2-mile jog can be sustained
3. (High school physical education) When using correct techniques, completes eight repetitions of (a) flat bench press of 75 percent of own body weight, (b) military press of 33 percent of own body weight, (c) leg press of 125 percent of own body weight, (d) calf raise of 150 percent of own body weight, (e) tricep pull-down of 15 percent of own body weight, (f) curl of 10 percent of own body weight, (g) lat pull-down of 60 percent of own body weight, and (h) behind-the-neck press of 5 percent of own body weight

Ability to Perform a Specific Skill An ability-to-perform-a-specific-skill objective requires students to *utilize voluntary muscle capabilities in executing a specified physical process*. The content of ability-to-perform-a-specific-skill objectives should indicate the physical process or routine to be demonstrated. The following are examples:

1. (Kindergarten language arts) Vocalizes the appropriate consonant sound when prompted to make the sound for *b, d,* or *g*
2. (Kindergarten handwriting) Manipulates a pencil well enough to follow the steps for printing an uppercase *A*
3. (Middle school recreation) Executes a legal tennis serve without faulting seven out of ten times
4. (High school physical education) Demonstrates the correct procedures for executing a flat bench press, military press, leg press, calf raise, tricep pull-down, standing curl with curl bar, seated lat pull-down, and behind-the-neck press

How to assess student achievement of psychomotor objectives is the focus of Chapter 7.

USING THE SCHEME FOR CLASSIFYING BEHAVIORAL CONSTRUCTS

As a teacher, you (1) develop or select curricula, (2) plan and conduct lessons to help students achieve the goals of those curricula, and (3) evaluate how well students achieve those goals. Goals should be defined before you attempt to assess achievement. Thus, it is *not* the purpose of this book to influence your decisions regarding what you intend your students to learn. The purpose of this book is to help you accurately assess how well students achieve the goals and objectives *you* decide are appropriate.

The scheme (summarized in Table 1.1) for classifying the behavioral constructs of the objectives you set was presented in previous sections of this chapter to provide a mechanism for

1. Organizing your thoughts about how you want your students to interact with the subject matter of the curricula
2. Clarifying and communicating the cognitive, affective, or psychomotor level of learning targeted by each objective

The behavioral construct you intend for even a well-written objective may not be communicated clearly until you actually label the objective according to the scheme for classifying behavioral constructs.

TABLE 1.1   Categories of Behavioral
Constructs Specified by Learning Objectives

Cognitive Domain

I. Knowledge level
   A. Simple knowledge
   B. Knowledge of a process
II. Intellectual level
   A. Comprehension of a communication
   B. Conceptualization
   C. Application
   D. Beyond application

Affective Domain

I. Appreciation level
II. Willingness-to-act level

Psychomotor Domain

I. Voluntary muscle capability
II. Ability to perform a specific skill

Goals for seven units from a range of grade levels and subject areas are used for examples throughout this chapter. The seven teachers responsible for teaching these goals defined them by objectives and, for further clarification, labeled each objective according to its behavioral construct. There is nothing sacred about how they defined the goals or labeled the objectives. The following simply reflects what they define as student achievement for the units.

1. (For a kindergarten language arts unit) Associates the appropriate consonant sounds with the letters *b, d,* and *g*
   A. Explains the general relationship between a word's letters and how that word "sounds" (*Cognitive: conceptualization*)
   B. Identifies the appropriate letter by sight upon hearing the consonant sound for *b, d,* or *g* (*Cognitive: simple knowledge*)
   C. Attempts to sound out the beginning sounds of words that begin with either *b, d,* or *g* (*Affective: willingness to act*)
   D. Knows how to vocalize the appropriate consonant sound when prompted to make the sound for *b, d,* or *g* (*Cognitive: knowledge of a process*)
   E. Vocalizes the appropriate consonant sound when prompted to make the sound for *b, d,* or *g* (*Psychomotor: ability to perform a specific skill*)
2. (For a second-grade citizenship unit) While in the classroom, displays respect and consideration for the rights and feelings of others
   A. Refrains from littering the classroom floor (*Affective: willingness to act*)
   B. If a classmate expresses a need for help, attempts to help, providing that she or he is able and that such help is acceptable to the teacher (*Affective: willingness to act*)
   C. Refrains from interrupting others who are speaking in the classroom (*Affective: willingness to act*)
   D. Takes care not to damage or waste the property of classmates (*Affective: willingness to act*)
   E. Refrains from stealing from classmates (*Affective: willingness to act*)
   F. Minimizes borrowing from classmates (*Affective: willingness to act*)
   G. Expresses appreciation to classmates for being helpful (*Affective: willingness to act*)
   H. Avoids physically contacting classmates in a way that would cause them pain or discomfort (*Affective: willingness to act*)
   I. Wants classmates to succeed in their efforts to learn (*Affective: appreciation*)
3. (For a fourth-grade social studies unit) Is aware of fundamental aspects of the U.S. Constitution, its history, and its influence on us today
   A. States that the purpose of the Constitution is to provide a general plan for governing the United States (*Cognitive: simple knowledge*)
   B. Lists the general parts of the original Constitution as the Preamble and seven articles (with the subject of each article) (*Cognitive: simple knowledge*)

    C. Lists facts from the following:
In 1787, 43 people wrote the Constitution in a four-month-long Constitutional Convention in Philadelphia. Forty of the 43 signed the document on September 17. The Bill of Rights was added in 1791. (*Cognitive: simple knowledge*)

    D. Explains George Mason's, Edmund Randolph's, and Elbridge Gerry's reasons for refusing to sign the document (*Cognitive: comprehension of a communication*)

    E. Explains the general provisions in the Bill of Rights (*Cognitive: comprehension of a communication*)

    F. Explains at least four amendments that have been added since the Bill of Rights (*Cognitive: comprehension of a communication*)

    G. Describes the general process for amending the Constitution (*Cognitive: knowledge of a process*)

    H. Given a description of a well-publicized current issue, determines what, if any, bearing the Constitution has on the resolution of that issue (*Cognitive: application*)

    I. Believes that the Constitution serves a valuable purpose (*Affective: appreciation*)

4. (For a sixth-grade math unit) Efficiently solves real-life problems that require finding sizes of surface areas

    A. Discriminates between the surface area of a figure and other quantitative characteristics of that figure (e.g., height and volume) (*Cognitive: conceptualization*)

    B. Explains why the area of a rectangle equals the product of its length and width (*Cognitive: conceptualization*)

    C. States the formula for the area of a rectangle (*Cognitive: simple knowledge*)

    D. Given the dimensions of a rectangle, computes its area (*Cognitive: knowledge of a process*)

    E. Explains how the formula for the area of a right triangle can be derived from the formula for the area of a rectangle (*Cognitive: conceptualization*)

    F. Given the dimensions of a right triangle, computes its area (*Cognitive: knowledge of a process*)

    G. Explains how the formula for the area of a right cylinder can be derived from the formula for the area of a rectangle (*Cognitive: conceptualization*)

    H. Given the dimensions of a right cylinder, computes its surface area (*Cognitive: knowledge of a process*)

    I. When confronted with a real-life problem, determines whether or not computing a surface area will help solve that problem (*Cognitive: application*)

5. (For a ninth-grade English unit) Critiques essays written to sway readers' opinions

    A. States the definitions of the following: *essay, fact, opinion, evidence, conclusion, rationale, background,* and *critique* (*Cognitive: simple knowledge*)

    B. From reading an essay (with the sophistication level of a *Newsweek* or *Sports Illustrated* article), distinguishes among the following in that essay: facts, evidence for conclusions, and conclusions (*Cognitive: beyond application*)

C. From reading an essay (with the sophistication level of the back page of *Newsweek* or *Sports Illustrated*), separately summarizes the author's conclusions and the evidence supporting them (*Cognitive: comprehension of a communication*)

D. Expresses and defends a personal value judgment about the validity of an argument presented in an essay (*Cognitive: beyond application*)

6. (For a high school biology unit) Understands the fundamental elements and operations of food webs

A. Lists the fundamental elements of a food web (*Cognitive: simple knowledge*)

B. Distinguishes examples of food webs from other mechanisms within an ecosystem (*Cognitive: conceptual*)

C. States the definitions of the following terms: *food web, pyramid, biomass, tertiary consumer, secondary consumer, primary consumer, producer,* and *decomposer* (*Cognitive: simple knowledge*)

D. Given a description of interlinking food chains, sketches the resulting simplified food web (*Cognitive: knowledge of a process*)

E. Given a description of an example of a food web, predicts the impact of each of a number of possible disruptions to that web (*Cognitive: application*)

7. (For a high school physical education unit) Plans and follows a weight-lifting program for maintaining muscle strength

A. Upon hearing the name of a major muscle group, points to the location of that group on her or his own body (*Cognitive: simple knowledge*)

B. Describes the steps for executing a flat bench press, military press, leg press, calf raise, tricep pull-down, standing curl with curl bar, seated lat pull-down, and behind-the-neck press (*Cognitive: knowledge of a process*)

C. Demonstrates the correct procedures for executing a flat bench press, military press, leg press, calf raise, tricep pull-down, standing curl with curl bar, seated lat pull-down, and behind-the-neck press (*Psychomotor: ability to perform a specific skill*)

D. In the weight room, displays consideration for others, uses equipment in a safe manner, and puts weights in their proper places after using them (*Affective: willingness to act*)

E. Explains the fundamental relationships among (1) weight work, (2) rest, and (3) nutrition (*Cognitive: conceptualization*)

F. Designs a personal weight-training program for maintaining overall, balanced muscle strength (*Cognitive: application*)

G. Follows a plan for maintaining overall, balanced muscle strength (*Affective: willingness to act*)

H. When using correct techniques, completes eight repetitions of (1) flat bench press of 75 percent of own body weight, (2) military press of 33 percent of own body weight, (3) leg press of 125 percent of own body weight, (4) calf raise of 150 percent of own body weight, (5) tricep pull-down of 15 percent of own body weight, (6) curl of 10 percent of own body weight, (7) lat pull-down of 60 percent of own body weight, and (8) behind-the-neck press of 5 percent of own body weight (*Psychomotor: voluntary muscle capability*)

SELF-ASSESSMENT OF YOUR ACHIEVEMENT OF CHAPTER I'S OBJECTIVES

The self-assessment sections at the end of each chapter (exercises for Chapter 1 begin below) provide exercises to help you:

1. Evaluate your achievement of the chapter's objectives so that you can identify your areas of proficiency and the areas you need to review;

2. Reinforce and extend what you've learned from the chapter.

    I. Examine each of the following activities and categorize it as (1) a formative evaluation of student achievement, (2) a summative evaluation of student achievement, (3) *not* an evaluation of student achievement:

      A. Ms. Kincaid decides that Richard has learned enough about scientific principles and procedures to receive a B for the semester.

      B. Mr. Meeks judges that students got very little from the social studies unit he just completed.

      C. Mr. Warren notices that Andy correctly computed eight out of 17 arithmetic exercises.

      D. Because he noticed that Andy only computed eight out of 17 arithmetic exercises, Mr. Warren decides to reteach the process with a modified lesson.

      E. Ms. Hernandez judges that most of her students have learned the beginning of a unit on the scientific process well enough that she can abbreviate the time she had planned to spend with that unit.

        Compare your answers to these: Ms. Kincaid and Mr. Meeks made summative evaluations. In example C, Mr. Warren did not evaluate student achievement; he only made an observation that may have been a test of Andy's achievement. In example D, Mr. Warren did make a formative evaluation: He used his observation of Andy's work to *conclude* that Andy's lack of achievement with the computations warranted a strategy change in the lessons for the unit. In example E, Ms. Hernandez made a formative evaluation.

    II. In writing, describe an example in which you, in your role as a teacher, would make a formative evaluation. Describe an example in which you would make a summative evaluation. Explain why the differences in the two examples make the first a formative and the second a summative evaluation. Show what you've written to another teacher and discuss it.

III. Ms. Greer is a preservice history teacher in the early stages of her student teaching experience. Her cooperating or directing teacher gradually assigns instructional tasks to her. One day the cooperating teacher leaves Ms. Greer the following note: "Please construct a valid test that I can use in determining what the pupils understand about the Industrial Revolution. Bring the test in tomorrow. Thanks."

Ms. Greer is competent in developing valid history tests. However, without further information from the cooperating teacher, her task is impossible. Explain in a paragraph why the task is impossible and what additional information she needs from the cooperating teacher. Compare your paragraph to those of others who responded to this exercise. The paragraphs should include an indication that the goal of "understanding the Industrial Revolution" needs to be defined with learning objectives by the cooperating teacher.

IV. From a textbook or some other type of curricula material in your teaching specialty, identify a teaching unit appropriate for students you might teach. Write a goal for the unit and define it with a set of learning objectives. Label each objective according to the behavioral construct you intend for it to specify. Also, list the content specified in the objectives. Exchange your work on this exercise with someone and critique one another's papers. Be sure to save your work from this exercise as you will need it to complete exercises in other chapters.

V. For each of the following multiple-choice items, select the one response that best answers the question or correctly completes the statement:

A. Willingness to do something is subsumed by which of the following domains?
1. cognitive
2. affective
3. pyschomotor

B. A learning objective requiring students to *know* the steps in a physical activity is _____.
1. cognitive
2. affective
3. psychomotor

C. A learning objective requiring students to use reasoning is _____.
1. cognitive
2. affective
3. psychomotor

D. A cognitive objective requiring students to make decisions that go beyond what they remember is _____ .
   1. knowledge of a process
   2. simple knowledge
   3. affective
   4. intellectual

E. Which one of the following types of objectives requires students to reason deductively?
   1. knowledge of a process
   2. appreciation
   3. application
   4. conceptualization
   5. comprehension of a communication

F. When a teacher conducts a lesson targeting an affective learning objective, that teacher is attempting to get students to _____ .
   1. understand their own values
   2. understand the values of others
   3. be able to recognize values
   4. embrace values

G. By writing her name in legible cursive, Nancy has displayed achievement of an objective with cursive writing as a content and _____ as a behavioral construct.
   1. cognitive: comprehension of a communication
   2. psychomotor: ability to perform a specific skill
   3. cognitive: conceptualization

H. By writing her name in legible cursive, Nancy has displayed achievement of an objective with cursive writing as a content and _____ as a behavioral construct.
   1. affective: willingness to act
   2. cognitive: beyond application
   3. cognitive: application

I. By writing her name in legible cursive, Nancy has displayed achievement of an objective with cursive writing as a content and _____ as a behavioral construct.
   1. cognitive: comprehension of a communication
   2. cognitive: conceptualization
   3. cognitive: knowledge of a process

J. By accurately translating the American signed English of a hearing-impaired person into spoken English, Jan displays achievement of an objective with American signed English as the content and _____ as a cognitive behavioral construct.
   1. knowledge of a process

2. conceptualization
3. comprehension of a communication

K. What cognitive level of achievement does Juan display by accurately computing the quotient of 55.087 and .09669?
1. simple knowledge
2. knowledge of a process
3. conceptualization
4. application

Compare your choices to the following key: A-2, B-1, C-1, D-4, E-3, F-4, G-2, H-1, I-3, J-3, K-2.

The Measurement of Student Achievement

GOAL OF CHAPTER 2

Chapter 2 describes (1) what distinguishes accurate from inaccurate evaluations of student achievement and (2) some of the fundamental terminology used in communicating methods for accurately assessing student achievement. More specifically, Chapter 2 will help you to

1. Distinguish between the measurements and evaluations you make and clarify the role they play in assessing student achievements (*Cognitive: conceptualization*)
2. Describe the distinguishing features and common uses of three types of measurements of student achievement: commercially produced, standardized, and teacher-produced tests (*Cognitive: simple knowledge*)
3. Explain why a measurement's *relevance* depends on how well its items reflect the contents and behavioral constructs specified in the learning objectives (*Cognitive: conceptualization*)
4. Explain why a measurement's validity depends on its relevance and reliability (*Cognitive: conceptualization*)
5. Explain why the cost-effectiveness of a measurement depends on its validity and usability (*Cognitive: conceptualization*)
6. State the definitions of the following: *measurement, test, test item, evaluation, commercially produced test, standardized test, teacher-produced test, validity, relevance, content relevance, construct validity, reliability, internal consistency, test-retest reliability, intrascorer reliability, interscorer reliability, validation study, item analysis, usability,* and *cost-effectiveness* (*Cognitive: simple knowledge*)

TABLE 2.1   Examples of Teachers' Measurements and Evaluations

A	B
Ms. Morgan hears Jeannie, one of her kindergarten students, say, "My name sounds different from Mary's 'cause it's got different letters."	Ms. Morgan decides that Jeannie is beginning to achieve conceptualization of the relationship between a word's letters and how it sounds.
In one day, Ms. Parino notices seven incidents in which her second-graders tossed litter on the the classroom floor. Only six times did she note any of them using the wastebasket without first being prompted.	Ms. Parino judges that she needs to work harder at teaching her students to refrain from littering the classroom floor.
Mr. Little notes that Judith scored 37 points out of a possible 44 on the unit test on the Constitution he administered to his fourth-grade class.	Mr. Little decides that Judith achieved the goal of the unit on the Constitution well enough to receive a B.
While going over some work her sixth-graders completed in math class, Ms. Curry sees that 22 of the 26 students correctly answered the exercise relevant to conceptualization of the area-of-a-cylinder formula.	Ms. Curry decides that her sixth-graders are ready for her application-level lesson on area problems.
Mr. Alvarez looks at his ninth-graders' scores from the unit test on how well they critique persuasive essays.	Mr. Alvarez assigns five A's, nine B's, eight C's and six F's for the unit.
Ms. Bung-Lee overhears one of her eleventh-graders say, "Nobody understands this stuff about food webs!"	Ms. Bung-Lee decides to ask the students if they are having more trouble with the vocabulary or with the concepts associated with food webs.
Mr. Ascione counts how many times Debra bench-presses 80 pounds during one set.	Mr. Ascione judges that Debra is progressing satisfactorily.

MEASUREMENTS AND EVALUATIONS

Examine the activities of the teachers listed in the two columns of Table 2.1.

What do the activities in column A have in common? What do those in column B have in common? How do the activities in column A differ from those in column B? How do those in column A influence those in column B?

Column A lists activities in which teachers make empirical observations (e.g., by hearing or seeing something). Column B lists activities in which teachers make qualitative judgments about student achievement. The teachers collected facts in column A and formed opinions in column B. The teachers' knowledge of those facts probably swayed their opinions. Ms. Morgan, for example, judged Jeannie's achievement in light of what she heard Jeannie say. Similarly, the fact that Judith scored 37 on the unit test influenced Mr. Little to give her a B.

The teachers' data-gathering activities listed in column A are examples of *measurements*. The decision-making activities listed in column B are examples of *evaluations*.

MEASUREMENT

A measurement is the *process by which facts or data are gathered through empirical observations*. To assess student achievement, teachers measure by reading what students have written, watching their performances, listening to what they say, and in general, using the senses (i.e., sight, hearing, touch, smell, and taste) to gather information relevant to stated goals.

When people think of teachers' measurements, they typically think of *tests*. Tests are *planned measurements by which teachers attempt to create opportunities for students to display their achievement relative to specified goals*.

Tests are composed of *items*. Each item of a test (1) confronts students with a task and (2) provides a means for observing their responses to the task. Here, for example, are three of the items on the unit test that Mr. Little administered to Judith and his other fourth-grade students.

1. *Task presented to the students:*
   Circle the city where the Constitutional Convention was held:
   New York   Boston   Plymouth   Philadelphia
   Scoring key: +1 if only *Philadelphia* is circled; otherwise, 0 points.
2. *Task presented to the students:*
   In a one-to-one interview, Mr. Little directs the student as follows: "In 30 seconds, tell me, in your own words, what the Bill of Rights added to the original Constitution." If the student simply begins listing the first ten amendments, Mr. Little should interrupt and direct the student to summarize rather than list.
   Scoring key: (4 points possible) +1 for each of the following: (a) assurances of certain freedoms, (b) certain individual rights, and (c) limits on the power of government; also, +1 if nothing is included in the response that indicates a misconception about the Constitution.
3. *Task presented to the students:* Suppose our class were going to start a music club. The purpose of the club would be to give people a chance to play and listen to music. Write a paragraph telling what the class should do to get the music club organized.
   Scoring key: (2 points possible) +1 if the answer includes some indication that some sort of governing or management structure should be established; +1 if the answer indicates that the regulations for governing the club should be explained in a document.

EVALUATION

An evaluation is a *value judgment*. Evaluations are influenced by the results of measurements. Mr. Little, for example, evaluated when he decided that Judith achieved the goal of the unit on the Constitution well enough to receive a B. That *summative* evaluation was influenced by a measurement result (i.e., Judith scored 37 on the 44-point unit test). Whether or not Mr. Little's evaluation of Judith's achievement was accurate depends on the answers to two questions: (1) Did the measurements used by Mr. Little (i.e., the 44-point test) provide *valid* evidence of Judith's achievement of the unit's goal? (2) Did Mr. Little use wise judgment in interpreting the test scores (and any other measurements he might have used)?

Concern for measurement validity is a principal focus of this textbook. Mr. Little intended the first of the three test items to reflect the students' achievement of objective C listed in Chapter 1 for the second-grade citizenship unit. The second and third items were intended to reflect objectives E and I, respectively. The test's validity depends on how well the performances on these and other items reflect student achievement of the unit's goal.

Mr. Little measures achievement of the goal by reading Judith's responses to test items and figuring her score. But the score doesn't *tell* him her level of achievement. It only provides him with evidence to help him make an informed evaluation about achievement level.

To review an idea from Chapter 1, examine column B of Table 2.1 and categorize the evaluations as either *formative* or *summative*. Compare your responses to the following: Mr. Little and Mr. Alvarez provided examples of summative evaluations; the others appear to be formative.

COMMONLY USED MEASUREMENTS OF ACHIEVEMENT

COMMERCIALLY PRODUCED TESTS

Achievement tests for general content areas (e.g., geography and English grammar) at every grade level can be purchased from commercial publishers. Such tests often accompany a textbook series and some are produced as part of "packaged" curricula that schools and school systems sometimes purchase.

Unlike tests that are packaged as part of a textbook series or curricula, some commercially produced tests are administered on a school-wide basis once or twice a year. These are the "big event" tests that some people *naively* think of as true measures of students' intellectual achievements. Although capable of providing some evidence of what students have achieved in some broad general areas, big-event commercially produced tests do not yield data relative to the specific achievements of individual students.

STANDARDIZED TESTS

The more commonly known, big-event, commercially produced tests (e.g., Stanford Achievement Tests, Metropolitan Achievement Tests, Iowa Test of Basic Skills, and California Achievement Tests) are *standardized*. A standardized test is one that has been field-tested for the purpose of collecting data on (1) measurement reliability and (2) normative standards to be used in interpreting scores.

TEACHER-PRODUCED TESTS

Although both standardized and nonstandardized commercially produced tests can suggest your students' general achievements, tests you design yourself can provide the most important data for formative and summative evaluations. By following sound measurement design principles and techniques (e.g., those illustrated in Chapters 3 through 7), you can tailor your tests to the specific goals and objectives of the units you teach.

VALIDITY

Once again, consider the example in which Mr. Little used the results of a 44-point test to evaluate his fourth-graders' achievement of the goal for the unit on the Constitution. Judith and a classmate, Rico, scored 37 and 30, respectively. Should this fact lead Mr. Little to decide that Judith's level of achievement is greater than Rico's?

How accurately the difference of seven points in the two test scores actually reflects a difference in how well Judith and Rico achieved the goal depends on the *validity* of that 44-point test. If that test, as it was administered to those fourth-graders and scored by Mr. Little, produced highly valid scores, the results reasonably indicate that Judith's achievement was higher than Rico's. On the other hand, if the test scores were significantly affected by measurement error caused by poorly designed items, distractions during the administration, poor sampling of content, unclear directions, "give-away" items that could be answered without having achieved the unit's objectives, cheating, or any one of many other possible contaminants, the results may have very little to do with actual achievement.

The validity of a measurement depends on its (1) *relevance* and (2) *reliability*.

MEASUREMENT RELEVANCE

A test is *relevant* to the same degree that the following two questions can be answered affirmatively:

1. *Do the test's items match the stated objectives?*
2. *Is the test designed so that emphases are placed on objectives according to their relative importance to goal achievement?*

A test item matches the objective for which it is designed if a correct response to the item requires students to operate with the objective's content at the objective's behavioral construct level. For example,

To help her evaluate sixth-graders' achievement of the goal for a math unit on surface areas, Ms. Curry begins to design a test. The unit has nine objectives, which she has designated A through I. Here is objective I:

I.   When confronted with a real-life problem, determines whether or not computing the area of a surface will help solve that problem (*Cognitive: application*)

Ms. Curry develops the following three items for objective I:

1.   *Task presented to the students:*
     (Multiple choice) Computing a surface area will help you solve one of these three problems. Which one is it?
     a.   We have a large bookcase we want to bring into our classroom. Our problem is to determine if the bookcase can fit through the doorway.
     b.   As part of a project to fix up our classroom, we want to put stripping all along the crack where the walls meet the floor. Our problem is to figure how much stripping to buy.
     c.   As part of a project to fix up our classroom, we want to put carpet on the floor. Our problem is to figure how much carpet to buy.
     Scoring key: +1 for c only; 0 otherwise.
2.   *Task presented to the students:*
     (Multiple choice) What is the surface area of one side of this sheet of paper you are now reading? (Use your ruler to help you make your choice.)
     a.   93.5 square inches
     b.   93.5 inches
     c.   20.5 square inches
     d.   20.5 inches
     e.   41 square inches
     f.   41 inches
     Scoring key: +1 for a only; otherwise 0.
3.   *Task presented to the students:*
     (Multiple choice) As part of our project for fixing up the classroom, we need to buy some paint for the walls. The paint we want comes in two different sizes. A 5-liter can costs $16.85, and a 2-liter can costs $6.55. Which one of the following would help us decide which can is the best buy?
     a.   Compare 5 × $16.85 to 2 × $6.55.
     b.   Compare $16.85 ÷ 5 to $6.55 ÷ 2.
     c.   Compare $16.85 − $6.55 to 2/5.
     Scoring key: +1 for b only; otherwise 0.

How well do Ms. Curry's items match objective I? The first one seems to be relevant. Objective I specifies real-life problems involving surface areas as the content and cognitive applications as the behavioral construct. Students who select c in response to item 1 would be displaying evidence of application-level achievement with surface-area problems.

Item 2 does not seem to match objective I very well. Students could select a simply by remembering how to compute a surface area and not necessarily by being able to decide *when* to compute surface areas. Thus, although item 2 is relevant to the content of objective I (i.e., surface areas), it requires students to operate only at the knowledge-of-a-process level and thus doesn't match the behavioral construct of objective I.

Item 3 requires students to operate at the application level as specified by objective I. However, it fails to match objective I because the content is not relevant to surface areas.

Methods for developing items that match stated objectives are presented in Chapters 4 through 7.

Once Ms. Curry manages to obtain items that match the nine objectives, she should systematically compile those items into a test so that achievement of more important objectives affects test scores more than achievement of less important objectives. Techniques for accomplishing this task are presented in Chapter 3.

Content Relevance   How well the content covered by a test matches the content of the stated objectives is referred to as the test's *content relevance*. Items 1 and 2 have content relevance to objective I because both items involve students with the content specified by objective I. Ms. Curry's item 3 is not relevant to objective I because it lacks content relevance.

Construct Validity   How well the behavioral constructs covered by a test match those specified in the stated objectives is referred to as the test's *construct validity*. Items 1 and 3 have construct validity because both require students to exhibit application-level achievement as specified by objective I. Item 2 lacks construct validity relative to objective I because it requires knowledge-of-a-process-level achievement rather than application.

To be relevant a test must have both content relevance and construct validity.

MEASUREMENT RELIABILITY

To be valid, a test must not only be relevant but also reliable. A test is *reliable to the same degree that it can be depended on to yield consistent, noncontradictory results.*

As you design or select tests to measure your students' achievements, you should be concerned with four types of reliability: (1) internal consistency, (2) test-retest reliability, (3) intrascorer reliability, and (4) interscorer reliability.

Internal Consistency   Ms. Curry discovered contradictory results in the test she administered on surface area:

Ms. Curry labeled the nine objectives for the unit A through I. Items 7 and 19 on Ms. Curry's 22-item unit test were intended to be relevant to the sixth-graders' achievement of objective F:

F.   Given the dimensions of a right triangle, computes its area (*Cognitive: knowledge of a process*)

Items 7 and 19 are as follows:

7.   *Task presented to the students:*
     What is the area bounded by a right triangle with dimensions 5 cm, 4 cm, and 3 cm? (Display your computations and place the answer in the blank.)

     _____

     Scoring key: (4 points possible) +1 if the response indicates that the correct formula was used; +1 if a computation using 4 and 3, but not 5, is exhibited; +1 if 6 is given as the area; +1 if the answer is expressed in square cm.

19. *Task presented to the students:*
     What is the area of the interior of triangle *ABC* if angle *B* is a right angle, *AB* = 6 cm, *BC* = 8 cm, and *AC* = 10 cm? (Display your computations and place the answer in the blank.)

     _____

     Scoring key: (4 points possible) +1 if the response indicates that the correct formula was used; +1 if a computation using 6 and 8, but not 10, is exhibited; +1 if 24 is given as the area; +1 if the answer is expressed in square cm.

Curious about how well her students achieved objective F, Ms. Curry notes the performances on items 7 and 19 by five of her students.

STUDENT	POINTS ON ITEM 7	POINTS ON ITEM 19
Roxanne	4	4
Luanne	1	0
Izar	0	4
Mel	3	2
Jan	4	1

The data suggest that for objective F Roxanne has a high level of achievement, Luanne's achievement is low, and Mel's may be somewhere in between. However, Ms. Curry is perplexed by the performances of Izar and Jan on these two items. Does Izar know how to compute areas of right triangles? Item 7 suggests not, whereas item 19 indicates yes.

At least for Izar and Jan relative to objective F, Ms. Curry's test yielded some contradictory results. If the test results are dominated by such inconsistencies, the test lacks *internal consistency* and is, therefore, unreliable. On the other hand, if the results do not contain a significant proportion of contradictions and are more in line with what Ms. Curry obtained from Roxanne, Luanne, and Mel, the test is internally consistent.

A test is internally consistent to the same degree that its *results are noncontradictory.*

Test-Retest Reliability   If Ms. Curry administers the unit test to her students a second time, how closely would the second set of scores agree with the first? Would students who scored high the first time tend to score high again? Would those with low scores the first time also obtain low scores from the second administration? A retest *should* reflect gains and losses in student achievement that might have occurred since the initial administration of the test. However, significant fluctuations or inconsistencies between the test and the retest that are not attributable to actual changes in achievement are a consequence of poor reliability.

Students will score approximately the same on two administrations of the same test if (1) student achievement did not change between the two administrations (i.e., there was neither learning nor loss) and (2) the test has a high degree of test-retest reliability.

It is rarely necessary for you to administer a test twice to the same students. However, because test-retest reliability is a critical component of validity, you will need to design your tests so that they can be depended on to have test-retest reliability. Test-retest reliabilities of your tests can be enhanced by following techniques presented in Chapters 3 through 7.

Intrascorer Reliability   You will need to be concerned with intrascorer reliabilities of tests that include essays, performance observations, and other types of items with scoring keys that require an element of judgment. To illustrate the problem of obtaining intrascorer reliability, recall the second of the three items (from the subsection "Measurement" of this chapter) that Mr. Little included in the unit test on the Constitution:

As stipulated by the item, Mr. Little directs Judith in a one-to-one-interview as follows: "In 30 seconds, tell me in your own words what the Bill of Rights added to the original Constitution." Judith responds, "Well, ahh . . . okay. Like its name the Bill of Rights gave the people different rights. You know, like the rights of religion, that was the first one! Okay, and then we got the rights to bear arms and stuff. The Bill of Rights was something to help the people; it protected them from unfairness."

Judith returns to her desk and continues with the written-response items on the test as Mr. Little marks her score for the interview item. He thinks, "She really got to the heart of the question with that business about protection from 'unfairness.' Until then, she wasn't doing all that well. Let's see what she gets out of the four points possible. Did she include assurances of certain freedoms? Not really; she just called them 'rights.' Actually it should be 'freedom of religion,' not 'rights of religion.' But she must understand or she wouldn't have said that stuff about unfairness. Okay, plus one for freedoms, and plus one because she indicated something related to individual rights. But she said nothing about limits on government, so that's a zero. And she said nothing incorrect so that's a plus one. She gets three out of four."

After Judith, Mr. Little interviews 11 more fourth-graders and then Rico. Rico responds as follows to Mr. Little's prompt: "Gotcha! The Bill of Rights was real important. It gave everybody a lot of rights that they needed. Like religion and stuff. It gave religion rights to do what it wants. And it gave people rights to speak freely and the rights to jury trials and from being arrested when they shouldn't be. . . . Is my time up?"

Mr. Little answers, "Yes, thank you very much. You may return to your desk and finish with the test." Mr. Little thinks as he scores Rico's response to the item, "He didn't mention any assurances of freedoms, so zero for the first. He did include rights, so that's a plus one. Nothing for limiting governmental powers. The Bill doesn't give 'religion rights to do what it wants,' so he indicated a misconception. Rico gets one out of four."

Did Mr. Little apply the same scoring criteria to Rico's response that he did to Judith's? Did being impressed by Judith's statement regarding people being protected from unfairness lead him to be more liberal in his interpretations of her response than he was for Rico's? Did the 11 interviews Mr. Little conducted between Judith and Rico contribute to the inconsistencies in scoring? These are questions about the intrascorer reliability of Mr. Little's test. Such questions need not be raised for items (e.g., multiple choice) with scoring keys that leave no room for judgment.

A test cannot be valid without a satisfactory degree of intrascorer reliability. A test has intrascorer reliability to the same degree that the *teacher* (or whoever is scoring the test) *consistently follows the item scoring keys so that the test results are not influenced by when the test is scored* (or corrected).

Interscorer Reliability   A test has interscorer reliability to the same degree that *test scores are not influenced by which teacher scores the items*. If two teachers of the same subject and grade level score a student's response to an item differently, the item is marred by poor interscorer reliability.

Unless properly designed, essay and performance observation items almost always suffer from scoring inconsistencies. Chapter 4 contains suggestions for constructing items that will have high levels of intrascorer and interscorer reliabilities.

ASSESSING TEST VALIDITY

The principal focus of this text is to help you develop and select *reliable* tests that are *relevant* to evaluations you make about your students' achievements.

Methods for assessing the validity of tests exist. However, their use in formal validation studies does not fall within the scope of this text. This section is provided simply to (1) increase your awareness of how test validity is assessed in formal studies and (2) relate some general ideas to keep in mind as techniques for designing and selecting tests are explained in subsequent chapters.

EXAMINING A TEST'S RELEVANCE

Numerous models for examining measurement relevance are offered by the scholarly literature on educational and psychological measurement and evaluation. Virtually all these models provide some sort of systematic approach for analyzing how well the content and behavioral constructs of a test's items relate to what the test is supposed to measure.

Some models employ sophisticated statistical techniques (e.g., factor analysis and cluster analysis) that examine patterns of correlations among items. Judgments are then made concerning whether these patterns tend to support or refute assumptions on which the test was based. All models require the match between the test and its stated purpose to be judged by persons who understand the content, the behavioral constructs, and the students who are the subjects of the evaluation.

If you are interested in more information on models for assessing relevance, here are some sources:

Cangelosi, J. S. (1982). *Measurement and evaluation: An inductive approach for teachers* (pp. 243–253). Dubuque, IA: W. C. Brown.

Gronlund, N. E. (1985). *Measurement and evaluation in teaching* (5th ed., pp. 57–84). New York: Macmillan.

Hambleton, R. K. (1984). Validating the test scores. In R. A. Berk (Ed.), *A guide to criterion-referenced test construction* (pp. 199–230). Baltimore: Johns Hopkins University Press.

Kubiszyn, T., & Borich, G. (1987). *Educational testing and measurement: Classroom application and practice* (2nd ed., pp. 277–289). Glenview, IL: Scott, Foresman.

Mehrens, W. A., & Lehmann, I. J. (1984). *Measurement and evaluation in education and psychology* (3rd ed., pp. 288–309). New York: Holt, Rinehart & Winston.

Nunnally, J. C. (1978). *Psychometric theory* (2nd ed., pp. 327–435). New York: McGraw-Hill.

EXAMINING A TEST'S RELIABILITY

Assessing a test's reliability is typically easier than assessing its relevance. Statistical methods can be used to measure consistency within test results, consistency between two administrations of the same test, and agreement among scorers. Unlike assessments for relevance, reliability assessments are not concerned with making judgments about the match between what a test actually measures and what it is supposed to measure.

Assessing Internal Consistency   In general, two types of models are used for studying internal consistency:

First, some models use correlation statistics to measure the consistency between the scores a test yields from one-half of its items and the scores from the other half of its items. For example,

---

A 40-item test is administered to 50 students. To assess the internal consistency of the test, each student receives a score for only the 20 odd-numbered items (i.e., 1, 3 . . . 39) and a score from only the 20 even-numbered items (i.e., 2, 4 . . . 40). The results for the first five students are as follows:

STUDENT	FROM ODDS	FROM EVENS
Elaine	14	15
Ken	7	5
Marilyn	19	3
Marva	19	20
Frank	0	13

A statistical correlation coefficient is computed from the 50 pairs of scores. The correlation coefficient is a number between −1 and +1 that indicates the consistency between the scores from the odd items and those from the even items. If, for example, the vast majority of the pairs are closely aligned, such as Elaine's, Ken's, and Marva's, the correlation coefficient will be near 1 (e.g., .85). But if the vast majority of the pairs are inconsistent, such as Marilyn's and Frank's, the correlation coefficient will be nearer to −1 (e.g., −.40). If there are about as many consistent as inconsistent pairs, the coefficient will be near 0 (e.g., .15).

When correlation coefficients are used to assess test reliability, they are referred to as *reliability coefficients*. Ordinarily, a reliability coefficient should be at least .80 before the test is judged reliable.

The second kind of model is exemplified by Kuder and Richardson (1937), who published "The Theory of Estimation of Test Reliability," in which methods were introduced that accomplish basically the same thing as the previous models. However, models based on Kuder and Richardson's work are easier to use. Instead of correlating two sets of scores that have been extracted from a test, a reliability coefficient is computed directly from scores for the whole test. Different formulas are used depending on the test's characteristics. For example, (1) the coefficient alpha formula would be appropriate for a 30-point test made up of four essay items that was administered to 25 students; (2) the Kuder-Richardson Formula 21 could be used for a 30-point test made up of 30 one-point items administered to 25 students.

Assessing Test-Retest Reliability   Theoretically, test-retest reliability is assessed by (1) administering the test to a group of students, (2) somehow preventing student achievement of what the test is supposed to measure from fluctuating, (3) readministering the test to the same group of students, and (4) correlating the two sets of scores, resulting in a reliability coefficient.

However, because of the difficulty of step 2 (i.e., *maintaining* student achievement that is constant between the test and the retest), such a method is rarely practical. Fortunately, an argument can be made that a test with internal consistency will have test-retest reliability. Thus, assessments of internal consistency (e.g., a Kuder-Richardson method) commonly double as assessments of test-retest reliability.

Assessing Intrascorer Reliability   Acceptable methods for assessing intrascorer reliability vary. However, all of them contain the features illustrated by the following example:

Mr. Martinez administers a three-item essay test to his history class. Before scoring the students' responses, he duplicates the papers on a copy machine. He puts the duplicates aside and scores the original papers and returns them to the students. Two weeks later, he retrieves the duplicates and once again scores the test. He then computes a correlation coefficient of .78 from the two sets of scores.

Mr. Martinez decides to tighten up the scoring rules for his essay items because he feels that the correlation coefficient should have been higher.

Assessing Interscorer Reliability   Interscorer reliability is assessed in a similar way. However, instead of correlating the scores obtained by the same teacher at two different times, the scores obtained by two different teachers are correlated.

Sources for Further Information   If you are interested in learning how to assess reliability, here are some sources:

Berk, R. A. (1984). Selecting the index of reliability. In R. A. Berk (Ed.), *A guide to criterion-referenced test construction* (pp. 231–265). Baltimore: Johns Hopkins University Press.

Brennan, R. L. (1984). Estimating the dependability of scores. In R. A. Berk (Ed.), *A guide to criterion-referenced test construction* (pp. 292–334). Baltimore: Johns Hopkins University Press.

Cangelosi, J. S. (1982). *Measurement and evaluation: An inductive approach for teachers* (pp. 255–307). Dubuque, IA: W. C. Brown.

Ebel, R. L. (1965). *Measuring educational achievement* (pp. 308–343). Englewood Cliffs, NJ: Prentice-Hall.

Frisbie, D. A. (1988). Reliability of scores from teacher-made tests. *Educational Measurement Issues and Practice, 7,* 25–35.

Kubiszyn, T., & Borich, G. (1987). *Educational testing and measurement: Classroom application and practice* (2nd ed., pp. 291–301). Glenview, IL: Scott, Foresman.

Nunnally, J. C. (1978). *Psychometric theory* (2nd ed., pp. 225–255). New York: McGraw-Hill.

ITEM ANALYSIS

Besides assessing relevance and reliability, test validation studies often examine the quality of each item of the test. Data on individual items are used to improve the test by replacing or modifying faulty items.

Procedures for examining item quality are generally referred to as *item analysis*. There are many item analysis models. Some use advanced statistical routines; others require only fundamental arithmetic. Most models focus on how well an item discriminates between responses of students with high scores on the test and those with low scores. Items that correlate positively with the rest of the test tend to enhance the test's reliability.

Chapters 4 through 7 should help you design items that would stand up to item analysis. Sources of information on item analysis include the following:

Berk, R. A. (1984). Conducting the item analysis. In R. A. Berk (Ed.), *A guide to criterion-referenced test construction* (pp. 97–142). Baltimore: Johns Hopkins University Press.

Cangelosi, J. S. (1982). *Measurement and evaluation: An inductive approach for teachers* (pp. 309–340). Dubuque, IA: W. C. Brown.

Ebel, R. L. (1972). *Essentials of educational measurement* (pp. 383–405). Englewood Cliffs, NJ: Prentice-Hall.

Hambleton, R. K. & Swaminathan, H. (1985). *Item response theory* (pp. 1–52, 225–309). Boston: Kluwer-Nijhoff.

USABILITY

No matter how valid a test might be for measuring student achievements, it is of no value to you if it is too time-consuming to administer or score, costly to purchase, or threatens the well-being of your students. In other words, it must be practical for your needs. *A test is usable to the degree that it is inexpensive, brief, easy to administer and score, and does not interfere with other activities.*

COST-EFFECTIVENESS

A test is cost-effective if it is both satisfactorily valid and usable. The following example illustrates cost-effectiveness:

Mr. Alvarez wants to measure his ninth-graders' achievement of the goal for a unit on critiquing persuasive essays. (The objectives for this unit appear in Chapter 1 for the ninth-grade English unit.)

He considers developing a test in which each student would select an essay to read and then respond to questions from Mr. Alvarez in a one-to-one interview. He feels that this type of test would probably have high validity because each student would be critiquing an essay of her or his own choice and the one-to-one interview would allow Mr. Alvarez to probe the depth of students' achievements. However, he rejects this type of test because it would be too time-consuming to administer and too difficult to manage.

Next he locates a commercial test with items that seem to match the objectives. But when he discovers that the test costs $7.98 per student, he decides to find another avenue.

He decides to develop the test himself. He considers having only multiple-choice items relative to an essay that all students would be assigned to read before the test. Although, such a test would have excellent *usability*, he feels it won't be valid enough to provide meaningful evidence of achievement. He thinks students should have some choice in the essay they read and that two of the four objectives could not be effectively measured with multiple-choice items.

Finally, he settles on a test in which students select one of four possible essays and then respond to 16 multiple-choice items and two short, highly structured essay items. He believes this test will serve as an adequate compromise between the more valid interview and commercial tests and the more usable multiple-choice tests. In other words, he chooses the most *cost-effective* option.

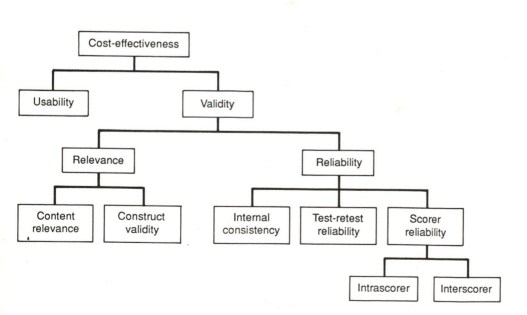

FIGURE 2.1   Components of a Cost-Effective Measurement

Figure 2.1 depicts the relationships among cost-effectiveness, usability, validity, reliability, internal consistency, test-retest reliability, intrascorer reliability, interscorer reliability, relevance, content relevance, and construct validity.

SELF-ASSESSMENT OF YOUR ACHIEVEMENT OF CHAPTER 2'S OBJECTIVES

I. Examine each of the following activities and categorize it as a (1) formative evaluation, (2) summative evaluation, or (3) measurement:
   A. Mr. Bromberg places the scores from a performance observation test in rank order.
   B. Ms. Spencer listens to Clifton recite lines from a play.
   C. Ms. Spencer decides that she should delay dress rehearsal until Clifton is more familiar with his lines.
   D. Ms. Parkinson reads students' responses to an essay item.
   E. Mr. Bromberg assigns A's to students who had the highest eight scores on a test.

Compare your answers to these: The teachers in examples A, B, and D measured. In C, Ms. Spencer made a formative evaluation. In E, Mr. Bromberg made a summative evaluation.

II. For each of the following multiple-choice items, select the one response that best answers the question or correctly completes the statement:
   A. If a test validation study has been completed on a test and norms have been established for interpreting its results, the test is _____ .
      1. valid
      2. cost-effective
      3. commercially produced
      4. standardized
   B. The intrarater reliability of a test is influenced most by which one of the following?
      1. the test's construct validity
      2. the clarity of the test items' scoring keys
      3. the internal consistency of the test scores
      4. the test's content relevance
   C. Every relevant measurement has _____ .
      1. construct validity
      2. validity
      3. reliability
      4. usability
   D. A test could be valid, but *not* _____ .
      1. have content relevance
      2. be reliable

    3. be cost-effective

    4. have construct validity

E. A *reliable* test might not be cost-effective because it lacks
_____ .

    1. internal consistency

    2. interscorer reliability

    3. test-retest reliability

    4. construct validity

F. Every evaluation _____ .

    1. involves a value judgment

    2. is based on a valid measurement

    3. is based on an invalid measurement

    4. involves a well-defined behavioral construct

G. Which one of the following has the greatest influence on the
relevance of a test?

    1. the usability of the test

    2. the internal consistency of the test's scores

    3. the match between the test's items and the stated objectives

    4. whether the stated objectives emphasize intellectual-level
achievement or only knowledge-level achievement

H. A test is valid if it _____ .

    1. is usable

    2. has been item-analyzed

    3. has a reliability coefficient greater than .85

    4. is cost-effective

I. A test validation study is supposed to _____ .

    1. provide data on the relevance and reliability of a test

    2. enhance the validity of a test

    3. determine whether or not a test is usable

    4. provide either a formative or summative evaluation

J. A test cannot be valid unless it _____ .

    1. is usable

    2. has undergone a validation study

    3. is internally consistent

    4. is cost-effective

K. A test item that requires knowledge-of-a-process behavior of
students but is used to measure achievement of an application
objective lacks _____ .

    1. content relevance

    2. internal consistency

    3. interscorer reliability

    4. construct validity

L. If test items that actually measure students' recall of addition
facts are used to measure their recall of historical facts, the items
lack which one of the following?

1. content relevance
2. internal consistency
3. intrascorer reliability
4. construct validity

Compare your choices to the following key: A-4, B-2, C-1, D-3, E-4, F-1, G-3, H-4, I-1, J-3, K-4, L-1.

III. Select one of the learning objectives you wrote for exercise IV in Chapter 1's self-assessment. Develop three test items with the following stipulations:
   A. The first item should be relevant to the objective you selected.
   B. The second item should have content relevance to your objective but lack relevance.
   C. The third item should have construct validity for your objective but lack relevance.

Be sure you include a scoring key for the three items. Finally, exchange your work on this exercise with someone and critique one another's papers.

CHAPTER 3

Creating Cost-Effective Achievement Tests

GOAL OF CHAPTER 3

Chapter 3 describes a process for designing and constructing cost-effective achievement tests. More specifically, Chapter 3 will help you to

1. List and explain the following seven steps in the process for designing and constructing an achievement test: (a) clarify the learning goal, (b) develop a test blueprint, (c) obtain relevant test item pools, (d) synthesize the test, (e) administer the test, (f) score the test, and (g) determine cutoff scores (*Cognitive: comprehension of a communication*)
2. Believe your time is more efficiently utilized when you follow the process suggested here for designing and constructing achievement tests rather than when you produce tests in a less systematic manner (*Affective: appreciation*)
3. Develop a table of specifications for each unit you teach and explain the rationale for your weighting of the objectives (*Cognitive: application*)
4. Develop a blueprint for each achievement test you plan to administer to your students (*Cognitive: application*)
5. Organize a system for maintaining item pools that enhances your capability of producing cost-effective tests (*Cognitive: application*)
6. Explain how the manner in which a test's items are organized, the test is administered, and the test is scored can influence the test's validity (*Cognitive: conceptualization*)
7. Develop a plan for administering tests to your students that minimizes distractions, misunderstanding of directions, cheating, and other potential contaminants to measurement reliability (*Cognitive: application*)
8. Explain how a criterion-referenced method for setting cutoff scores differs from a norm-referenced method (*Cognitive: conceptualization*)
9. Develop a plan for reviewing the results of tests with your students that provides productive learning experiences (*Cognitive: application*)

10. State the definition of the following: *table of specifications, power test, timed test, item format, easy item, moderate item, hard item, item pool, test blueprint, criterion-referenced method for setting cutoff scores,* and *norm-referenced method for setting cutoff scores* (*Cognitive: simple knowledge*)

A SYSTEMATIC APPROACH TO TEST CONSTRUCTION

Reread the example on page 4 in which Mr. Little constructs a test for his unit on the U.S. Constitution. Mr. Little's haphazard method for producing achievement tests is commonly practiced by many teachers, but it is unlikely to result in cost-effective tests that accurately reflect student achievement of learning goals. A more systematic approach is needed to produce achievement tests that are both valid and usable.

This chapter proposes a systematic test construction process. Once you have gained some experience using this process and have become adept at applying it, you will discover that (1) Your tests are more valid than those developed by your colleagues who use Mr. Little's method and (2) you have a mechanism for reducing the time it takes you to produce a test.

CLARIFYING THE LEARNING GOAL

THE FIRST STEP IN THE PROCESS

You can hardly be expected to create an achievement test if you don't understand what is meant by *student achievement*. Thus, the first step in the test design and construction process is to clarify the learning goal to which the test is supposed to be relevant.

SPECIFYING A SET OF OBJECTIVES

As indicated in Chapter 1, a learning goal is the composite of specific *learning objectives*. These objectives should, of course, be listed and categorized by behavioral constructs when a teaching unit is being planned. Thus, to begin clarifying what your achievement test is to measure, you simply retrieve the goal and objectives from the unit plan.

RELATIVE IMPORTANCE OF THE OBJECTIVES

Near the end of Chapter 1 there are seven lists of learning objectives, each list defining the goal of a teaching unit. The units range from kindergarten language arts to high school physical education. Select one of the seven learning goals that most closely resembles a goal for a unit that you might teach.

Do some of the objectives on the list you chose strike you as being more important to goal achievement than others? For example, what is more important in achieving the goal of the fourth-grade social studies unit on the Constitution, objective D or E? The answer, of course, is a matter of professional opinion. Mr. Little, who assembled objectives A through I for the unit in the first place, responded to the question as follows:

"It's important for my students to achieve both objectives D and E. I hadn't really thought about one objective being any more important than another before now. However, I must admit that objective E, explaining the general provisions of the Bill of Rights, is more critical to my fourth-graders' understanding of the Constitution than their abilities to explain Mason's, Randolph's, and Gerry's rationales—although I wouldn't want to neglect teaching for objective D!"

If one objective is more important to goal achievement than another, shouldn't a test for achievement of that goal be designed so that the more important objective is emphasized to a greater extent than the less important objective? To help Mr. Little design a test for the unit that would emphasize more important objectives, he was asked to rank the nine objectives of his unit according to importance. His rankings are as follows:

FIRST

H. Given a description of a well-publicized current issue, determines what, if any, bearing the Constitution has on the resolution of that issue (*Cognitive: application*)

THREE-WAY TIE FOR SECOND

A. States that the purpose of the Constitution is to provide a general plan for governing the United States (*Cognitive: simple knowledge*)

B. Lists the general parts of the original Constitution as the Preamble and seven articles (with the subject of each article) (*Cognitive: simple knowledge*)

E. Explains the general provisions in the Bill of Rights (*Cognitive: comprehension of a communication*)

FIFTH

F. Explains at least four amendments that have been added since the Bill of Rights (*Cognitive: comprehension of a communication*)

SIXTH

G. Describes the general process for amending the Constitution (*Cognitive: knowledge of a process*)

SEVENTH

I. Believes that the Constitution serves a valuable purpose (*Affective: appreciation*)

TWO-WAY TIE FOR EIGHTH

C. Lists facts from the following:

> In 1787, 43 people wrote the Constitution in a four-month-long Constitutional Convention in Philadelphia. Forty of the 43 signed the document on September 17. The Bill of Rights was added in 1791. (*Cognitive: simple knowledge*)

D. Explains George Mason's, Edmund Randolph's, and Elbridge Gerry's reasons for refusing to sign the document (*Cognitive: comprehension of a communication*)

WEIGHTING OBJECTIVES

Next, Mr. Little was asked to rate the relative importance of each of the nine objectives by *weighting* each as a percentage of the goal. His response was as follows:

"Objective H should have the highest weight because it's the most important. But I don't know how to start assigning it a percentage of the goal. . . . Oh! I've got an idea. There are nine objectives, so if each were equally important they'd each be about 11 percent of the goal (100/9 = 11.111). So, objective H will surely be weighted more than 11 percent and the least important objectives, C and D, will each be weighted somewhat less than 11 percent.

Objectives H, A, B, E, and F are all critical to understanding the impact of the Constitution. They are a lot more important than the others. Those five objectives make up about 75 percent of the goal. So I could start with that idea, having those five average around 15 percent each (75/5 = 15) with H counting the most and F the least of those five. Okay, I'll weight A, B, and E 15 percent each, H 18 percent, and F 12 percent.

That leaves 25 percent for the last four objectives. I'll make it 9 percent for G, 8 percent for I, and 4 percent each for C and D."

The example illustrates how a teacher should *weight* the objectives in planning an achievement test. The method may appear somewhat unscientific

TABLE 3.1 Table of Specifications for
Mr. Little's Test

Objective	Weight (percentage)
A	15
B	15
C	4
D	4
E	15
F	12
G	9
H	18
I	8

and off-the-cuff. However, it provides a mechanism for teachers to reflect on and control what their tests will emphasize. If you haphazardly construct a test without first weighting objectives, you are likely to neglect some important objectives and overemphasize others.

TABLE OF SPECIFICATIONS

A list of weighted objectives to be measured by a test is referred to as a *table of specifications*. Table 3.1 shows the *table of specifications* that resulted from Mr. Little's weighting of the objectives for his unit on the Constitution.

DEVELOPING A TEST BLUEPRINT

THE SECOND STEP IN THE PROCESS

After the learning goal is clarified with a list of objectives and a table of specifications, the next step is to develop a test blueprint. The blueprint lists the features planned for the test.

THE COMPLEXITY OF THE TEST DESIGN

Whether your test blueprint should describe a complex or a simple test design depends in large measure on (1) how sophisticated your students are in taking tests and (2) the nature of the learning goal.

Obviously, the type of items planned for a test is limited by the reading and writing levels of students and by their previous test-taking experiences. For example,

Ms. Morgan is planning to measure her kindergarten students' achievement from a language arts unit intended to help students associate the appropriate consonant sounds with the letters *b*, *d*, and *g*. She realizes that for such young, inexperienced children, the test will have to be administered to one student at a time. This requirement complicates her test design because provisions must be made for keeping the class occupied as one-to-one interview items are administered.

Ms. Morgan thinks to herself, "It's times like these when I think how nice it would be to have pupils who could already read and write and were used to taking tests. Then, I could test them all at once."

Tests for achievement of objectives that specify only the simpler behavioral constructs (e.g., simple knowledge and knowledge of a process) do not typically need plans that are as elaborate as those for more complex behavioral constructs (e.g., conceptualization and willingness to act). Examine any one of the lists of objectives just before the Self-Assessment exercises near the end of Chapter 1. Imagine how much simpler it would be to plan tests if only the knowledge-level objectives were included.

ADMINISTRATION TIME

Validity considerations must be compromised with usability considerations. Generally speaking, longer tests are more likely to have greater validity than shorter tests. However, longer tests usually take more time to administer and are consequently less usable. Plans for your tests are influenced by how much time you are willing to take away from classroom learning activities and devote to testing. Thus, the test blueprint should indicate how much time can be allotted for administering the test.

More time must be allotted for your test if it is to be primarily a *power* rather than a *timed* test. *Power tests* are those that provide ample time for all students to respond to all items. *Timed tests* place a premium on students' abilities to respond to items quickly and do not generally provide enough time for all students to respond to all items. As explained in Chapters 4 and 5, timed tests are often appropriate for measuring objectives that specify knowledge-level behavioral constructs, whereas power tests are more appropriate for intellectual-level behavioral constructs.

For some testing situations, especially when the learning goal is complex or when the students are young and shouldn't be expected to sit for an extended test administration, consider administering the test in a number of short sessions over several days. Do not limit your test plans by thinking that each test must be confined to a single class period.

SCORING TIME

Just as there are limits on how much time your students have for taking tests, so you must also consider the amount of time you have to devote to scoring a test. Your blueprint should indicate how much time you have available for test scoring. This factor will determine the number of items and the type of items (e.g., essay items are more time-consuming to score than multiple-choice items).

ITEM FORMATS

Chapter 4 provides hints for constructing various types of items according to the item *format* (e.g., short answer, multiple choice, true/false, matching, essay, performance observation, and interview). Chapters 5 through 7 will help you relate the appropriateness of different items formats with the behavioral constructs you want measured.

Thus, as you plan the test, examine the objectives and the table of specifications and indicate in your blueprint the formats for items you expect to include.

NUMBER OF ITEMS

It is generally desirable to include as many items as you can after you've considered (1) the time you've allotted for administering the test, (2) the time you've scheduled for scoring the test, (3) whether it is a power or a timed test, (4) the item formats, and (5) the table of specifications. The test blueprint should include an estimate of the number of items.

DIFFICULTY OF ITEMS

For reasons explained in a subsequent section of this chapter, you should be concerned with how many of the test's items should be relatively easy, how many should be moderately difficult, and how many should be especially challenging even for students with advanced levels of achievement. The blueprint should communicate the desired distribution of items in the test according to their difficulty.

ESTIMATE OF THE MAXIMUM NUMBER OF POINTS ON THE TEST

Many teachers automatically set the total number of points for each test at 100. This practice is generally discouraged by educational measurement specialists, who prefer the maximum point total to be determined by the number and complexity of the items. If all items are scored either $+1$ or 0, as would be appropriate for multiple-choice items, the maximum number of points for the test would equal the number of items. However, some types of items (e.g., essay items) provide for responses that are not simply "right" or "wrong"; they have scoring keys that allow for a wider range of scores (e.g., 0, +1, +2, +3, or +4). Item 7 from Ms. Curry's 22-item test in Chapter 2 is one such item.

While developing the test blueprint, you should estimate the maximum possible test score by multiplying the number of items planned for the test by an approximation of the average maximum score per item. Only an approximate figure is needed for the blueprint.

NUMBER OF POINTS FOR EACH OBJECTIVE

Because you want your test to emphasize more important over less important objectives, you should distribute the maximum number of test points according to the table of specifications. Suppose for example, that Mr. Little estimated that his unit test on the Constitution would have a maximum score of 60. He should then use the table of specifications from Table 3.1 to determine the proportion of the 60 that should relate to each objective. The results appear in Table 3.2.

The number of points planned for each objective is critical information for the enhancement of test relevance. Thus, it should be included in the test blueprint.

METHOD FOR DETERMINING CUTOFF SCORES

Suppose Mr. Little plans to use his 60-point test on the Constitution to make summative evaluations that influence students' grades. He's faced with decisions regarding how scores (e.g., 44, 31, 50, 29, 44, 17, and 35) should be converted to grades (e.g., A, C, and D). Such decisions raise issues regarding how *cutoff scores* should be identified. Methods for determining cutoff scores are alluded to in a subsequent section of this chapter and are dealt with in some detail in Chapter 9.

The method for determining cutoff scores should be identified in the test blueprint.

TABLE 3.2   Point Distribution for Test Based on Mr. Little's Table of Specifications

Objective	Weight (percentage)	Computation	Test Points
A	15	.15 × 60	9
B	15	.15 × 60	9
C	4	.04 × 60	2 or 3
D	4	.04 × 60	2 or 3
E	15	.15 × 60	9
F	12	.12 × 60	7 or 8
G	9	.09 × 60	5 or 6
H	18	.18 × 60	10 or 11
I	8	.08 × 60	4 or 5
	100		About 60

TEST OUTLINE

Finally, the test blueprint should include an outline indicating the sections and subsections of the test and where such things as directions will occur.

Figure 3.1 is a sample test blueprint that might help Mr. Little in the planning of his test on the Constitution.

OBTAINING ITEM POOLS

THE THIRD STEP IN THE PROCESS

An *item pool is a collection of test items that are all designed to be relevant to the same learning objective.* The *third step* in the test design and construction process is to obtain an item pool for each objective to be measured. This step can be the most difficult one in the process if the test you're creating is to be relevant to objectives that you've never before attempted to measure. However, once you have built a collection of items for each objective, you may only need to retrieve preexisting item pools.

THE ADVANTAGES OF ITEM POOLS

There are five reasons to utilize item pools:

1. The act of building item pools focuses your attention on one objective at a time, stimulating you to expand your ideas on how student achievement of each objective can be demonstrated.
2. Each item in a pool is designed to focus on the content and behavioral construct specified by an objective. Thus, a test constructed with items drawn from pools is more likely to be relevant than a test with items that are designed as the test is being put together.
3. Having an item pool available for each objective before items are actually chosen for a test makes it easier to construct the test according to the table of specifications.
4. If test items from item pools, student performances on various items provide specific information on *which objectives* were achieved. Being able to associate each item with a particular objective provides the diagnostic information needed for formative evaluations.
5. It is easier to create and improve tests after a system for maintaining and expanding item pools has been implemented.

DESIRABLE CHARACTERISTICS OF AN ITEM POOL

ITEM COMPONENTS

Each item in a pool is made up of a (1) *task for students to confront* and (2) *scoring key* indicating how students' responses to the task will be observed and quantified. Here are some examples:

UNIT: Fourth-Grade Social Studies: U.S. Constitution

ADMINISTRATION TIME: In 2 sessions:

1. Parts I & II on Wed., Jan. 25, 1:10–2:00.
2. Parts III & IV on Thurs., Jan. 26, 1:10–1:35.

SCORING TIME:

1. Part I to be scored by aide Wed. between 2:45 and 3:15.
2. Part II to be scored by me as administered.
3. Parts III & IV scored by me Thursday between 3:15 and 5:00.

ITEM FORMATS:

Objective	Format of Items
A	multiple choice & short answer
B	multiple choice & short answer
C	multiple choice
D	multiple choice
E	multiple choice & interview
F	multiple choice
G	essay
H	multiple choice
I	essay

NUMBER OF ITEMS: 40–45

DIFFICULTY OF ITEMS:

Average test score should be about half the maximum total, with approximately 33% of the items easy, 33% moderate, and 33% hard. These ratios should be nearly consistent across all 9 objectives.

MAXIMUM NUMBER OF POINTS: 60

FIGURE 3.1   Sample Test Blueprint

Objective H of Mr. Little's unit on the Constitution reads, "Given a description of a well-publicized current issue, determines what, if any, bearing the Constitution has on the resolution of that issue (*Cognitive: application*)."

After discovering the efficiency of using item pools in test construction, Mr. Little stored the following items in his pool for objective H:

1. *Task presented to the students:*
   (Multiple choice) Annie is a ten-year-old U.S. citizen. She says, "Since the Nineteenth Amendment gives females the right to vote, it's against the U.S. Constitution to make me wait until I'm 18 years old to vote." Select the answer that best explains why Annie is incorrect.
   a. Annie would be correct if this were 1920, when the Nineteenth Amendment was ratified. But she lives now, so her rights under the Nineteenth Amendment aren't being violated.

MAXIMUM NUMBER OF POINTS FOR EACH OBJECTIVE:

Objective	Points
A	9
B	9
C	2 or 3
D	2 or 3
E	9
F	7 or 8
G	5 or 6
H	10 or 11
I	4 or 5

METHOD FOR DETERMINING CUTOFF SCORES:

The *compromise method* (explained in Chapter 10) will be used to convert test scores to letter grades.

TEST OUTLINE:

First Session

Part I: 38 multiple-choice items, 1 point each. Directions given orally to the group as a whole. Items distributed among the 9 objectives as follows:

A-5, B-5, C-3, D-3, E-5, F-7, G-0, H-10, I-0

Part II: One 4-point interview item relevant to objective E. Individually administered one to one while group takes Part I.

Second Session

Part III: Two 4-point short-answer items, 1 relevant to objective A, the other to objective B. Directions to be read by students.

Part IV: Two 5-point essay items, 1 relevant to objective I, the other to objective G. Directions to be read by students.

FIGURE 3.1   (continued)

 b. Annie is not allowed to vote for the same reason that ten-year-old males are not allowed to vote. So her rights under the Nineteenth Amendment aren't being violated.

 c. The Constitution and its amendments provide adult U.S. citizens with rights and freedoms. Annie is a minor, and thus the Constitution does not apply to her.

Scoring key: +1 only if b is selected; otherwise 0.

2. *Task presented to the students:*

(Short answer) Some members of a town council want to pass a law requiring people to pass a gun-safety test *before* they are allowed to own a gun. Write two sentences explaining how the U.S. Constitution *discourages* such a law. Write two more sentences explaining how the U.S. Constitution *encourages* such a law.

Scoring key: (4 points possible) +1 if the first two sentences include a reference to the Second Amendment; +1 if the first two sentences suggest that such a law might mean that citizens will lose their rights to bear arms; +1 if the last two sentences include a reference to the constitutional right of local governments to pass laws to protect citizens;

+ 1 if the last two sentences include a reference to the responsibility of governments to pass laws to protect citizens.

Objective F of Ms. Curry's sixth-grade math unit on surface areas reads, "Given the dimensions of a right triangle, computes its area (*Cognitive: knowledge of a process*)."

The following items are included in Ms. Curry's pool for objective F:

1. *Task presented to the students:*
   What is the area of the following triangle?

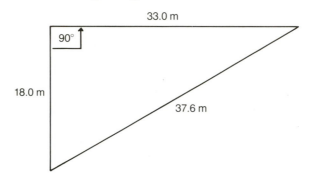

   Display your computations here.
   Scoring key: (5 points possible) +1 if the formula for the area of a right triangle is used; +1 if 33 and 18 are the only given dimensions used in the formula; +1 if 33 and 18 are properly substituted for variables in the formula; +1 if 297 is the answer; +1 if the answer is expressed in square meters.

2. *Task presented to the students:*
   The sides of a right triangle measure 11.2 inches, 12.2 inches, and 4.9 inches. What is the triangle's area in square inches?
   a. 27.44   **b.** 28.30   **c.** 59.78
   d. 68.32   **e.** 334.77   **f.** 669.54
   Scoring key: +1 for a only; otherwise 0.

VARIETY OF ITEM FORMATS

Some students are particularly adept at responding to essay items. Others may respond better to multiple-choice or performance-observation items. However, you want your achievement tests to provide information relevant to your students' achievement of learning goals, not be a measure of how well they take certain types of tests.

A test with a greater variety of item formats (e.g., multiple choice, essay, one-to-one interview, and performance observation) provides students with more opportunities to display their achievement levels for the test's objectives than a test with fewer types of item formats (e.g., multiple choice only). Thus, you should consider a mixture of item formats in each of your item pools.

ITEM DIFFICULTY

Compare the three items in the following example:

Objective I of Ms. Curry's sixth-grade math unit on surface area reads, "When confronted with a real-life problem, determines whether or not computing a surface area will help solve that problem (*Cognitive: application*)."

Three of the items included in Ms. Curry's item pool for objective I are the following.

1. *Task presented to the students:*
   (Multiple-choice) Carpet is to be bought for the rectangular-shaped floor of a room. The room is 8 feet high, 12 feet wide, and 15 feet long. Which of the following computations would be the most helpful in deciding how much carpet to buy?
   a. $12' + 8' + 15'$
   b. $2' \times (12' + 15')$
   c. $12' \times 8' \times 15'$
   d. $12' \times 15'$
   Scoring key: +1 for d only; otherwise 0.
2. *Task presented to the students:*
   Suppose we want to build book shelves across one wall of our classroom. The shelves are to be 18 inches apart. Which one of the following numbers would be most helpful in figuring how many shelves we can fit on the wall?
   a. area of the wall
   b. width of the wall
   c. height of the wall
   d. perimeter of the wall
   Scoring key: +1 for c only; otherwise 0.
3. *Task presented to the students:*
   (Multiple choice) The 13 steps of a staircase are to be painted. Each step is 36 inches wide, 12 inches deep, and 7 inches high. Which of the following computations would be most helpful in determining how much paint will be needed?
   a. $[(12'' \times 13) \times (7'' \times 13)]/2$
   b. $36'' \times [13 \times (12'' \times 7'')]$
   c. $(13 \times 7'') \times (36'' + 12'')$
   d. $13 \times [(36'' \times 7'') + (36'' \times 12'')]$
   Scoring key: +1 for d only; otherwise 0.

Which of the three items in the example do you think will be the easiest for Ms. Curry's sixth-graders? Which will be the hardest?

Easy Items   From her experience in testing students, Ms. Curry predicts that between 75 percent and 100 percent of her students will respond correctly to the first of the three items in the example. An item is defined as *easy* for a group of students if *more than 75 percent of the group accurately responds to that item* on a test. A test needs a number of easy items to measure relatively low levels of achievement. Such items provide information about students with less than average levels of achievement.

Moderate Items   If *between 25 percent and 75 percent of the students in a group accurately respond to an item* on a test, the item is considered *moderate*. Moderate items are valuable sources of information on the achievement of the majority of students. Ms. Curry predicts that the second item in the example will be a moderate item.

Hard Items   Ms. Curry expects only her students who have achieved objective I at an advanced level to respond correctly to the third item in the example. A *hard* item is one in which *fewer than 25 percent of the students correctly answer* on a test. Hard items are needed to measure relatively advanced levels of goal achievement. Unless a test has some hard items to challenge even advanced students, the achievement level of those students is undetected.

Because you want tests to provide information on what all your students have and have not achieved, you should build easy, moderate, and hard items into each item pool. With these three types of items, you can create tests for a wide range of achievement levels.

MAINTAINING ITEM POOLS

You will need to organize a secure and efficient system for maintaining and expanding item pools. The system should provide ready access to items, varying in difficulty and format, for each objective you want to measure. Your system should allow you to construct efficiently multiple tests that measure the same set of objectives.

Traditionally, item pools are maintained in file boxes or file drawers, but in recent years that task has been taken over by computer disks.

FILE BOX SYSTEM

Here is an example of a traditional system for maintaining item pools:

Over the past 11 years, Ms. Curry has taught mathematics, physical education, and health science at two junior highs and one middle school. She has accumulated a large file of item pools. The pools are secured in four drawers labeled as follows:

Drawer 1:   Sixth- & Seventh-Grade Math
Drawer 2:   Eighth- & Ninth-Grade Math
Drawer 3:   Physical Education & Health Science
Drawer 4:   Miscellaneous Units

The first three drawers are sectioned by courses that Ms. Curry has taught. For example, Drawer 1 is separated into four parts:

I.   General Sixth-Year Math
II. Fundamental Arithmetic
III. Pre-Algebra
IV. General Seventh-Year Math

Each course is subsectioned into teaching units. For example, Part I, General Sixth-Year Math, contains 28 units. Each subsection is clearly labeled with the number and name of the unit. Here is a sample of the units for Part I:

1. Numerals for Whole Numbers
5. Adding and Subtracting Fractions
7. Expressions for Rational Numbers
11. Measurement
13. Surface Area
14. Volume
22. Integers

The learning goal for a unit is written on the file separator at the beginning of its subsection. The unit subsection is further subdivided by learning objectives for the unit. Unit 13, for example, is subdivided into objectives A through I (see Figure 3.2).

Each objective's subdivision contains the item pool for its learning objective on a collection of 8-by-5-inch index cards (see Figure 3.3). Each card contains the following:

1. A reference code indicating the course, unit, and objective for which the item is designed
2. The task to be presented to the students
3. The scoring key
4. A note indicating whether the item is designed to be easy, moderate, or hard
5. A note on the history of the item if it has been used on one or more tests (e.g., percentage of students correctly responding to the item)

Whenever Ms. Curry constructs a test, she refers to the test blueprint for the number and type of items she needs from each relevant item pool. If she needs a type of item that her item pools lack, she develops new items or pools and adds them to the file. She also routinely modifies and improves items based on what she learns from including them in tests.

Ms. Curry's students are amazed at how readily she produces equivalent forms of tests for retesting or for making up tests for those who were absent.

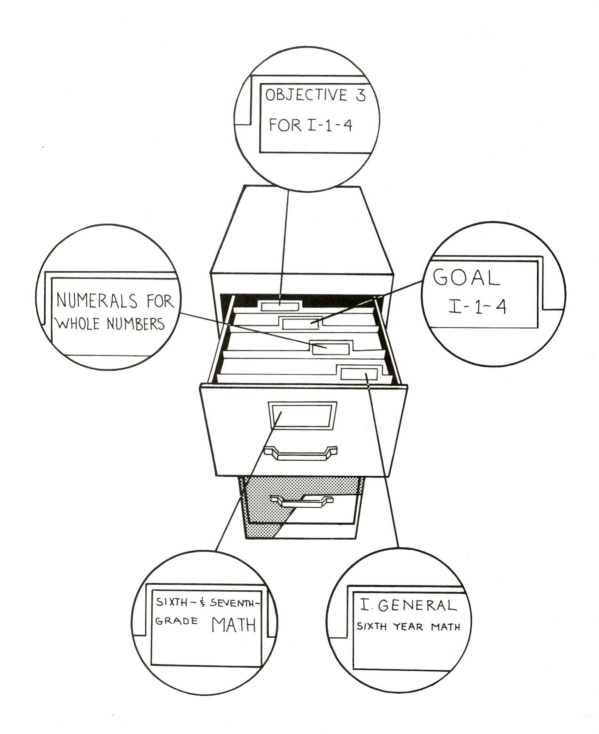

FIGURE 3.2 Drawer I of Ms. Curry's Item Pool File

(front)

I–5 Objective 4

Task presented to the students:

Bart makes a mistake and gets 21/20 when he adds 13/9 and 8/11. Write Bart a note explaining why his answer is wrong for the same reason that 10 apples plus 7 oranges is *not* "17 apple– like oranges." Use about five sentences for your note and write it here:

Scoring key:

(3 points possible) +1 for pointing out that in Bart's problem 1/9 and 1/11 are units just as an apple and an orange are the units in the analogous problem; +1 for expressing a need for a common unit (e.g., by contrasting a common denominator to "fruit"); +1 for showing that by using the sum of the denominators as the common unit, Bart made a logic error similar to treating the 17 pieces of fruit as if each is some combination of an apple and an orange.

(back)

Intended difficulty: Hard

History: 10/18/89. With 3rd & 4th periods
      – Item discriminated well & stimulated
        lively discussion during review
      20% scored 3
      15% scored 2
      60% scored 1
      5% scored 0
    1/27/90. With 2nd period
      25% scored 3
      15% scored 2
      45% scored 1
      15% scored 0

FIGURE 3.3 One of Ms. Curry's Item Pool Cards

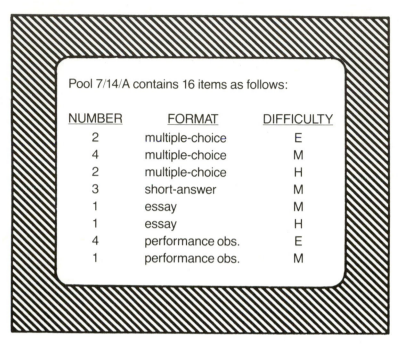

Pool 7/14/A contains 16 items as follows:

NUMBER	FORMAT	DIFFICULTY
2	multiple-choice	E
4	multiple-choice	M
2	multiple-choice	H
3	short-answer	M
1	essay	M
1	essay	H
4	performance obs.	E
1	performance obs.	M

FIGURE 3.4   A Display from Mr. Little's Computerized Item Pools

COMPUTERIZED SYSTEM

The teacher in the following example uses a microcomputer to manage item pools (see Figure 3.4).

After six years as an elementary school teacher, Mr. Little supplanted a haphazard method of constructing tests with a systematic one that utilizes item pools. His item pool file is organized similarly to Ms. Curry's. However, instead of using file drawers or boxes, Mr. Little stores the items on diskettes, accesses them with his microcomputer, and produces tests on his printer.

Mr. Little uses a commercially produced software program that facilitates organizing the file, setting up the item pools, expanding pools, retrieving items in accordance with test blueprints, synthesizing tests, and printing tests. The following is an example of how Mr. Little adds a new item to a pool:

The computer asks, "What function do you want?" Mr. Little keys in, "Add item."

COMPUTER: In what pool do you want this item (respond with course/unit/objective code)?

MR. LITTLE: 7/11/C.

COMPUTER: What is the difficulty of this item (e/m/h)?
MR. LITTLE: m.
COMPUTER: Type in the task as you want it presented to the students.
MR. LITTLE: In what year was the Bill of Rights added to the Constitution?
COMPUTER: Type in the scoring key.
MR. LITTLE: +1 for 1791 only; otherwise 0.
COMPUTER: Type in any notes you want included about this item.

Mr. Little strikes the return key.

COMPUTER: Your new item has been stored in the 7/11/C pool as Item 12. Do you want to add another item?
MR. LITTLE: n.

Mr. Little is in the process of constructing a test:

COMPUTER: What function do you want?
MR. LITTLE: Access items.
COMPUTER: From what pool (course/unit/objective)?
MR. LITTLE: 7/14/A.
COMPUTER: Do you want a table of contents for that pool?
MR. LITTLE: y.

The computer displays the table of contents shown on screen in Figure 3.4.
Mr. Little strikes the return key.

COMPUTER: Do you want to (1) view items from pool, (2) have items randomly selected for you according to parameters you specify, (3) select items yourself, or (4) move to another function?
MR. LITTLE: 3. . . .

Mr. Little continues with the program until his test is printed according to the specifications contained in the blueprint.

Software packages designed especially for maintaining item pools and constructing tests are readily available from both commercial and noncommercial sources. Computer software catalogues, computer retail stores, computer magazines, professional journals for teachers, and school district resource and media centers for teachers have information on how such software can be obtained.

Of course you do not have to have special software to maintain and manage your item pools efficiently with a computer. Many teachers use standard word-processing programs, storing each pool in a separate text file. Others prefer to write their own programs.

SYNTHESIZING THE TEST

THE FOURTH STEP IN THE PROCESS

The fourth step in the test design and construction process is to select, organize, and compile the items into a test as directed by the test blueprint. The blueprint indicates the number of items to be selected from each pool, their formats, and the difficulty levels.

ITEM INTERACTION

Consider the following example:

Following the blueprint given in Figure 3.1, Mr. Little selects items for his unit test on the Constitution so that the tasks for multiple-choice items 3 and 4 are as follows:

3. How many people signed the Constitution at the Constitutional Convention?
   a. 40   **b.** 42   **c.** 43   **d.** 45
4. George Mason was one of the three authors of the Constitution who refused to sign it. According to his statements, he probably would have signed the document if it had included which one of the following:
   a. the Twentieth through the Twenty-fifth Amendments
   b. a more clearly stated Preamble
   c. the first ten amendments
   d. assurances that the delegates would be paid for their work

When she gets to item 3, Judith, one of Mr. Little's students, thinks, "I don't remember how many signed it. But 43 wrote it, so the answer must be c." For item 4 Judith thinks, "I don't have a clue about which one of these is right. But, oh look! It says three authors didn't sign it, so I'll change my answer on number 3 to a."

Although Mr. Little followed the test blueprint, he contaminated test validity by selecting an item that *interacts* with another. Judith had a correct response to item 3, not because she had achieved its objective, but because she drew information from item 4.

When compiling items into a test, select and arrange them so that one item does not interfere with how well another measures its objective.

SEQUENCING ITEMS

Look at the test outline section of the test blueprint in Figure 3.1. Items are grouped by format. The test is organized so that students can dispense with items that have less time-consuming formats (e.g., multiple choice) before confronting items with more time-consuming formats (e.g., essay). Grouping together items with the same format simplifies the directions for the test and prevents students from having to reorient their thinking frequently because of a change of format.

At least for timed tests, items within the same part of a test (e.g., Part I from the test outline of Figure 3.1) should generally be sequenced from easiest to hardest. This format helps students avoid spending so much time on difficult items that they never get to some of the easier items. The easy-to-hard arrangement isn't necessary for power tests.

DIRECTIONS TO STUDENTS

Because you want your test to discriminate among various levels of goal achievement and not among various abilities to follow the test directions, it is critical for directions to be easy for all students to follow. Directions need to be written *below* the reading comprehension level of *all* students; oral directions need to be below their listening comprehension levels.

Suggestions for designing items so that directions are simple and unlikely to be misunderstood are included in Chapter 4.

ADMINISTERING THE TEST

THE FIFTH STEP IN THE PROCESS

A scientific experiment is the application of systematic procedures for the purpose of uncovering evidence that helps answer a specified question. An achievement test is a type of scientific experiment in which the question to be answered is how well students have achieved a particular learning goal. The experimental conditions (e.g., time and environment) of a test should be controlled to prevent results from being influenced by variables other than student achievement. Proper control of test conditions is a function of how the test is administered, the fifth step in the test design and construction process.

MINIMIZING DISTRACTIONS

Failure to manage the test environment properly leads to distractions that threaten measurement reliability in the following example.

Mr. Little is administering the first session of the test whose blueprint appears in Figure 3.1. He is seated at his desk in the front of the room just finishing the one-to-one interview item with Marjorie as the other students work on the multiple-choice part. Dan is trying to answer multiple-choice item 11, related to objective C, as Mr. Little announces, "Okay, next let me have Kevin up here. The rest of you go on." The announcement breaks Dan's trend of thought about item 11, and he chooses an incorrect response. However, he is not distracted as he thinks about item 12, also relevant to objective C, so he selects the correct response.

As Kevin walks to the front for the interview item, he jabs Kristine with his pen as she is about to circle an incorrect choice for item 23. This rude act disrupts her so much that she unintentionally circles the correct response to that item. Items 23 and 27 are both relevant to objective F. Kristine fails to answer item 27 correctly.

Nine students have completed the multiple-choice items with 15 minutes remaining for the test. Some of them entertain themselves with talking and movement that are distracting to those still taking the test.

Distraction-caused inconsistencies in Dan's, Kristine's, and other students' test results tend to contaminate measurement *reliability*. Had Mr. Little applied some very basic classroom management strategies to the administration of this test, distractions could have been avoided. Here are some suggestions for minimizing distractions during the administration of tests:

1. Anticipate times and locations when interruptions (e.g., public address announcements, band practice, outside visitors, building construction, and custodial work) are likely to interfere with test administration. Work out compromises between your testing schedule and the scheduling of potentially disruptive events.

2. Establish and enforce rules and procedures for conduct that minimize disruptive behaviors (e.g., Kevin jabbing Kristine with a pen) during test administrations. Practical suggestions for such rules and procedures are included in the following references:

    Cangelosi, J. S. (1986). *Cooperation in the classroom: Students and teachers together* (pp. 28–37). Washington, DC: National Education Association.

    ———. (1988). *Classroom management strategies: Gaining and maintaining students' cooperation* (pp. 111–128). White Plains, NY: Longman.

    Emmer, E. T., Evertson, C. M., Sanford, J. P., Clements, B. S., & Worsham, M. E. (1984). *Classroom management for secondary teachers* (pp. 15–38). Englewood Cliffs, NJ: Prentice-Hall.

    Evertson, C. M., Emmer, E. T., Clements, B. S., Sanford, J. P., & Worsham, M. E. (1984). *Classroom management for elementary teachers* (pp. 15–35). Englewood Cliffs, NJ: Prentice-Hall.

    Jones, V. F., & Jones, L. S. (1986). *Comprehensive classroom management: Creating positive learning environments* (2nd ed., pp. 396–416). Boston: Allyn & Bacon.

3. Have constructive activities planned for students who complete tests ahead of schedule. Students should be conditioned to begin these

activities (e.g., a homework assignment or reading) without disturbing those still being tested. Mr. Little, for example, might put a note at the end of the multiple-choice section of the test directing each student to quietly (a) remain seated, (b) turn the test paper over and place it on his or her desk, and (c) work on Exercises 7, 8, 9, and 12 from page 188 until Mr. Little announces that the test is over.

4. Model nondisruptive behaviors yourself during test administrations. Emphasize the serious, businesslike nature of test conditions. Instead of repeatedly disturbing the whole class by asking students to come up to his desk for the interview item, Mr. Little should have organized a less disturbing system, such as the following:

> The student who sits in the first desk of the first row is interviewed first. When she finishes, she quietly walks over to the second student in the row and gently taps him on the shoulder. He recognizes this as his cue to be interviewed. The procedure continues until the whole class has taken the interview item.

Mr. Little models appropriate, businesslike behavior for students in the following example:

> During the test, Mr. Little's principal comes to the doorway and asks Mr. Little, "Do you know about the change in time for tonight's meeting?" Instead of answering from across the room, Mr. Little frowns and silently gestures with his hands that he doesn't want to disturb the students while they are taking a test. He then quickly writes the principal a note and quietly brings it to her at the door.

5. Proofread the test before distributing copies. You do not want to disturb students during the test to correct errors (e.g., typographical).

FOLLOWING DIRECTIONS FOR TEST ADMINISTRATION

A test should be designed to be administered in a particular fashion. Deviations from the administration plan threaten measurement reliability. For example, the items on Mr. Little's test on the Constitution were all designed for students to answer without the benefit of hints or prompts. Mr. Little would probably be risking the consistency of test results if he "generously" responded to students' queries about items with hints.

MONITORING STUDENTS

Students need to be supervised while taking tests just as they should be during any other school-related activity. Proper monitoring is essential to protect students from being disturbed by others and to prevent some students from cheating. Besides being an unethical, distasteful practice, cheating reduces measurement reliability by creating inconsistencies in students' responses. For example, two items may both be relevant to the same objective, and a student cheats on one but not the other. Consequently, the test results provide conflicting evidence on the student's achievement of that objective.

PREVENTING CHEATING

Consider these nine incidents of student cheating:

Angee gets up from her desk, walks over to the classroom pencil sharpener, and returns to her desk to complete the multiple-choice science test she and the rest of her sixth-grade classmates are taking. During her walk, Angee looked on several other students' papers to find out how they responded to certain items that she couldn't answer.

A calculus teacher, Mr. Kruhl, scores test papers by writing down the number of "points off" by each item a student doesn't correctly answer. Mr. Kruhl does not mark anything by correctly answered items; he simply subtracts the number of points for incorrect items from the maximum possible score of 100. Jack, one of Mr. Kruhl's students, realizes this after his first calculus test is returned. When Jack is about to begin taking the second calculus test, he thinks, "I'll never have time to complete this 12-page monster in the 90 minutes Kruhl's allowing us. I'll just rip out pages 6 and 9 and discard them. He'll probably just pass over them and not realize they're missing. If he does catch it, I'll just say they were never there." Several days later, Mr. Kruhl returns Jack's paper with a score derived by subtracting the number of points off for incorrect items from 100. Jack's score is the same as it would have been if Jack had correctly responded to all of the items on pages 6 and 9.

June did not study for the history exam that Ms. Tolbert is giving today. Instead, June memorized the answers to an old unit test that Ms. Tolbert had administered to one of June's friends in a previously held class. June is overjoyed when Ms. Tolbert hands her a test identical to the one her friend shared.

Twelfth graders Kraemer, Tom, and Arthur engage Ms. Hubert in a lively conversation before school as their co-conspirator, Mary Ellen, steals four copies of the final physics exam scheduled for that afternoon off of Ms. Hubert's desk. During the morning study hall, the four students jointly figure out the answers and each fills out a copy of the test. They make sure that there are some minor discrepancies among their papers. When Ms. Hubert administers the test, the four carefully substitute their completed copies for the ones distributed by Ms. Hubert.

Sonia, an eighth-grade student, runs a popular service for her schoolmates at Abraham Lincoln High School. Sonia searches trash containers for used duplicating carbons and masters that have been discarded in the faculty lounge or school office. From her growing "test file," she provides test information to her many "friends." Sonia feels very popular with her peers.

"May I please be excused to go to the restroom?" Mickey asks Mr. Green during a fourth-grade spelling test.

MR. GREEN: "Yes, but hurry so you will have plenty of time to finish your test."
MICKEY: "I will. Thank you very much." In the restroom, Mickey extracts a spelling list that earlier in the day he had hidden under a toilet. He quickly checks the spelling of the four words from the test that he does not know.

As Mr. Duetchman supervises a large group of high school students taking a two-day-long achievement test battery, he finds it curious that Donna frequently brings her elbows together and stares down the neckline of her dress. Not knowing what to do, he dismisses her behavior as a reflection of adolescent self-consciousness. Actually, Donna has a "cheat sheet" attached to the inside of her bra.

Ms. Bolden instructs her first graders to keep their test papers covered and not to let classmates see their answers while taking a math test. Ashley and Monica are sitting at the same table taking the test when Monica turns to Ashley and, pointing to one of her test items, says,

"I forgot what this one is."
ASHLEY: Ms. Bolden said you weren't supposed to show me your paper! Cover it up.
MONICA: Sorry! But I need some help on this one.
ASHLEY: Okay, don't show me your paper. Just read it to me.
MONICA: What's this called?

Monica draws a rectangle in the air with her finger.

ASHLEY: Let me see what I just put for that. But don't look on my paper while I look. It's not allowed.

Ashley turns back to Monica, still carefully covering her paper, and says, "It's a rectangle."

Freda takes a lengthy psychology test and leaves several short-answer, written-response items blank. Her teacher, Mr. Zabriski, scores the test and returns them to the class the following day. The items Freda left blank are marked with zeroes, but she quickly fills in the answers and approaches Mr. Zabriski, "Mr. Zabriski, don't I get any credit for these? I thought they were at least partially correct!"

Students would have no inclination to cheat on a test if they believed that *accurate* information about their achievement in the hands of their teachers is more beneficial to them than is misinformation that deceives their teachers. Once again, three vital principles become apparent:

1. The self-worth students perceive and the respect, love, and esteem others (including teachers) feel for them should never be dependent upon their achievements.
2. Formative evaluations of students' achievements should be emphasized to a far greater degree than should summative evaluations.
3. Grades should only be used to communicate summative evaluations; they should not be used as a reward for achievements.

Given the unfortunate fact that there is almost universal violation of these principles, you are virtually assured of encountering students with an inclination for cheating on tests. But even with these students, cheating is unlikely when

1. *You set a businesslike tone and dispay an attitude that communicates that students are expected not to cheat.*
2. *Test administrations are closely supervised.* (Please note, however, that, as indicated by the example involving first graders Monica and Ashley in Ms. Bolden's class, the concept of cheating is not well developed in young children (e.g., under the age of nine). Primary school children do not differentiate between obtaining a correct response with unauthorized aid and obtaining it without unauthorized aid (Pulaski, 1980). Teachers should observe whether or not young children respond on their own or with unauthorized aid. Steps should be taken so that such aid is not attainable. However, warning young students not to cheat or punishing them for behaviors that adults consider to be cheating is, for them, a frustrating experience that only teaches them they are not trusted. Even with older students, warnings not to cheat are futile and

should be avoided. However, students should not be given reasonable opportunities to cheat.)

3. *The same form of a test is not used repeatedly.*
4. *You account for each copy of a test that is duplicated (copies can be numbered) and materials, such as duplicating masters, are secured.*
5. *You mark test papers so that points are added for correct responses rather than subtracting points for incorrect ones.*
6. *You annotate, as well as score, test papers.* (Not only does this practice provide helpful feedback to students, but it also helps you remember why you scored items as you did. Students are less likely to manipulate answers after the tests are returned if you have already commented on their answers.)
7. *Students are directed to check on whether or not their test copies contain all pages and are properly collated before they begin.*
8. *Students are not tested on their recall of material that seems unnecessary to mèmorize.* (When obtaining a grade on a test is the *sole* perceived purpose students have for memorizing what they know will be forgotten after the test, using crib notes seems like a sensible thing to do.)

Because a student cheats on a test is not a reason for recording a low score. Cheating does not reflect learning goal attainment (except in the rare case in which the learning goal is for the student to be honest). Thus, if a teacher knows that a student has cheated on a test, then the test results are not valid and *no score* should be recorded as if the student never took the test at all. A student's understanding of biology, for example, should not be judged by whether or not that student cooperated with the test-taking procedures. Judgments of how well learning goals are achieved should be withheld until after the student no longer displays the dishonest behavior and a valid measurement of achievement can be obtained.

The following are three examples of teachers' responses to student cheating:

While scoring a unit test he had administered to his tenth grade first-aid class, Mr. Broussard notices some inconsistencies in Joe's test responses. Joe's answers to a couple of the more difficult items on the test are correct, while he missed a number of items that measured simple rudimentary knowledge. Mr. Broussard asks himself, "How could he get these correct without knowing this?" Later, while scoring Remy's paper, Mr. Broussard notices that Remy answers the same difficult items using words very similar to those in Joe's responses. Mr. Broussard then compares their two sets of responses and notices some peculiar similarities. On the multiple-choice portions of the test, Joe's choices nearly always agree with Remy's. He finds it curious that the two would consistently choose the same distractors or foils for multiple-choice items that they both missed.

Convinced that Joe copied from Remy's paper, Mr. Broussard begins planning how to deal with the situation. He thinks, "I should confront them both with this. Scare the hell out of them! But if I'm wrong, I'll only teach them they're not trusted. That could be damaging. They just might cheat from now on because they figured there'd be no trust to lose. But I really can't put any stock in Joe's test results and I need to know what he got out of this unit. I need an accurate score on him. Also, I don't want Joe to get away with this. I don't think he's cheated before. I should block any positive reinforcement so this doesn't become a pattern. I know! I'll 'lose' his test paper and schedule a retest for him with an equivalent form."

The next day, Mr. Broussard distributes the scored and annotated test papers.

JOE (from his desk): Mr. Broussard, you didn't give my test back.
MR. BROUSSARD: I didn't? Please come up here.

Joe arrives and Mr. Broussard says softly, "You didn't get your paper back. What do you think happened?"

JOE: I don't know. I took the test.
MR. BROUSSARD: Yes, I know. I remember going over it.

Mr. Broussard pulls out his grade book and says, "Here, Joe, let's see if I recorded a score for you. No, there's no score here. Look." Joe sees the empty square.

MR. BROUSSARD: We'll just schedule a retest. How about tomorrow? I'll give you a test tomorrow.
JOE: That's not fair for me to have to take another test.
MR. BROUSSARD: Yes, I know. Now, let's see when we can schedule it. . . .

═══

Mr. Stoddard validates each sociology test that he administers to his classes before allowing the test results to influence evaluations he makes regarding students' achievement levels. From analysis of one set of test results and from his observations of some curious student behaviors during the administration of that test, Mr. Stoddard suspects that student cheating contaminated the accuracy of the test results. At the next class meeting, Mr. Stoddard announces, "The results I received from the test are invalid. There are some major discrepancies among the scores. Statistical analyses indicate the test was too unreliable to accurately indicate your levels of achievement. Therefore, I discarded the results and we will take a refined version of the test under more controlled conditions on Wednesday."

═══

Ms. Maggio administers a problem-solving test to her fourth graders in which they are directed to work out "in their heads" a sequence of tasks that are presented on pages

39 and 40 of one of their textbooks. She instructs them to look at only those two pages in their books while working out the solutions and expressing answers on a sheet of paper. Ms. Maggio notices one student, Nettie, keeping an eye on her during the test. Nettie seems to manipulate her book suddenly whenever Ms. Maggio comes near or looks at her. Ms. Maggio suspects that Nettie has surreptitiously turned to the back of the book in which answers to the problems are given.

After the test, Ms. Maggio examines Nettie's answer sheet. Most of the responses are correct. She then engages Nettie in a private conference and presents one of the problems that Nettie answered on the test and asks her to solve it. Nettie is unable to come up with a solution this time. Nettie fails twice more to reproduce answers which she had written on the test earlier in the day.

> MS. MAGGIO: "Nettie, I do not understand why you cannot figure out these answers now if you solved the problems during the test."
> NETTIE: "I don't know."
> MS. MAGGIO: "I will not check off that you can do these types of problems until you demonstrate to me that you can."

SCORING THE TEST

THE SIXTH STEP IN THE PROCESS

The sixth step is using the test scoring key (compiled from item scoring keys) to (1) quantify each student's response to each item and (2) record each student's test score as the sum of his or her item scores. Do not confuse the *scoring* of a test with *grading*. Scoring is part of the measurement process in which you follow item scoring keys and add the item scores to produce test results. Grading, on the other hand, is a summative evaluation process in which you make value judgments about students' levels of achievements. Methods for converting test scores to grades are explained in Chapter 9.

CONCERN FOR USABILITY

Scoring tests is one of the less popular aspects of teaching. Many teachers indicate that they do not test student achievement as frequently as they should because they cannot spend more time on scoring tests (Duke, Cangelosi, & Knight, 1988).

Of course, supplanting tests dominated by item formats (e.g., essay) that are time-consuming to score with tests dominated by items (e.g., multiple choice) with quick-scoring formats diminishes the time needed to score tests. Scoring time is further reduced by having students record responses on separate answer sheets that can be machine-scored or scored with a test key stencil or overlay. Even more efficient are computer-administered tests with programs that take care of the scoring chore for you.

However, items with quick-scoring formats do not always lend themselves to the objectives you want to measure. For example,

---

Mr. Alvarez teaches three sections of ninth-grade English and two sections of Spanish at Southside High. As he designs the blueprint for a test for an English unit on critiquing essays, he thinks, "I've got 28 in second period, 24 in third, and 23 in fifth. Gracious! I'll have 75 papers to score all at the same time! I'd better avoid essay and other kinds of items that are hard to score. Let's see what I have in my item pools. . . . I'm okay for objective A, I've got plenty of easy-to-score items relevant to how well they can define *essay*, *fact*, and so forth. But it's bad news for objective B! I don't have any easy-to-score items relevant to how well they distinguish among facts, evidence, and conclusions in a written article. All my pool items are either essays or other items requiring them to write a couple of sentences. It will take me a long time to read all that. But I can't figure how to measure objective B without asking them to write or tell me their thoughts."

Mr. Alvarez decides to use essay items for objective B. However, he also begins devising ways to reduce the time he will spend scoring those essay items. He examines the following item from the objective B scoring pool.

Task presented to the students:
Read the attached magazine article. Write an essay explaining how one of the author's conclusions is supported by facts contained in the article.
Scoring key: (5 points possible) +1 if the student chooses one of the following as a conclusion: (1) The death penalty doesn't deter crime, (2) Prisons can be used to change behaviors, or (3) Research on crime prevention is needed; +1 for each of the two facts the student properly identifies as supporting the conclusion; 0, +1, or +2 depending on how well the student explains why the facts are related to the conclusion.

Mr. Alvarez thinks, "I like that item, but I'll spend hours reading their essays, hunting through the words for conclusions and facts chosen. Some of them will write four pages; others won't give me three sentences. I'll modify the item to make it easier for me to pull out the pertinent information from their writing and not have to make so many judgments during the scoring. Oh, yes! I'll also tell them how much to write. That'll prevent the four-pagers I don't have time to read and the one-sentencers where I have to guess about what they mean."

After further thought, Mr. Alvarez replaces the original item with the following:

Task presented to the students:
Read the attached magazine article. Now, select *one* of the author's *conclusions* and write it in this blank: _____

Now, list two *facts* the author used to support *that* conclusion and write them here:

1. _____
2. _____

In one paragraph of three to six sentences, explain why the two facts you listed actually do support the conclusion. Use the space below for your paragraph.

Scoring key: (5 points possible) +1 if the student lists the equivalent to one of the following in the first blank: (1) The death penalty doesn't deter crime; (2) Prisons can be used to change behaviors; (3) Research on crime prevention is needed. +1 if the correct two facts that support the conclusions are listed. 0, +1, or +2 according to the following scale: 0 if the response does not even allude to any relation between the two facts listed and the conclusion; +1 if it intimates a relationship between the listed facts and the conclusion, but the relationship is either an understatement or an overstatement of the author's position; +2 if the relationship is explained in a manner consistent with the article.

Even when quick-scoring item formats are appropriate for the objectives, some of the time-saving scoring devices may be inappropriate for certain student groups. For example, Gaffney and Maguire (1971) concluded that the task of recording answers on separate answer sheets markedly contaminates the reliability of tests administered to students below the fourth-grade level. Even for older students, allowances should be made to accommodate the use of separate answer sheets: (1) Practice using answer sheets is needed before they are used for the first time. (2) Test administration time should be extended for the added minutes spent manipulating the sheets.

CONCERN FOR INTRASCORER AND INTERSCORER RELIABILITIES

Maintaining consistency in scoring tests is a major concern whenever tests include essay, performance observation, interview, or any other type of item in which scoring keys leave room for judgment. How to build intrascorer and interscorer reliabilities into even these types of items is a major focus of Chapter 4.

DETERMINING CUTOFF SCORES

THE SEVENTH STEP IN THE PROCESS

Test results are the fruit of your efforts in designing, constructing, administering, and scoring a test. Typically, test results provide one number, or score, for each student tested. But how high should a student's test score be before it is considered to be evidence that the student has satisfactorily achieved the learning goal? How low must the score be to indicate that the goal should be retaught? What score should be the cutoff between a C grade and a B grade? These questions display a need for cutoff scores to help bridge the gap between test results and the formative and summative evaluations you must make. Determining cutoff scores is the seventh and final step in the test design and construction process.

CRITERION-REFERENCED METHODS

Teachers use *criterion-referenced methods for determining cutoff scores* by applying standards that (1) are set prior to the administration of the test and (2) involve no comparisons between the scores of different test-takers. One of the more commonly used but ill-advised criterion-referenced methods is *traditional percentage grading*. For example,

---

Ms. Bung-Lee, a high school science teacher, applies traditional percentage grading in making summative evaluations. At the beginning of a semester, she displays the following on the board for her biology class:

94%–100% for an A
86%– 93% for a B
78%– 85% for a C
70%– 77% for a D
 0%– 69% for an F

She announces, "Your grades are objectively determined. Your tests will be graded according to this scale. Under this system, no one has to fail. In fact, there's nothing to stop everyone from making an A. But I do not lower the standards for anyone. If no one gets 94 percent, there will be no A's."

Later, Ms. Bung-Lee administers a 40-point unit test on food webs and applies her grading standard. The test results and grades are reported in Table 3.3.

Although Ms. Bung-Lee's method for determining cutoff scores and grades is fairly common, it has two major weaknesses:

1.   Establishing such high percentages (e.g., 94% for an A and 70% for passing) precludes the use of hard and moderate items. Thus, with a test composed of predominately easy items, Ms. Bung-Lee fails to measure the more advanced levels of achievement. The test, for example, fails to discriminate among Linda's, Allison's, Kelly's, Clifton's, Kathleen's, and Juanita's achievement levels. They all scored 100 percent, but surely there are some differences in how well they learned about food webs. Ms. Bung-Lee should include harder items on her test and

TABLE 3.3   Results from Ms. Bung-Lee's Test

Student	Score	Percentage Correct	Grade
Linda	40	100	A
Allison	40	100	A
Kelly	40	100	A
Clifton	40	100	A
Kathleen	40	100	A
Juanita	40	100	A
Ron	38	95	A
Bernie	37	93	B
Oral	34	85	B
Jan	33	83	B
Casey	33	83	B
Lawrence	32	80	C
Stuart	30	75	C
Stacey	30	75	C
Nicole	30	75	C
Kevin	29	73	D
Joe	28	70	D
Jacob	26	65	F
Lydia	25	63	F
Coleen	25	63	F
Rich	10	25	F

adjust the scoring scale so that lower percentages merit higher grades (e.g., 50% earns a C).

2. Students with scores that are not significantly different obtain different grades. For example, Ron's 38 converted to an A; Bernie's 37 converted to a B. Although Bernie's score is closer to Ron's than it is to Casey's 33, both Bernie and Casey received B's.

Alternative methods for converting test scores to grades are explained in Chapter 9. For now, it is only necessary for you to understand that determining cutoff scores is an important step in the test design and construction process.

NORM-REFERENCED METHODS

Teachers use *norm-referenced methods for determining cutoff scores* by applying standards based on the test performance of a group of students. For example,

Ms. Curry administers a 55-point math test, obtaining the scores in Table 3.4. The test was designed to have about 20 easy, 20 moderate, and 15 hard items. She notes that the average of the scores is about 30 and decides to assign the grade of C to scores near the

TABLE 3.4   Results and Grades from Ms. Curry's Test

Student	Score	Grade
Leroy	51	A
Valerie	49	A
Katie	49	A
Mary	48	A
Chuck	44	B
Jeannie	40	B
Frank	40	B
Otis	39	B
Damien	39	B
Amad	33	C
Mark	32	C
Charog	30	C
Erica	28	C
Emile	23	C
John	23	C
Bonnie	20	D
Justin	20	D
Caroline	20	D
Delia	19	D
Charles	14	F
Pauline	12	F
Seritta	11	F
Rosalie	9	F
Vincent	9	F

average, B's to scores somewhat above the average, D's somewhat below the average, A's to scores well above the average, and F's to scores well below the average.

Norm-referenced methods for establishing cutoff scores are used with standardized tests. For example,

To qualify for a special remedial reading program, students at Blackhawk Elementary must score below the thirtieth percentile on the comprehension reading subtest of the Metropolitan Achievement Test. A score at the thirtieth percentile is a score that is greater than 30 percent and less than 70 percent of the scores obtained by a group of students on which the subtest was field-tested (i.e., the norm group).

If you are interested in examining some of the more sophisticated methods for determining cutoff scores, the following works will help:

Berk, R. A. (1986). A consumer's guide to setting performance standards on criterion-referenced tests. *Review of Educational Research, 56,* 137–172.

Cangelosi, J. S. (1984). Another answer to the cutoff score question. *Educational measurement: Issues and practice, 3,* 23–25.

Livingston, S. A., & Zieky, M. J. (1982). *Passing scores: A manual for setting standards of performance on educational and occupational tests.* Princeton, NJ: Educational Testing Service.

THE MOST TAXING TASK

Designing items to fill your item pools is the most creative aspect of test development. The art of creating items relevant to the content and behavioral construct specified by a given objective is not easily learned. Chapters 4 through 7 are designed to help.

REVIEWING TEST RESULTS WITH STUDENTS

Students engage in extremely productive learning experiences when teachers promptly return scored and annotated test papers, review the results, and discuss the responses. For example,

The 55-point test whose results appear in Table 3.4 was administered on a Friday. The following Monday, Ms. Curry tells her students as she returns their test papers, "You can locate your test's score and grade by turning up the bottom right corner of page three. After you've noted that, please spend the next eight minutes silently reading the comments I've written throughout your paper."

Ms. Curry avoids judgmental comments such as "Good" and "Poor" that label rather than inform. Instead, she writes *descriptive,* informative statements on students' test papers. Figure 3.5 shows some of the comments Ms. Curry wrote on one student's paper.

At the end of the eight minutes, Ms. Curry organizes the class into six groups of four students each. The students then discuss their responses to the test items within the small groups. After 20 minutes, Ms. Curry directs the students to reassemble as a large group. In the remaining time, she responds to students' questions and provides additional instruction for objectives that the test results indicated should be retaught.

During the session, many of the students seem to begin grasping ideas for the first time. At one point, Erica comments to Ms. Curry, "This stuff makes sense now. Why didn't you teach it so we could've understood it before the test?" Other students echo Erica's sentiments. Ms. Curry smiles as she quietly thinks to herself, "They don't understand that they had to go through the experience of taking this test—being confronted with these tasks—before they could be *ready* to really understand."

6th Grade Math ** Test for Unit 5

NOTE: Calculators may not be used on this test.

I. What is your name _Otis Johnson_

II. Bart makes a mistake and gets "21/20" when he adds 13/9 and 8/11. Write Bart a note explaining why his answer is wrong for the same reason that 10 apples plus 7 oranges is *not* "17 apple-like oranges." Use about five sentences for your note and write it here:

(2 pts)

+0 because you didn't explain why its wrong to just add denominators.

+1 because you suggested a need for a common unit.

$13/9 + 8/11 = \frac{143+72}{99} = \frac{215}{99}$. Bart should have got $\frac{215}{99}$ not $\frac{21}{20}$. He didn't find a common denominator. You can't add apples and oranges so you can't add ninths to 11 ths like Bart. He did it wrong.

(1 pt.) Until you redo this one - then it'll be (2 pts.)

III. Express each of the following as a fraction in lowest terms (Do your scratch work in the box by the problem. Write your final answer clearly in the blank):

a) $(30/12) + (5/14) =$ (25/2) .

$\frac{30}{3\cdot2\cdot2} + \frac{5}{7\cdot2} =$

$\frac{30\cdot7}{3\cdot2\cdot2\cdot7} + \frac{5\cdot3\cdot2}{7\cdot2\cdot3\cdot2} = \frac{(30\cdot7)+(5)(3\cdot2)}{3\cdot2\cdot2\cdot7} = \frac{175}{14} = \frac{25\cdot7}{2\cdot7} = \frac{25}{2}$

What is 35+5? Not 175. Everything else is correct. Redo this one adding 35 and 5 instead of multiplying them.

b) $(9/33) - (3/5) =$ (-18/55) .

$9/33 - 3/5 =$

(2 pts)

This one is correct.

$\frac{9\cdot5}{3\cdot11\cdot5} - \frac{3\cdot3\cdot11}{3\cdot11\cdot5} = \frac{45-99}{3\cdot11\cdot5} = -\frac{54}{3\cdot11\cdot5}^{18} = -\frac{18}{155}$

c) $(89/89) - (56/57) =$ (89/5073) .

$\frac{(89\cdot57)-(56\cdot89)}{89\times57} =$

(1 pt)

$\frac{5073-4984}{5073} = \frac{89}{5073}$ — I don't know if this can be reduced.

although this is not reduced, it is the correct answer. BUT, why didn't you do this:

$\frac{89}{89} - \frac{56}{57} = 1 - \frac{56}{57} = \frac{1}{57}$?

FIGURE 3.5 A Sample of Ms. Curry's Comments on One Test Paper

SELF-ASSESSMENT OF YOUR ACHIEVEMENT OF CHAPTER 3'S OBJECTIVES

I. For each of the following multiple-choice items, select the one response that best answers the question or correctly completes the statement:

A. Clarifying the learning goal is the first step in the test design and construction process. Which one of the following is part of that first step?
   1. maintaining item pools
   2. determining the scoring rules for test items
   3. accounting for item interaction
   4. weighting objectives

B. Synthesizing the test is the fourth step in the test design and construction process. Which one of the following is part of that fourth step?
   1. monitoring students
   2. sequencing items
   3. determining grades
   4. making formative evaluations

C. Developing the test blueprint is the second step in the test design and construction process. Which one of the following is part of that second step?
   1. determining the learning goal
   2. expanding item pools
   3. converting scores to grades
   4. listing the sections of the test

D. The purpose for using a table of specifications in the creation of a test is to enhance _____.
   1. intrascorer reliability
   2. measurement usability
   3. measurement relevance
   4. test-retest reliability

E. To control the influence of various objectives on a test, a table of specifications should be used, with weights assigned _____.
   1. according to the relative importance of each objective
   2. according to the relative amount of class time that was spent on each objective
   3. so that there are the same number of items as there are objectives
   4. so that all behavioral construct levels are covered by the test

F. A hard item, as defined here, is an item that _____.
   1. measures at a higher cognitive level (e.g., application)
   2. fewer than 25 percent of the test group correctly answer

3. measures an objective that fewer than 25 percent of the test group have achieved
4. only students scoring in the top 25 percent of the test group will correctly answer

G. The purpose of including hard items on achievement tests is to _____ .
1. measure at the lower achievement levels
2. measure at the higher achievement levels
3. reward students who studied
4. reduce the number of high grades

H. During an application-level science test, one student whistles and taps a pencil loudly. Such noises are likely to influence the test's _____ .
1. construct validity
2. content relevance
3. interscorer reliability
4. internal consistency

I. During an application-level science test, several students cheat by occasionally looking on one another's papers. This misbehavior is likely to influence the test's _____ .
1. usability
2. intrascorer reliability
3. test-retest reliability
4. relevance

J. Which one of the following rules is based on a criterion-referenced method for cutoff scores?
1. Any score lower than 15 converts to an F.
2. To obtain a grade of A, the test score must be in the top 8 percent.
3. Anyone scoring below the average of last year's class will be retaught.
4. Morica scored 7 points higher than anyone else in the class; thus she gets an A.

Compare your choices to the following key: A–4, B–2, C–4, D–3, E–1, F–2, G–2, H–4, I–3, J–1.

II. Retrieve the set of objectives you listed for Exercise IV, Chapter 1. Begin the process of designing and developing an achievement test for the goal that those objectives define by (1) weighting the objectives and developing a table of specifications and (2) developing a test blueprint. Exchange your work on this exercise with someone and critique one another's blueprints.

III. Organize a system, either computerized or file box, for maintaining item pools.

Item Development Hints

GOAL OF CHAPTER 4

Chapter 4 describes a process and provides hints for designing effective test items. More specifically, Chapter 4 will help you to

1. Explain the five critical steps of item design (*Cognitive: conceptualization*)
2. Apply sound item design principles to the development of each of the following types of items: (a) short answer, (b) completion (c) multiple choice, (d) true/false, (e) multiple answer multiple choice, (f) matching, (g) weighted multiple choice, (h) essay, (i) oral discourse, (j) product rating, (k) performance observation, and (l) interview (*Cognitive: application*)
3. State the definition of the following: *short-answer item, dichotomously scored, weighted item, globally scored, analytically scored, completion item, multiple-choice item, rating scale, Likert scale, correction for guessing, true/false item, multiple-answer multiple-choice item, matching item, essay item, product-rating item, performance-observation item, interview item, linear interview sequence, branching interview sequence,* and *computer-administered item* (*Cognitive: simple knowledge*)

FIVE CRITICAL STEPS OF ITEM DESIGN

Consider what goes through Mr. Ascione's mind as he designs items to add to the item pools for a physical education unit on weightlifting:

Mr. Ascione thinks, "Okay, I need some items for objective A. I'll read it once again." He reads,

"**A.**   Upon hearing the name of a major muscle group, points to the location of that group on her or his own body (*Cognitive: simple knowledge*)"

Mr. Ascione continues thinking, "It's simple knowledge, so I only have to test if they can remember the names that go with the locations on their bodies. I can whip some items out pretty quick. To get organized, I'll list the major muscle groups to include. . . . But just how sophisticated should I make this list? . . . I know! I'll make a list of the ones that should be obvious to anyone who has ever heard of weightlifting. From those well-known muscles, I'll build some easy items. Then I'll list some lesser known muscles to build some moderate and hard items."

He lists the following:

MUSCLE GROUPS FOR EASY ITEMS

Pectorals, abdominals, hamstrings, quadriceps, biceps, and triceps

MUSCLE GROUPS FOR MODERATE ITEMS

Trapezius, deltoids, gastrocnemius, gluteus, latissimus dorsi, and scapula

MUSCLE GROUPS FOR HARD ITEMS

Sternocleidomastoid, pectoralis minor, pectoralis major, extensor carpi radialis, serratus anterior, vastus lateralis, rectus femoris, vastus medialis, bicep femoris, semitendinosus, semimembransous, glueteus maximus, glueteus medius, and external oblique

He ponders while developing an easy item: "I need to set the task. An obvious item would have a one-to-one interview format where I'd just ask the student to point to his or her pectorals, abdominals, hamstrings, quadriceps, biceps, and triceps. Then the item could be scored one point for each part that the student pointed to correctly."

Mr. Ascione types the item into his computerized item pool file. He thinks, "I'd like another easy item for objective A with a more usable format, one I can administer to everyone at once. . . . I'll present them with a list of the muscle groups and a sketch of the outline of the body and have them associate the muscles with their locations. That wouldn't be exactly like the objective, but it would require the same knowledge as the objective. It would set up a task that *correlates* with the task specified in the objective." In a few minutes, the item shown in Figure 4.1 is entered into Mr. Ascione's item pool file.

As he continues to design items, Mr. Ascione reaches objective E, which is

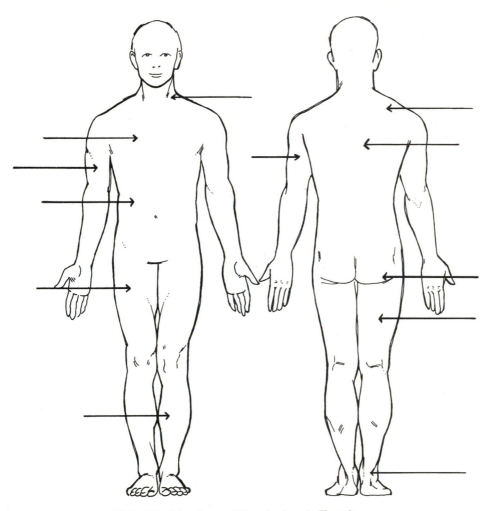

FIGURE 4.1   One of Mr. Ascione's Test Items

E. Explains the fundamental relations among (a) weight work, (b) rest, and (c) nutrition (*Cognitive: conceptualization*)

He thinks, "Oh-oh, conceptualization! Designing items for objective E will be more complicated than for objective A. I can go with an essay item that directs them to do just what's stated in the objective. The scoring key will have to be worked out. Let me think. . . ."

In a few minutes, Mr. Ascione has entered the following item into his pool for objective E:

Task presented to the students:
Use about two-thirds of a page to explain the fundamental relations among (a) weightlifting exercise, (b) rest, and (c) nutrition.
Scoring key: (5 points possible) +1 for *each* of the following that is somehow indicated in the student's response:

1. Weightlifting "tears down" muscle tissue.
2. Muscles regenerate during rest periods.
3. Energy for muscle regeneration is supplied from ingested food.
4. Muscles recover stronger than before from being "torn down" in weight work.
5. The effectiveness of these three elements working together to strengthen or maintain muscles depends on whether the exercise, rest, and nutrition are properly planned and coordinated.

Mr. Ascione thinks, "This essay item should be moderate to easy in difficulty. But I need some items for objective E that don't require an essay, ones that don't depend so much on the students' writing skills. I know! I can go back through the essay's scoring key and pick out some things they have to understand to achieve the objective. Then I can build multiple-choice items from those. . . . But that would be moving away from the objective, which says they should *explain*. Hmmm! But *if* the multiple-choice items presented them with mental tasks that *correlated* with the task of explaining the relations among weight work, rest, and nutrition, the multiple-choice items would have some relevance to objective E, just like the essay item. . . . I'll try some."

Twelve minutes later, Mr. Ascione has designed three multiple-choice items and added them to objective E's item pool. Here's one:

Task presented to the students:
Why were you advised in class to wait 48 hours between bench-press routines?

   A. To prevent you from being bored with repetitive routines
   B. To give you enough time to work other parts of the body besides the chest and arms
   C. To give your chest and arm muscles time to build up again
   D. To give you enough time for intake of adequate amounts of nutrition

Scoring key: +1 for C only; otherwise 0.

To design an item that's relevant to a given objective, you must

1. *Focus on the content and behavioral construct of the objective.* When Mr. Ascione designed items for objective A, he concentrated on what it meant for a student to function at the simple-knowledge level with respect to the names and locations of muscle groups. He organized lists of muscle groups to help him focus on just what the objective required students to remember. On the other hand, when working on items for objective E, he directed his thinking toward ways in which students

demonstrate not what they remember but rather their understanding of why the relationship among weightlifting, rest, and nutrition exists. This first critical step serves to maintain your attention on the learning objective as you design the item's task and scoring key.

2. *Answer the first of the following questions for a cognitive or a psychomotor objective; answer the second for an affective objective: (a) What task can students perform as a result of having achieved the objective? (b) What behaviors do students exhibit as a result of having achieved the objective?* Because objective A is so straightforward and clearly worded, Mr. Ascione had little difficulty with this step. By pointing to the correct location on their bodies of the muscle group, students perform a task that's indicative of achievement of objective A. In objective E, the task is to "explain the fundamental relation . . ." but Mr. Ascione had to analyze what he meant by a satisfactory explanation before formulating the scoring for his essay item.

3. *If the task identified in step 2 is not practical for a usable item, devise an alternative task that (a) requires students to exhibit the same type of skills, abilities, or attitudes required by the task identified in step 2, and (b) is practical to incorporate in a usable item.* Mr. Ascione identified such an alternative task when he decided that directing students to locate muscles on a sketch presented them with a task that would reflect how well they could point to those muscles on their own bodies. Similarly, he identified tasks that would correlate with the one presented in the essay item for objective E when he developed the more usable multiple-choice items.

4. *Devise a usable means for presenting students with the task identified in steps 2 or 3.* This step involves deciding how to stimulate students to attempt the task. In other words, you select the item's format and decide how you will give the directions.

5. *Formulate the item's scoring key.*

DESIGNING SHORT-ANSWER ITEMS

An item that presents a task to which the student is to respond with a brief expression (usually verbal) is a short-answer item. Short-answer items require students to *provide* expressions rather than select them from given lists (e.g., with a multiple-choice format). Students' responses are expected to be briefly written, spoken, or signed expressions ranging from a single symbol or word for some items to a few sentences for others. Here are five examples of short-answer items:

1. *Task presented to the students:*
   Who discovered America? _____
   Scoring key: +1 for Columbus; otherwise 0.

2. *Task presented to the students:*
   (Oral directions and response in one-to-one format) Teacher tells student, "Translate the sentence I give you into signed English. Here's the sentence: 'I want to go home, but I don't know if I should!'"

Scoring key: (10 points possible) +2 if the complete literal meaning of the sentence is signed; +2 if the response doesn't include anything that doesn't belong in the sentence; +2 if there are no syntax errors; +2 based on the following rating for facial expression and emphasis: 0 if inappropriate, +1 if neutral, and +2 if appropriate; +2 based on the following rating for pacing: 0 for hesitation before any of the signs, +1 if there are not major pauses but pace is slow, and +2 for continuous signing.

3. *Task presented to the students:*
   Abraham Lincoln was the sixteenth president of the United States. List, in order, the names of the seventeenth, eighteenth, and nineteenth presidents.
   seventeenth: _____
   eighteenth: _____
   nineteenth: _____
   Scoring key: (6 points possible) +1 for each of the following names (spelling is not a factor): Andrew Johnson, Ulysses Grant, and Rutherford Hayes; +1 if Johnson appears before Grant, +1 if Johnson appears before Hayes, and +1 if Grant appears before Hayes.

4. *Task presented to the students:*
   Suppose that you have a friend who never smoked marijuana. Further suppose that this friend invites you to join him or her in smoking a joint. In one or two sentences tell what you would do.
   Scoring key: (2 points possible) +1 if the response indicates that the student would not smoke the joint; +1 if there is an indication that the student would attempt to discourage the friend from smoking it.

5. *Task presented to the students:*
   Tickets for last year's spring dance sold for $5 per couple and $3 for individuals; 37 tickets for couples and 42 for individuals were sold. It was estimated that 15 people sneaked into the dance without tickets. How much money was brought in by the sale of the tickets? Display your work in the space provided.
   Scoring key: (3 points possible) +1 if the response includes an expression equivalent to $(37 \times 5) + (42 \times 3)$; +1 if the response indicates no attempt to utilize irrelevant information (e.g., 15 persons sneaking in); +1 if the answer is $311.

Here are some ideas for you to consider regarding the selection and design of short-answer items.

PROVIDE-TYPE OBJECTIVES

Short-answer items are particularly appropriate for objectives that require students to *furnish* or *provide* expressions rather than simply selecting expressions from a given list. For example, the teacher who designed the second of the five items just listed intended for that objective to be relevant to the following objective:

> From hearing a sentence that uses only English words within the student's signing vocabulary, translates the sentence into signed English. (*Cognitive: application*)

Since translating from spoken to signed English requires one to provide, not simply select, a communication pattern, the teacher prefers a short-answer format for this objective to a multiple-choice format.

STRAIGHTFORWARD DIRECTIONS

To find out if students can solve a particular type of problem, direct them to solve an example of that type of problem. Evidence of what students remember from a lesson can be obtained by asking them a question that can be answered only by recalling information from that lesson. To assess how students would act in a given situation (e.g., for an affective objective), present the situation and ask them what they would do. Such direct approaches to item design lead to short-answer items that typically present students with tasks that don't require as complex directions as other types of items (e.g., essay, multiple choice, and performance observation).

DANGER OF AMBIGUITY

The simplicity and straightforwardness of the directions for short-answer items are illustrated by the first of the five preceding items. That item simply asks, "Who discovered America?" However, the advantage of simplicity can be accompanied by the disadvantage of ambiguity unless the item is carefully designed. For example,

A fifth-grader, Pauline, reads the question on the social studies test she is taking: "Who discovered America?" Pauline thinks, "Christopher Columbus sailed to the New World in 1492. But there were native Americans already there. I wonder what answer she wants. It could be those Vikings that sailed over before Columbus. Or does she want that guy John Cabot who got to America; Columbus only made it to the Caribbean."

Often, it is difficult to present a short-answer item that is not open to a variety of interpretations. You want the item to discriminate among various levels of objective achievement, not discriminate according to how the students interpreted the question or directions. Pauline's sophisticated level of understanding of the content hindered, instead of helped, her performance on the item.

The wording in the following item is a less ambiguous but more complex and difficult to read alternative:

Task presented to the students:
Who was the first person, now known by name, to sail from Europe to what is now known as the Americas? _____
Scoring key: +1 for Columbus; otherwise 0.

A multiple-choice item could be designed that is not as ambiguous as the original item and not as complex as the one just given. For example,

Task presented to the students:
Who discovered America?
A. Amerigo Vespucci
B. George Washington
C. Vasco de Balboa
D. Christopher Columbus
Scoring key: +1 for D; otherwise 0.

This multiple-choice item keeps the simple wording of the question but avoids the ambiguity because defensible responses such as "Native Americans," "Vikings," and "John Cabot" are not included among the alternatives. Note three disadvantages of the multiple-choice item in comparison to the short-answer items: (1) The multiple-choice item won't work as well if the objective requires the student to provide rather than just to identify the answer, (2) the directions for a section of multiple-choice items will need to be more complex, and (3) students are more likely to *guess* correctly the answer to the multiple-choice question.

GUESSING

Ideally, students' performances on an item depend on how well they have achieved the item's objective. But unfortunately, achieving students (e.g., Pauline in the example) may miss an item because of a weakness in its design (e.g., ambiguous wording), and nonachieving students may correctly respond to the item (e.g., by simply guessing).

When students respond correctly to items because of guessing rather than achievement, the validity of the test is weakened. Short-answer items have the advantage of not being as susceptible to student guessing as multiple-choice items.

TAXING COMMUNICATION SKILLS

Typically, successful responses to short-answer items do not require as sophisticated communication skills (e.g., writing or speaking) as essay items. However, some short-answer items (e.g., the fourth of the five items to be found on pages 83 through 84) depend on students being able to communicate information *concisely*. Because the short-answer format places tight limits on the length of students' expressions, students need to be highly selective in their choice of words.

STRUCTURE AND DETAIL

For some objectives, it is difficult to design a short-answer item that (1) is more a measure of students' achievement of the objective than of their communications skills and (2) unambiguously communicates the intended task. Here are two examples of that problem:

Mr. Little is designing a short-answer item to be relevant to a knowledge-of-a-process objective on how the U.S. Constitution is amended. He keys the following item into his computer-managed item pool file:

Task presented to the students:
How is the Constitution amended?
Scoring key: (5 points possible) +1 for each of the following: (1) a Constitutional convention, (2) two-thirds of both houses or two-thirds of state legislatures vote to hold the convention, (3) proposing amendments, (4) passing proposed amendments, and (5) ratification of amendments by three-fourths of the states.

As Mr. Little analyzes the item, he thinks, "Some of my students will give me the shortest possible answer. Something like 'By voting.' Others will rise above the knowledge-of-a-process level I want and explain all kinds of subtleties about the process. A whole library could be devoted to answering that question, but I couldn't argue with the answer 'by voting.' I need to add more specific directions and structure to the way the task is presented. They need to know that I expect them to describe the steps simply and briefly."

After further reflection, Mr. Little revises the item so that the task will be presented as follows:

Article V of the Constitution gives rules for amending the Constitution. Here are three questions about those rules. Answer each question in one sentence.

1. What must happen *before* a constitutional convention can be held? _____
_____

2. What must happen *during* a constitutional convention before an amendment to the Constitution is passed? _____
_____

3. What is the *last* thing that must happen before an amendment is added to the Constitution? _____

_____

_____

Mr. Little is concerned that the revised item appears more complicated than the original one. However, he prefers it because the presentation of the task is clearer and the item does not require as high a level of writing skill.

Most of the items in Ms. Parino's item pools for the objectives of her unit on classroom citizenship use a performance-observation format. However, she is toying with the idea of developing a test with written-response items as one measure of how well her second-graders are progressing with the unit.

One of the unit's objectives, objective B, is stated as follows:

If a classmate expresses a need for help, attempts to help, providing that she or he is able and that such help is acceptable to the teacher. (*Affective: willingness to act*)

Ms. Parino considers including the following short-answer item for objective B.

Task presented to the students:
(Oral directions with students responding in writing on an answer sheet) The teacher tells the class, "Write a sentence telling me what you would do if one of your friends asked you to help them with a math problem."
Scoring key: (2 points possible) +2 based on the following rating: 0 if the response indicates that the student would refuse to help, +1 if the response is unclear about whether or not help would be attempted, and +2 if it clearly states that the student would attempt to help.

Ms. Parino examines the item and thinks, "I wonder if this item is open to different interpretations. Tomorrow, I'll try it out on a couple of the second-graders and then ask them to talk with me about what they wrote. That way I'll know whether I should use these kinds of items in the future."

The next day, Ms. Parino field-tests the item on Dustin and Tyler. From Dustin's paper she reads, "I won't help." Ms. Parino asks, "Dustin, what were you thinking when you wrote that?"

DUSTIN: I was thinkin' 'bout Riley. He said he didn't ever want me to help him again.
MS. PARINO: Would you like to help him?
DUSTIN: Sure, but he's mad at me and doesn't want me to. I'd help anybody else.

Ms. Parino asks Riley to talk about the answer he wrote, which was, "No way I'd help."

RILEY: I'm the worse in the class on math. I'd try, but it wouldn't help.

Ms. Parino now realizes that the item is ambiguously worded. She decides to present the students with a more specific situation and, thus, changes the presentation of the task to the following:

> (Oral directions with students responding in writing on an answer sheet) The teacher tells the class, "I'm going to tell you a story and then ask you to tell me what you would do if that story were true. Here's the story: *'A girl who has just moved to town joins our class. You have never met her before. But at recess she asks you to tell her what our class has been doing in math.'* That's the end of the story. Now I want you to write two sentences telling me what you would do."

VARIETY OF BEHAVIORAL CONSTRUCTS

Short-answer items are thought by many as being appropriate for knowledge-level objectives. Items 1, 2, and 3 from the examples of short-answer test items listed on pages 83 through 84 are relevant to knowledge-level objectives. However, short-answer items (e.g., item 5) can be designed to measure cognitive intellectual objectives. Item 4 illustrates that short-answer items can also be designed for affective objectives.

DICHOTOMOUSLY SCORED ITEMS

For the five test items listed on pages 83 through 84, note that the scoring key for item 1 specifies one point for the correct response and zero otherwise. *Items to which responses are scored either right or wrong (i.e., no partial credit possible) are called dichotomously scored.*

As illustrated by the five items, short-answer items may or may not be dichotomously scored. Items that are not dichotomously scored (e.g., items 2 through 5) are referred to as *weighted items*. Typically, multiple-choice items are dichotomously scored, whereas essay, performance-observation, and interview items are usually weighted.

WEIGHTED ITEMS

ANALYTICALLY SCORED WEIGHTED ITEMS

Item 3 from the list on pages 83 through 84 is weighted six points. However, its scoring key specifies that one point should be awarded for each of six features that appear within a student's response. *Weighted items with scoring keys that associate one point of the maximum possible score with a particular feature of students' responses are analytically scored.*

GLOBALLY SCORED WEIGHTED ITEMS

Item 2 from the list on pages 83 through 84 is weighted 10 points. Unlike an analytically scored item, its scoring key does not associate each one of its maximum possible points with a particular feature of students' responses. To score item 2, the teacher must *rate* certain aspects of students' responses according to a scale defined by the scoring key.

The number of features the teacher is to look for in responses to an analytically scored item equals the maximum number of points possible for the item. On the other hand, *items with scoring keys that list fewer features than the item's maximum possible score are globally scored.*

Dichotomously scored items and analytically scored weighted items tend to have better intrascorer and interscorer reliabilities than globally scored weighted items.

DESIGNING COMPLETION ITEMS

Completion items are a variety of short-answer items. *A short-answer item that presents students with the task of filling in the missing parts of an incomplete statement is a completion item.* Here are three examples:

1. *Task presented to the students:*
    America was discovered by _____.
    Scoring key: +1 for Columbus, otherwise 0.
2. Task presented to the students:
    Complete the sentence so that it expresses a feeling of guilt, but without using a form of the word *guilty*: If anything happens to Amy, I will never _____

    _____
    Scoring key: +1 if the response completes the sentence without using a form of the word *guilty* but does indicate either feelings of remorse and responsibility ("forgive myself") or a desire to punish oneself (e.g., "smile again").
3. *Task presented to the students:*
    37.97 + _____ = 19.111
    Scoring key: +1 for −18.859; otherwise 0.

Here are some more ideas for you to consider regarding the selection and design of completion items.

ADVANTAGE OF STRUCTURE

The structure of the completion format allows students to make responses that don't require as sophisticated communication skills as do other types of short-answer items. For example, the second of the three completion items just listed does not require students to write as much nor to structure their expressions as does the following item.

Task presented to the students:
Write a sentence that expresses a feeling of guilt but without using a form of the word *guilty*:
Scoring key: +1 if the response is a sentence that does not use a form of the word *guilty* but does indicate either feelings of remorse and responsibility ("forgive myself") or a desire to punish oneself (e.g., "never smile again").

TOO LITTLE INFORMATION

The additional structure of the completion format does not overcome the problem of ambiguity. "Men in a ship," "Vikings," "Native Americans," "people seeking riches," "the nineteenth century," and "explorers" are all tenable responses to item 1 on page 90. However, none of these answers is what the teacher had in mind when the scoring key was devised.

Like item 1, the following item does not contain enough information to define the task clearly:

Task presented to the students:
In _____, _____ wrote the _____ in a four-month-long _____ in _____ .
Scoring key: (5 points possible) +1 for each blank filled as follows: (1) 1787, (2) 43 people, (3) Constitution, (4) constitutional convention, and (5) Philadelphia.
The way the item is worded, students are required to guess at the teacher's intent. How should the teacher score a response that completes the sentence as follows: "In *a building, delegates* wrote the *plan for government* in the four-month-long *time* in *America*"?

TOO MUCH INFORMATION

Completion items should be designed so that, unlike the previous item, enough information is provided so that students understand the task, but unlike the item in the following example, information isn't included that gives the answer to students who haven't achieved the objective:

Ms. Bung-Lee included the following completion item in a test on food webs:

Task presented to the students:
The main problem with an exclusive wheat diet is the lack of _____; selected _____ or _____ should be added for protein.

Scoring key: (3 points possible) +1 for each blank correctly filled ("protein" in the first and "vegetables" and "meat" in the other two).

As Sue reads the item, she thinks, "Let's see, 'The main problem with an exclusive wheat diet is a lack of' . . . What? I don't have the foggiest! I'll put 'nutrition.' Okay, 'selected blank or blank should be added for protein.' *Voilà!* Now, I know what goes in that first blank!"
Sue erases "nutrition" and writes "protein."

FREQUENT MISUSE

A frequently used, but ill-advised, technique for designing completion items is to take sentences word-for-word from a textbook and replace some of the words with blanks. For example,

---

Ms. Bung-Lee is considering using one of the commercially produced achievement tests supplied by the publisher of her ninth-grade biology textbook. The first item on the test is

Task presented to the students:
Men have been studying living things for thousands of years in an
    attempt to ——————————————————— .
Scoring key: +1 for "better understand themselves."

Initially, her attention is drawn to this item because she thinks the sentence contains sexist terminology. A second look at the item leads her to question what it actually measures. Suspicious that the item actually measures recall of verbiage from the textbook rather than understanding of why people study biology, Ms. Bung-Lee conducts the following experiment: She administers the item to five of her biology students whom she is confident have poor levels of understanding of why biology is studied but who have read the passage from the textbook containing that sentence. All five score +1 on the item. She then has five biology professors from the college where she attends graduate school answer the item. All five score zero. Their responses included "explain phenomena," "solve problems," and "further knowledge."
Ms. Bung-Lee decides against using any part of the test and resolves not to design completion items by lifting sentences from textbooks.

Creating completion items out of sentences from reading matter assigned to students is such a widespread practice that completion items have the reputation of being only relevant to simple knowledge behavioral constructs. Item 2 on page 90 illustrates that completion items relevant to intellectual-level objectives can be designed.

DESIGNING MULTIPLE-CHOICE ITEMS

An item that presents a task to which the student is to select a response from a given list of alternatives is a multiple-choice item. A multiple-choice item presents its task in two parts:

1. A *stem* that asks a question, gives a direction, or gives an incomplete statement
2. A number of *alternatives* from which the student is to select the one that answers the question, follows the direction, or completes the statement presented in the stem.

The alternatives, except for the correct one, are referred to as *distractors* or *foils.*

A short-answer item can be converted into a multiple-choice item by using the short-answer item's presentation of the task for the multiple-choice stem and listing a correct response with some plausible, but incorrect, responses for the alternatives.

Here are three examples of multiple-choice items:

1. *Task presented to the students:*
   Which one of the following types of items is most likely to have satisfactory intrascorer reliability?
   a.   short-answer
   b.   essay
   c.   performance observation
   d.   multiple choice
   e.   one-to-one interview
   Scoring key: +1 for d only; otherwise 0.
2. *Task presented to the students:*
   Select the correct form of the verb to complete the sentence:
   Last year, there _____ more people at the concert than the year before.
   a. were   b. are   c. is   d. be
   Scoring key: +1 for a only; otherwise 0.
3. *Task presented to the student:*
   (Oral directions and response in a one-to-one format) The teacher displays the uppercase letters A, F, T, G, Q, R, U, and W to the student and says, "Point to the W."
   Scoring key: A check on the chart by W if the student points to it without hesitation.

Here are some ideas for you to consider regarding the selection and design of multiple-choice items.

DIRECTIONS

Ordinarily, a test with any multiple-choice items at all has at least ten of them grouped into one section, and directions are given for the entire section. The directions should clearly specify (1) how students are to communicate their selections (e.g., by circling the letter of each choice or filling in ovals on a separate answer sheet), (2) how many alternatives per item can be selected (ordinarily one and only one), (3) whether the alternative of choice for each item represents the only accurate answer or the most accurate answer, and (4) any other pertinent information (e.g., whether or not guessing is permissible).

Sometimes it is difficult to develop brief and simple directions that communicate all students need to know. Here is an example of directions that are complete but too long and complex:

> This section of the test contains 27 multiple-choice items. Each contains either a question or an incomplete statement followed by four possible answers to the question or ways to complete the statement. Only one of these four choices correctly answers the question or completes the statement so that it is true. You are to circle the letter (A, B, C, or D) in front of the one correct choice. If after carefully considering each choice for an item, you are still unsure which one to choose, make an educated guess and move on to the next item. There is no penalty for guessing. You should allow yourself about 30 minutes for this section. Each item is worth 1 point.

Students need to know all the information that these directions contain. But teachers tend to use less complete, simpler directions such as

MULTIPLE CHOICE

The appropriate compromise between the two extremes may be achieved by (1) instructing students on how to take the test and having them practice with similar items on a day before the test is administered and (2) complementing written directions with oral explanations when the test is administered.

DESIGN DIFFICULTIES

Their advantages (e.g., ease of scoring) have made multiple-choice items extremely popular. However, writing a stem, a correct alternative, and distractors that clearly and concisely confront students with a relevant task takes talent, thought, and organization. Consequently, many flawed multiple-choice items appear on both commercially produced and teacher-produced tests. For example,

---

Mr. Ascione is designing a multiple-choice item to add to his item pool for the following objective from a unit on weightlifting:

> Explains the fundamental relations among (1) weight work, (2) rest, and (3) nutrition (*Cognitive: conceptualization*)

He thinks, "I'll see if they recognize the importance of balancing the weight work with rest and nutrition for a sound program." For the stem he writes, "The plan for your weight program should include _____ ."

He thinks, "Okay, the correct response should be something like, 'a balance among weight work, rest, and nutrition.' But I think that would just measure if they remember the principle, not conceptualize it. For conceptualization, I'll have to make the answer an example of the principle. But that'll add to the wording; I don't want to make this too long. I'll narrow it down to the relation between nutrition and weight work; then the wording won't be so complicated. Hmm. . . ."

For the correct response, Mr. Ascione settles on "a diet that is in balance with the amount of energy expended lifting weights."

He doesn't give much thought to designing distractors, assuming they can be any incorrect way of completing the sentence, and he quickly finishes the item.

Task presented to the students:
The plan for your weight program should include _____ .
- **A.** an increase in caloric intake
- **B.** a decrease in caloric intake
- **C.** a diet that is in balance with the amount of energy expended lifting weights
- **D.** daily weightlifting for all major muscle groups

Scoring key: +1 for C only; otherwise 0.

Later, when the item is included on a unit test, two students have the following thoughts as they respond to it:

CHERYL: What should the plan for *my weight* program include? Let's see, A is increase caloric intake . . . I don't know. B, decrease in calories, not for *me*, I'm so skinny already. C, that one would be okay if I didn't want to gain weight, but to gain weight my diet should be greater, not equal to, the energy I burn up. I know D is wrong; muscles need rest after weight work. A is correct.

DAVID: I have no idea what my weight program should include. None of this stuff makes sense to me. So, which one of these should I pick? . . . No doubt, Ascione wants C. I don't know what it means, but it's the longest and most impressive choice and *balance* is surely a good thing.

Mr. Ascione failed to heed some of the suggestions for designing multiple-choice items that are included in the remainder of this section. Consequently, Cheryl misinterpreted the intent of the stem's wording and David used test-taking cleverness instead of objective achievement to select the correct response.

PARALLEL ALTERNATIVES

What is the content of the objective to which the following item is relevant?

Task presented to the students:
The game of table tennis _____ .
   A. originated in the United States
   B. is an effective exercise for strengthening the hamstrings
   C. is played so that only the server can score points
Scoring key: +1 for A only; otherwise 0.

The item generally deals with the game of table tennis. But more specifically, alternative A will have students thinking about the history of the game, B about its value as an exercise, and C its rules. What does the designer of this item want it to measure? The scoring key suggests that the intent is to measure students' knowledge of the history of table tennis. Why, then, should alternatives be included that pertain to content areas other than the history of table tennis?

The item should be redesigned so that the alternatives are *parallel* to one another. Alternatives are parallel if they all present ways of responding to the same task within a well-defined content area. Each of the following three multiple-choice items has only parallel alternatives:

1. *Task presented to the students:*
   In what country did table tennis originate?
   a. United States   **b.** China   **c.** Israel
   d. Japan   **e.** Iraq   **f.** Soviet Union   **g.** Korea
   Scoring key: +1 for a only; otherwise 0.
2. *Task presented to the students:*
   Table tennis, as played at the international championship level, is an especially effective exercise for _____ .
   a. strengthening the hamstrings
   b. increasing lower back flexibility
   c. increasing sprinting speed
   d. improving cardiovascular endurance
   Scoring key: +1 for d only; otherwise 0.
3. *Task presented to the students:*
   The rules of international table tennis _____ .
   a. are different for male and female players
   b. allow only the server to score
   c. penalize the server for committing a second fault
   d. provide for a change of service every fifth point
   Scoring key: +1 for d only; otherwise 0.

CONTROLLING ITEM DIFFICULTY

One method for controlling whether a multiple-choice item is easy, moderate, or hard is to manipulate the similarity among the alternatives. Which of the following two items is more difficult?

1. *Task presented to the students:*
   Who was the president of the United States when the era of southern reconstruction was officially terminated?
   a. John Tyler
   b. James Garfield
   c. Rutherford B. Hayes
   d. Ulysses S. Grant
   e. Andrew Johnson
   Scoring key: +1 for c only; otherwise 0.
2. *Task presented to the students:*
   Who was the president of the United States when the era of southern reconstruction was officially terminated?
   a. John Tyler
   b. Benjamin Franklin
   c. Rutherford B. Hayes
   d. Ralph Bunche
   e. Franklin Roosevelt
   Scoring key: +1 for c only; otherwise 0.

   More persons would probably correctly respond to the second item than to the first. The alternatives in the first are all presidents who held office between 1841 and 1881. The alternatives in the second are not all presidents, and they appear in U.S. history from colonial times well into the twentieth century. Both items are relevant to a knowledge-level objective on historical facts about the United States. However, the first is better for measuring higher levels of objective achievement, whereas the second is better for lower levels.

CORRECT RESPONSES FOR THE WRONG REASONS

Measuring Class Attention   The first of the five critical steps of item design enumerated in the beginning of this chapter is to *focus on the content and behavioral construct of the objective.* Sometimes teachers lose sight of their objectives and develop items that measure students' attention to lessons more than achievement. For example,

---

Otis reads the following item while taking one of Mr. Hansen's psychology tests:

Research studies on the effects of corporal punishment _____.
   A. show that parents who were spanked as children will spank their own children
   B. indicate that fewer than 25 percent of the parents in the United States have ever spanked their children
   C. are inconclusive

Otis thinks, "Although there's a high correlation between parents who were spanked as children and parents spanking children, A isn't really true because there are exceptions.

Obviously B isn't true. C *should* be the right answer, but Hansen wants us to put A. How many times has he said, 'violence begets violence.' No doubt, he thinks A is right because he's pushed that point so hard in class."

The next example illustrates how a student's attention in class allows him to succeed on an item without having achieved the item's objective.

Professor Lancy is evaluating a project in which children whose parents recently migrated to the United States participate in a special social studies class about their parents' native countries. As part of her data-collection procedures, Professor Lancy is administering the following multiple-choice items she drew from the project's item pool file to Ramon, a Cuban-born five-year-old.

Task presented to the students:
(Oral directions and response in a one-to-one format) The teacher places a globe (nations distinguished by colors and printed names) in front of the first-grade student and spins it around (randomly). Then the teacher tells the student, "Point to Cuba."
Scoring key: (3 points possible) +1 if the student first turns to the Western hemisphere; +1 if the student points in the vicinity of the Gulf of Mexico, Bahamas, and Caribbean Sea; +1 if the student points to Cuba.

The item is supposed to be relevant to how well the student can locate on a globe the country from which his or her parents emigrated. A project teacher told Professor Lancy that Ramon had achieved this objective because he had taken the item once before and scored 3.

Using a globe she brought from her office, Professor Lancy displays it to Ramon and says, "Point to Cuba." Unhesitatingly, Ramon turns the globe. Frowning, Ramon looks up and down as if he knows exactly what he is looking for but can't find it. Finally, Ramon tells Professor Lancy in a surprised voice, "It's not here!" Pointing to Cuba, Professor Lancy responds, "That's okay, Cuba is right here." "Oh!" said Ramon, "I thought Cuba was yellow."

Professor Lancy realizes that Ramon correctly responded to that item before because his teacher used the same globe that was used in teaching for the testing. Ramon had not achieved the objective but only associated Cuba with a color.

Most people don't think of items like the one Professor Lancy administered as multiple choice. However, please note that it fits the definition of multiple choice, with the stem being the display and the oral directive and the alternatives being the various countries on the globe.

Overlapping Alternatives   The students in the next two examples help their chances of performing well on multiple-choice items by using logical deductive reasoning, not their achievement of the items' objectives:

Ruth is taking a test on societies of central Asia as she confronts the following item, designed to measure her knowledge of the culture of Afghanistan:

The majority of the people of Afghanistan today are members of which one of the following religious faiths?
  A. Christian   **B.** Protestant   **C.** Islam
  D. Jewish   **E.** Catholic   **F.** Buddhist

Ruth thinks: "I don't know what religions they have in Afghanistan. I've got one chance in six to guess this right. That's not very good. Maybe, I can improve my chances. Let see. . . . Ah-ha! Only one answer can be right. So, I can eliminate B and E because if either of those were right, A would have to be right also. That would make two correct answers. So now my chances are up to one in four."

Amad is taking a test for a teacher-education course when he confronts the following item:

Which one of the following would prevent a *valid* test from being cost-effective?
  A. The test lacks relevance.
  B. The test lacks reliability.
  C. The test does not pertain to what is being evaluated.
  D. The test takes too much time to administer.

He thinks, "What does this guy mean by 'cost-effective'? I'll just guess A. Oh, wait! *A* can't be right because the definition of relevance is C. If either A or C is right so is the other. So the answer has to be either B or D. I've improved my chances from one in four to 50-50.

Ruth and Amad would not have been able to improve their chances through logic rather than objective achievement if the items did not include *overlapping* alternatives. Two alternatives overlap if one cannot be correct unless the other is also correct. Overlapping alternatives should be avoided except for items that are supposed to be relevant to how well students can solve logic puzzles.

Grammatical Mismatches   Examine the following item:

Task presented to the students:
The modes of 7, 3, 3, 8, 1, 7, 5, 3, 11, 7 are _____ .
  A. 7   **D.** 3 and 7
  B. 1, 3, and 7 **E.** 1 and 3
  C. 1
Scoring key: +1 for D only; otherwise 0.

A student who does not know the meaning of *mode* might well eliminate A and C because those alternatives do not match the grammatical structure of the stem. That weakness could be eliminated by rewording the stem as follows:

The mode(s) of 7, 3, 3, 8, 1, 7, 5, 3, 11, 7 is (are) _____ .

Naturally, you want your items to model proper grammar, sentence structure, and spelling. Unless you are using an item to measure knowledge of these skills, be sure all alternatives are grammatically consistent with the stem.

Standout Alternatives   Select the response that provides the most accurate answer to the following question:

According to Johnson's book, why did the Treaty of Macrabreaux fail between the tribes of Hebrueau and Yugatania?
  A. Not enough time was spent planning the treaty.
  B. Few tribespeople really wanted peace.
  C. The religious beliefs of the Yugatanians prevented them from conceiving that coexistence with "nonbelievers" (e.g., Hebrueaus) was even possible.
  D. The illiteracy rate among the Hebrueaus was too high.

If your response was typical, you guessed C. Actually, this is a nonsense item without a scoring key. But most people guess C because C's length and complexity cause it to stand out from the other alternatives.

INCORRECT RESPONSES FOR THE WRONG REASONS

Ambiguity   When designing multiple-choice items, as with any type of item, you should imagine the various ways your students might interpret the task. Ambiguity problems can be identified, and subsequently solved, by informally trying out items on one or two persons before they are included on a test. In the following example, a student confronts an item with ambiguous wording:

The following item appears on the standardized language arts test that Liz is taking:

Choose the correct verb:
My brother and friend _____ here.
  A. is   B. are

Liz thinks, "It could be either one depending on what the sentence is supposed to mean. If 'my brother and friend' is the same person, A is correct. If they're different people, B is correct."

Too Advanced for the Item   Liz, in the previous example, apparently achieved the objective that the item would have measured had it not been ambiguous. Here is an example of a student whose advanced achievement of the objective is penalized by a poorly designed item.

Ms. Lowe includes the following items among those on a test to measure her pre-algebra students' achievement of a simple knowledge objective on set language:

Task presented to the students:
How many elements are there in {a, b, e, q, w}?
A. 1   **B.** 3   **C.** 5   **D.** 7
Scoring key: +1 for C only; otherwise 0,

When Leona comes to that item while taking the test, she thinks, "You really can't tell the exact number of elements in the set. There are no more than five, so D can't be right. But we don't know whether or not $a = b$ or $b = e$ or which, if any, of the symbols represent the same element. So there could be anywhere from one to five elements in the set. A is the only correct answer because there's at least one element in the set if the *exact* number is one, two, three, four, or five."

Leona's thinking is absolutely correct, but Ms. Lowe was not thinking at that sophisticated level when she designed the item.

All alternatives should be approximately equal in length and complexity.

PLAUSIBLE DISTRACTORS

Examine the following item.

Task presented to the students:
The People's Republic of China was established in 1949 under the leader-
   ship of_____.
   A.   Chou En-lai
   B.   people who wanted to reinstate a monarchy
   C.   Babe Ruth
   D.   Jiang Quing
   E.   Marlin Printer
   F.   Mao Tse-tung
Scoring key: +1 for F only; otherwise 0.

In addition to B not being parallel to any of the other alternatives, C and E would hardly serve to distract even students with virtually no knowledge of China's history. The item designer may have been trying to be humorous by including C, but why waste students' time and disrupt their thinking about the content of the test with such a joke? E should be replaced with a Chinese name.

If students who have not achieved the objective never select a particular distractor, that distractor should be eliminated or modified.

PLACEMENT OF THE CORRECT RESPONSE

Where should the correct response be placed among an item's alternatives? The correct response should be *randomly* located. Sometimes teachers are tempted to place correct responses among alternatives so that answers form a pattern on the test key that will make the test easier to score. Students soon realize this and waste their test-taking time searching for, and often discovering, the pattern. Correct responses to the multiple-choice items on a test should appear in each alternative position about the same number of times. An inordinate number of B alternatives being correct, for example, will affect the guess factor.

Another temptation to resist is trying to "hide" the correct response somewhere in the middle of the alternatives. This practice is particularly tempting when responses are numerical, such as in the following example.

Task presented to the students:
What number if w if $w + 12 = 30$?
A. 12   **B.** 18   **C.** 28   **D.** 42
Scoring key: +1 for B only; otherwise 0.

When students guess on these types of items, they select "in-between" alternatives more often than extreme ones.

NUMBER OF ALTERNATIVES

Up to this point, you've seen a multiple-choice item with only two alternatives (p. 100) and one with as many alternatives as there are countries on a globe (p. 98). The use of four or five alternatives is conventional.

In deciding the number of alternatives for an item, keep in mind the following: (1) Guessing by students is more difficult for items with fewer alternatives than for items with more alternatives; (2) it is easier to design an item with a few rather than many parallel and plausible alternatives; (3) the fewer the alternatives, the more usable the item.

CORRECTION FOR GUESSING

By using nothing more than random guess, a student has one chance in four of selecting the correct response to a multiple-choice item that has four alternatives. It is not unlikely for students to guess correctly one multiple-choice item and guess incorrectly another although both items are designed to measure the same objective. Thus, the guessing factor tends to contaminate the internal consistency of the test results.

To combat this threat to measurement reliability, teachers and test publishers sometimes use a *correction-for-guessing* technique. When such a technique is used, students are directed to select *only* alternatives to multiple-choice items that they are reasonably certain to be correct. For items that they do not know how to answer, they are directed either not to answer or to select an alternative worded "I do not know." Test scores are then figured by using one of several correction-for-guessing formulas. One popular formula is

$$S = C - (W/(A - 1))$$

where C = the number of items to which the student correctly responded,
 W = the number of items to which the student incorrectly responded (not including those not answered or for which "I don't know" was selected), and
 A = the number of alternatives per item.

Obviously, this formula applies only when the multiple-choice items have the same number of alternatives and are dichotomously scored.

The issue of whether or not correction-for-guessing should be used was quite a controversial issue at one time (Sax, 1980). In recent years, measurement specialists tend to agree that it is a mistake to use correction-for-guessing techniques (Cangelosi, 1982). Although discouraging some students from guessing, the practice introduces a question for students to answer on each item that is *irrelevant* to their achievement of objectives. They must decide whether or not to attempt the item. Consequently, scores are influenced by students' propensities to take chances.

The guessing factor can be better controlled by including a large number of items in the multiple-choice section of the test. When many items (e.g., more than 20) are used, the influence of guessing on scores is equitable and predictable across a group of students. The smaller the number of alternatives per item, the more items will be needed to combat the guessing factor.

DIAGNOSTIC POTENTIAL

The teacher in the following example designs multiple-choice items with parallel and plausible alternatives that provide diagnostic information for formative evaluations.

Mr. Chapley, a fourth-grade teacher, is expanding his item pool file for the following objective:

Computes the product of a three-digit and a one-digit whole number for cases where regrouping is necessary and none of the digits is 0 (*Cognitive: knowledge of a process*)

Mr. Chapley attempts to build items that will provide information not only on how well students can execute computations but also on exactly what they are doing when they compute incorrectly. Over the years, he has identified a number of common error patterns that students make while executing the computation specified in this objective. Thus, he thinks, as he designs one item, "For the stem I'll use 423 × 7. That fits the content of the objective. If that's multiplied out correctly it's ahh . . . , 2,961; so that'll be one of the alternatives. Okay, I'll get the distractors by using some of the common error patterns. Let's see, if I multiply from left to right and do the carrying, I get, let's see . . . 2,323. Executing the algorithm correctly except adding the carried digit before multiplying gets, ahh . . . , 4,281. One more; sometimes they just multiply two unit's digits and bring the rest down. That comes out to be . . . , 4,221." The following item is entered into the item pool:

Task presented to the students:
423 × 7 = _____
A. 2,323   **B.** 4,281   **C.** 4,221   **D.** 2,961
Scoring key: +1 for D only; otherwise 0 and record the chosen distractor.

When this item is used on a test, Mr. Chapley will record the percentage of students who select each alternative. This information is then used in planning subsequent lessons.

TAXING COMPREHENSION SKILLS

Although students don't have to formulate expressions in response to multiple-choice items as they do for short-answer, essay, and interview items, multiple-choice items do require students to possess fairly sophisticated comprehension skills. Writing multiple-choice items so that they are simple for students to read often leads to ambiguity.

While taking one of Ms. Bung-Lee's biology tests, Pace reads the following item:

Human cells have _____ chromosomes.
A. 18   **B.** 26   **C.** 46   **D.** 58

Pace thinks, "All normal cells have 46 chromosomes except, of course, egg cells in females and sperm cells in males—they have only 23. And I'll bet there're billions of abnormal cells that have extra or missing chromosomes. So the only choice that is always correct is A, 18. All cells have at least 18 chromosomes; all don't have 46. Is this a trick question? If Bung-Lee's testing reasoning, the answer is A. If it's memory, it's C."
Pace informs Ms. Bung-Lee of his dilemma. She apologizes and tells him to mark C. Afterward, she returns to her item pool and rewords the item's stem as follows:

What is the maximum number of chromosomes that a human cell has, providing that the cell is normal and is not a sex cell?

Ms. Bung-Lee is pleased that the revised version of the item is not ambiguous like the original one, nor should it discriminate against students for being advanced. However, she's unhappy that the new wording requires a higher level of reading comprehension skills. She worries that some students will now miss the item, not because they haven't achieved the objective but because they have difficulty understanding the question.

RANGE OF BEHAVIORAL CONSTRUCTS

Multiple-choice items can be designed for affective behavioral constructs and for cognitive behavioral constructs from simple knowledge through application. Chapters 5 and 6 contain suggestions for designing items for specific cognitive and affective levels. Multiple-choice items are not appropriate for objectives that require students to synthesize expressions, think divergently, or display creative behaviors.

EFFICIENT USE OF WORDS

Respond to the following item:

Select the answer that correctly answers the question; write down the letter of your choice.
What is the purpose of a table of specifications?
A. A table of specifications enhances the internal consistency of a test by providing guidelines for having at least two points for each objective.
B. A table of specifications provides a guideline for distributing the points of a test so that objectives are emphasized according to their relative importance.
C. A table of specification provides guidelines for making a test's items relevant to the objectives that they are designed to measure.
D. A table of specifications enhances the construct validity of a test by providing guidelines for having test scores influenced by all behavioral construct levels in *Bloom's Taxonomy*.

As you determined your choice of responses to the item, did you feel you wasted time and energy repeatedly reading the same words (e.g., "a table of specifications," "test," and "guidelines")? The item could be streamlined so that those confronting it could spend more time thinking about the purpose of a table of specifications and less time mired in words. Here is one possibility:

Select the option that makes the statement true; write down the letter of your choice.
The purpose of a table of specifications is to provide guidelines for distributing the points on a test so that _____ .
A. internal consistency is enhanced by having at least two points for each objective
B. objectives are emphasized according to their relative importance

C. the items are relevant to the objectives that they are designed to measure
D. construct validity is enhanced by including all behavioral construct levels in *Bloom's Taxonomy*

The item is easier to read when words common to all alternatives are transferred to the stem. The differences among alternatives are more apparent when information about the task is concentrated in the stem and the wording for alternatives is brief.

DESIGNING TRUE/FALSE ITEMS

A multiple-choice item that presents students with the task of judging a statement as either true or false is a true/false item. The *statement* is the item's stem; *true* and *false* are the alternatives.

Two examples of true/false items follow.

1. *Task presented to the students:*
    Circle T if the statement is always true and F if it is *not* always true:
    T   F   According to the Constitution, it is illegal to prevent a U.S. citizen from serving as president of the U.S. solely because of his or her age.
    Scoring key: +1 for circling F only; otherwise 0.
2. *Task presented to the students:*
    (Oral directions; student responds by circling T or F on the answer sheet) The teacher reads the statement: 7 is less than *or* equal to 15
    Scoring key: +1 for circling T only; otherwise 0.

Here are some more ideas for you to consider regarding the selection and design of true/false items.

THE MEANING OF "TRUE" AND "FALSE"

True/false items cannot be depended on to provide valid information on students' achievements unless the students are first taught the meaning of the phrases *true statement* and *false statement*. To illustrate the concern, judge each of the following three statements as either true or false:

1. All valid measurements are reliable.
2. If X is a number, then X is less than X^2.
3. Carnivores eat plants.

Statement 1 is true because, by definition, a measurement would not be valid unless it is reliable. Reliability is a necessary condition for validity. However, some people would argue that to be valid, a measurement must *also* be relevant, so it's not sufficient to say a valid measurement is reliable. By making that argument, people don't display a lack of understanding of validity, relevance, and reliability; they display a misunderstanding of what is meant by a "true statement." Thus, a true/false item using statement 1 fails to indicate much about their understanding of validity.

Statement 2 is false because there are numbers (e.g., 0 and 0.5) that are not less than their squares (e.g., $0 = 0^2$ and $0.5 > 0.5^2$ because $0.5 > 0.25$). However, some people would argue that the statement is true because numbers exist (e.g., 3) that are less than their squares ($3 < 3^2$ since $3 < 9$). But the standard logicians' definition of "true" and "false" statements provides that a statement is true only if it is true for all cases and false if it is false for at least one case. Students should not be exposed to true/false items before they are taught these conventions.

Whether statement 3 is true or false depends on how it is interpreted; thus, it is ambiguous. By definition carnivores, such as dogs, eat *primarily* meat. But this doesn't exclude them from also eating some plants (as many dogs do). If the statement is interpreted *"some* carnivores eat plants," then it's true. If it's interpreted *"all* carnivores eat plants," then it's false.

Teachers sometimes choose a true/false format because they think the items will be easy to score and the statements can be readily developed. Surely true/false items are easy to score, but developing the statements and training students to take true/false items are difficult tasks.

LITERALLY TRUE STATEMENTS

The day after administering a biology test, Ms. Bung-Lee returns the scored papers and begins reviewing the results with her class. Phil raises an issue about one true/false item Ms. Bung-Lee had included to measure their knowledge of the definition of *ecosystem.*

PHIL: The statement says, "An ecosystem can be defined as a group of organisms." I marked true because an ecosystem *could* be defined that way or any other way for that matter.

AMALYA: But it's not. The answer is false because our definition of an ecosystem said that it included relationships among organisms and their environments, not just as . . .

PHIL (interrupting): I know what *our* definition said, but you're not reading the statement right. It says, *"can* be defined." The word *can* means "it is possible to do so" and it is *possible* to define ecosystem as "a green hotdog with warts"!

AMALYA: Oh, you know what Ms. Bung-Lee meant!

MS. BUNG-LEE: Thank you, Amalya, for trying to defend my item, but I really can't argue with Phil.

STAN: "Oh, no! Does that mean you're going to mark the rest of us wrong for putting false?

MS. BUNG-LEE: No, I won't do that. But next time I will be more careful how I word these statements.

PHIL: This one would have been okay if you had put "According to the definition agreed to in class, an ecosystem is a group of organisms." Then the statement would be *literally* false.

Ground rules for true/false items should be established and taught to students. Only nonambiguous statements whose literal meanings can be verified as either true or false should be used. Students shouldn't be burdened with the task of judging whether they should interpret the statement literally or "read

TABLE 4.1   Literal Meanings of Some Common Terms

Term	Meaning
all:	every member of a group; 100 percent; without exception
always:	every time; occurs 100 percent of the time; never fails to occur
and:	in addition to (e.g., "Erica, Amanda, and Kelly played basketball" is a *true* statement if and only if *all three* of those named played basketball. If one did not, the statement is false. A compound statement consisting of two clauses joined by the conjunction *and* is true if and only if both clauses are true. See parallel example and statements for the definition of the word *or.*)
because:	for the reason that (One event occurs *because* of another if and only if the first would not happen in the absence of the second.)
certain:	a probability of one
every:	all possible; without exception
few:	more than one but not many (e.g., between two and ten)
impossible:	cannot happen; probability of zero
independent:	not influenced by (Two events are independent if the occurrence of one has no bearing on whether or not the other occurs.)
likely:	has at least a 50 percent chance of occuring; probable
many:	a large number relative to the situation
more:	greater in number or amount
most:	the greatest number in a group
mutually exclusive:	impossible to occur at the same time (Two events are *mutually exclusive* if the probability of both events occurring simultaneously is zero.)
never:	at no time
none:	zero
only:	uniquely
only if:	cannot occur unless
or:	as an alternative to (e.g., "Erica, Amanda, or Kelly played basketball" is a *true* statement if and only if *at least one* of those named played basketball. The statement is false only if none of them played. A compound statement consisting of two clauses joined by the conjunction *or* is true if and only if at least one of the clauses is true. See parallel example and statements for the definition of the word *and.*)
possible:	can occur; a probability greater than zero
probably:	a probability of at least 50 percent
some:	at least one

between the lines" to figure out the teacher's intent. They should be taught before the test to interpret statements literally.

For students to comprehend literal meanings of statements, they need to be familiar with literal definitions of some commonly used, but frequently misunderstood, *quantitative* terms. Literal definitions for some of those terms are given in Table 4.1.

"If-then" statements can be useful in true/false items for measuring intellectual-level behavioral constructs. However, students should be taught how to interpret such statements before they are used in true/false items. The following example illustrates that need.

One of the true/false items on the mathematics test Barbara is taking reads,

T   F   If there were no negative numbers, then 15 could not be subtracted from 9.

Barbara thinks, "The answer is false, for two reasons. There really are negative numbers and 15 can be subtracted from 9.

Barbara missed the item, not because she failed to achieve the mathematics objective the item was designed to measure, but because she failed to comprehend the if-then statement.

AMBIGUOUS STATEMENTS

One of Mr. Little's tests on the Constitution includes a true/false item with the following statement:

Before the Nineteenth Amendment was adopted in 1920, women in the United States did not have the right to vote.

Bernie is quite familiar with the Nineteenth Amendment, but he responds "false" when Mr. Little's scoring key says "true" because Bernie thinks, "Morally, women always had the *right* to vote. They were just prevented from exercising that right before the Nineteenth Amendment."

Later, after discovering that several students interpreted "right" as "what is right," Mr. Little refined the item so that the statement read,

> Before the Nineteenth Amendment was adopted in 1920, the right of women to vote was not protected by the Constitution.

The statements listed in the left-hand column of Table 4.2 are too ambiguous for true/false items. Less ambiguous statements are in the right-hand column.

DESCRIPTIVE RATHER THAN JUDGMENTAL STATEMENTS

Descriptive statements are more appropriate for true/false items than judgmental statements. Judgmental statements tend to be ambiguous and cannot be verified as true or false. The statements listed in the left-hand column of Table 4.3 are judgmental; descriptive statements are to the right.

NUMBER OF ITEMS AND GUESSING

Keep in mind that true/false items are multiple-choice items with only two alternatives. Students are able to respond correctly to about half of true/false items simply by random guessing. To combat the guessing factor, *many* true/false items should be included on a test if any are included at all.

COMBINING TRUE/FALSE AND SHORT-ANSWER ITEMS

Some teachers use items for which students are to judge statements as true or false and then (1) reword false statements to make them true, (2) explain why

TABLE 4.2   Ambiguous and Improved Statements for True/False Items

Ambiguous	Improved
Snakes are poisonous.	The bites of some snakes are poisonous to people.
Snakes are poisonous.	The bites of all snakes are poisonous to people.
Jupiter is the largest planet.	The largest known planet in our solar system is Jupiter.
Drinking orange juice is unhealthy.	Orange juice contains none of the vitamins essential to a healthy human body.
Thomas Jefferson wrote the Declaration of Independence.	According to historical accounts, Thomas Jefferson wrote the initial draft of the Declaration of Independence.

TABLE 4.3   Descriptive Statements Are More Appropriate for True/False Items

Judgmental	Descriptive
Benjamin Franklin is one of the most significant figures in American history.	Benjamin Franklin's influence on the formation of the U.S. government is a major topic of many history books.
Citizens should cherish their right of free speech.	Many court cases have been heard over disputes involving individuals' right of free speech.
Good classroom citizens pick up after themselves.	One of our classroom citizenship rules is to pick up after ourselves.
It is not as important to have a high school diploma as it was 25 years ago.	According to the O'Connel survey of 25 years ago, a higher ratio of job openings required a high school diploma than is required today.

false statements are false, or (3) provide counter-examples to false statements. For example,

> *Task presented to the students:*
> T   F   When the Nineteenth Amendment to the U.S. Constitution took effect in 1920, no person in the United States could be legally denied the right to vote solely because of sex, race, or ethnic background.
>
> If you circled F, explain why in one sentence.
>
> _____
>
> _____
>
> *Scoring key:* +1 if F is circled *and* if a correct counter-example is provided (e.g., "Native-born Americans were excluded").

Unlike true/false items and other types of multiple-choice items, this type of item requires students to provide their own expressions and should be treated as a short-answer item.

DESIGNING MULTIPLE-ANSWER MULTIPLE-CHOICE ITEMS

A multiple-choice item that presents students with the task of determining whether or not each one of its alternatives is true is a multiple-answer multiple-choice item. For example,

1. *Task presented to the students:*
    Circle the letter in front of each alternative that correctly completes the statement. All, none, or a portion of the alternatives may be correct.

An exercise for strengthening the quadriceps is the _____ .
a. toe raise
b. leg press
c. bench press
d. leg curl
e. half squat
f. bench knee extension
g. leg lift

Scoring key: (7 points possible) +1 for each of the following that is circled: b, e, and f; +1 for each of the following that is *not* circled: a, c, d, and g.

2. *Task presented to the students:*
Draw a ring around each adjective in the sentence below:
    The hungry boy thought the big banana was ripe.
Scoring key: (10 points possible) +1 for each of the following words that is encircled: *hungry, big,* and *ripe;* +1 for each of the other seven words that is *not* circled.

The multiple-answer multiple-choice format simply provides a convenient way of combining a number of true/false items with a common stem. Item 1 supplants seven true/false items similar to

T   F   An exercise for strengthening the quadriceps is the toe raise.

At first glance, item 2 may not appear equivalent to ten true/false items. However, reflect on the thinking process students use as they respond to item 2. They judge ten statements as true or false in a way similar to the following:

The word *The* in the sentence "The hungry boy thought the big banana was ripe" is an adjective.

Some commercially produced and teacher-produced tests contain items that appear to use a standard multiple-choice format, but the items are really multiple-answer multiple-choice. For example,

Task presented to the students:
Langston Hughes wrote _____ .
   A. *Mulatto*
   B. *Day of Absence*
   C. *Native Son*
   D. both A and B
   E. both A and C
   F. both B and C
   G. A, B, and C
   H. none of the above
Scoring key: +1 for A only; otherwise 0.

You are advised against designing or selecting items of this sort. Students expend greater effort and time sorting out the item's puzzle of directions and words than they do with any task related to the objective.

The ideas presented here for true/false items should also be applied to the selection and design of multiple-answer multiple-choice items.

DESIGNING MATCHING ITEMS

Matching items are a common variation of the multiple-choice format. *A matching item presents students with two lists and the task of associating each entry of one list with an entry from the second list.* For example,

Task presented to the students:
Column A is a list of quantities. For each, determine the most convenient unit from Column B for measuring that quantity. "Most convenient," in this case, means the unit that will yield more familiar numbers (e.g., between 0 and 1,000 rather than numbers like .000000003 or 8,900,044,678). Express your choices by writing letters from Column B in the blanks of Column A. Any one unit from Column B may be used once, more than once, or not at all.

A	**B**
_____ 1. Your own weight	A. centimeter
_____ 2. The thickness of a cement slab	B. kilogram
_____ 3. The distance between New Orleans and Louisville	C. kilometer
_____ 4. The land size of South Dakota	D. square kilometer
_____ 5. The weight of an insect	E. square meter
_____ 6. The amount a house plant has grown in a year	F. gram
_____ 7. The size of a garden	
_____ 8. The floor space in a warehouse	
_____ 9. The altitude of a satellite orbiting the earth	

Scoring key: (9 points possible) +1 for each blank filled in as follows: 1–B, 2–A, 3–C, 4–D, 5–F, 6–A, 7–E, 8–E, 9–C.

The left-hand column of a matching item is a sequence of multiple-choice stems called *premises*. The right-hand column contains the *responses*, which form a list of alternatives for each premise.

Following is a very poorly constructed matching item. Administer it to yourself, analyze it, and discover its weaknesses.

Task presented to the students:

Match the elements of Column A with those of Column B by placing the letter of your choice from Column B. Use each letter once.

A	B
_____ 1. E. L. Thorndike	A. Developed the first mechanical device for self-instruction in 1924
_____ 2. associationists	B. Animals tend to repeat satisfying experiences
_____ 3. faculty psychology	C. Developed the first branching programmed-learning machine
_____ 4. law of readiness	D. Called the "Father of Behavioristic Psychology"
_____ 5. John Watson	E. Causes students initially to enjoy teaching machines and then lose interest in them over time
_____ 6. Norman Crowder	F. Concluded in 1890 that general memory was not a faculty that could be trained
_____ 7. pall effect	G. An individual will not be satisfied to act in a certain way until he or she is ready
_____ 8. William James	H. Includes the belief that transfer of training could occur between disciplines
_____ 9. Sidney Pressy	I. A student of William James who is largely responsible for connectionism theory
_____ 10. law of effect	J. A school of thought that maintained that memory is a process by which experiences are restated through reexcitement of a location of the brain

Scoring key: (10 points possible) +1 for each blank completed as follows: 1–I, 2–J, 3–H, 4–G, 5–D, 6–C, 7–E, 8–F, 9–A, 10–B.

Although the general content of this item appears to be learning theory, someone knowing virtually nothing about learning theory could figure out most of the matches. A student who only knows two key matches can use deductive reasoning to obtain the other eight.

Here are some more ideas for you to consider regarding the selection and design of matching items.

A COMMON BASIS FOR THE MATCHES

There should be one common basis for matching all premises with alternatives and that basis should be specified in the item's directions. In the faulty item just given, there isn't a common basis for all the matches. Five of Column A's elements are persons, three are laws, and two are schools of thought. This weakness could be remedied by having one item for matching names, another for laws, and one for schools of thought. The directions could specify the basis for the match (e.g., "Match each theory stated in Column A with the person, listed in Column B, who advanced that theory").

If there is a common basis for all matches, all alternatives should be plausible for each premise.

PROCESS OF ELIMINATION

To prevent students from narrowing down the possible responses to premises by deductive reasoning unrelated to objective achievement,

1. Design the item so that some responses are correct for more than one premise and others are not correct for any premise.
2. Do not use the same number of responses as there are premises.

BRIEF RESPONSES

Did you get tired of rereading the lengthy responses when you administered the faulty matching item to yourself? To keep students from wasting time rereading lengthy phrases, the responses should be shorter than the premises. The premises need be read only once, but students will need to look at the entire list of responses each time a premise is considered.

DESIGNING WEIGHTED MULTIPLE-CHOICE ITEMS

The scoring key for a *weighted multiple-choice item* specifies that different point values should be awarded depending on which alternative students choose. For example,

Task presented to the students:

Which one of the following would you most likely do if and when a friend of yours invites you to smoke a marijuana cigarette? (Assume no one else is present at the time.) Check only one:

_____ **A.** Accept the invitation and smoke.

_____ **B.** Refuse the invitation and not say much more about it.

_____ **C.** Refuse the invitation and try to convince my friend not to smoke one either.

_____ **D.** I'm too uncertain to know what I'd probably do.

Scoring key: Score on a 3-point scale: 0 for A, +1 for D, +2 for B, and +3 for C.

Weighted multiple-choice items are frequently used in conjunction with *Likert* (1932) *scales* to measure affective behavioral constructs. With a Likert scale, the multiple-choice stem is a statement and the alternatives are choices designed to reflect the students' degree of agreement with that statement. For example,

Task presented to the students:

Circle SA if you strongly agree with statement, A if you agree, NO for no opinion, D if you disagree, and SD if you strongly disagree:

Our fourth grade should attempt to write a document on how the class will be governed.

Scoring key: Score on a 4-point scale: 0 for SD, +1 for D, +2 for NO, +3 for A, and +4 for SA.

You should take into consideration the same ideas presented for multiple-choice items when you select or design weighted multiple-choice items. Particular attention needs to be paid to defining the task clearly, avoiding ambiguity, and having parallel alternatives.

DESIGNING ESSAY ITEMS

An item that presents a task to which the student is to respond by writing a literary composition of at least one paragraph, but normally not more than several pages, is an essay item. For example,

Task presented to the students:

Pretend that you have a friend in the fifth grade who writes you this note:

"In math class we were told how to find the area of a rectangle. I know how to use this formula:

Area = length × width.

But I don't understand *why* multiplying the length and width gives me the area. Our teacher didn't explain that to us. Since you're in the sixth grade, would you please explain to me why $A = l \times w$?"

Use about one sheet of paper to write your fifth-grade friend a note that explains *why* the area of a rectangle equals its length times its width. Include one or two pictures to help you with the explanation. But fill most of the page with sentences.

Scoring key: (8 points possible) Points distributed as follows:

+1 if the overall explanation accurately distinguishes area from other geometrical properties

+1 if the goal of determining the number of unit squares inside the bounds of the rectangle is established

+1 if the number of units in the length is related to the number of unit squares in the area

+1 if the number of unit squares in the width is related to the number of unit squares in the area

+1 if the idea of multiplication as repeated addition (e.g., as a way of counting by widths (or lengths) is used

+1 if the explanation uses at least one appropriate paradigm

+2 according to the following rating scale:

+2 if at least two-thirds of a page is filled and there are no mathematical errors in the explanation

+1 if at least two-thirds of a page is filled and there is one and only one mathematical error and it doesn't involve a misconception about area

0 if less than two-thirds of a page is filled, if there is an indication of a misconception about area, or if there is more than one mathematical error

Here are some ideas for you to consider regarding the selection and design of essay items.

TIME FOR ESSAY ITEMS

Students are expected to spend far more time responding to a single essay item than to a single short-answer or multiple-choice item. It will generally take you more time to score one essay item than a whole section of multiple-choice items. Consequently, it is rarely efficient to try to include an essay item for each objective to be measured by a test. The test blueprint from Figure 3.1, for example, outlines a test for nine objectives, only two of which are measured by essay items.

FLEXIBILITY OF EXPRESSION

Essay items allow students considerable flexibility in how they express responses. Such flexibility, not available with multiple-choice and short-answer items, is essential for measuring objectives that focus on students' abilities to structure and organize ideas.

Ability to structure and organize ideas is not a concern of cognitive knowledge and psychomotor objectives. The use of essay items should be limited to intellectual and affective objectives.

Taxing Writing Skills

The premium that essay items place on students' writing skills is advantageous when writing ability is important to objective achievement, as it would be for the following objective:

> Describes, in writing, a personal experience that evoked a feeling of frustration (*Cognitive: application*)

But for some objectives, students' lack of writing skills may prevent them from demonstrating, with an essay item, their level of achievement. Consider Tyrone's tragic case:

By the time Tyrone reached ninth grade, he had acquired a keen understanding and interest in history. Tyrone's ninth-grade history teacher, Ms. Dearborne, used essay tests almost exclusively. Although Tyrone achieved Ms. Dearborne's history objectives at an advanced level, he never scored high on her achievement tests, which taxed his writing skills. Consequently, both Tyrone and Ms. Dearborne became convinced that he understood little about history. In time, he became discouraged and lost interest in the subject.

Unfortunately, Tyrone's case is not unusual for a number of academic subjects. Please daydream for about five minutes and imagine that Tyrone had a different ninth-grade teacher and that the story had taken a different turn.

By the time Tyrone reached ninth grade, he had acquired a keen understanding and interest in history. Tyrone's ninth-grade teacher, Ms. Bernstein, used a variety of item formats including essay, multiple choice, short answer, and interview. Although Tyrone achieved Ms. Bernstein's history objectives at an advanced level, neither he nor Ms. Bernstein were convinced of his achievement because his test results were inconsistent.

An analysis of the results revealed that Tyrone scored poorly on items requiring written responses longer than several words. Tyrone scored much higher on other types of items. To assess her suspicion that Tyrone lacked writing skill, Ms. Bernstein administered an essay test to Tyrone that was designed to measure writing skills rather than history objectives. Because of the results of this writing test, Ms. Bernstein recommended that Tyrone enroll in a program for improving writing skills.

In the meantime, Ms. Bernstein found ways of measuring Tyrone's achievement of history objectives that did not depend on sophisticated writing skills. As his writing skills improved, she gradually reintroduced Tyrone to history tests containing essay items.

COMMON BUT UNNECESSARY WEAKNESSES

Vaguely Defined Tasks   Gronlund (1982) relates the following anecdote illustrating how differential writing skills among students can contaminate the relevance of essay items so that, unlike Tyrone, some nonachieving students score well.

A college bureau selected a student with special skills and sent him into a midsemester examination in place of a regular student in order to determine how well he could do on an essay test without preparation. The main question called for critical evaluation of a novel that the student had not read. His answer started out something as follows: "This is not the best novel I have ever read, but neither is it the worst. It has some real strengths, such as the detailed attention given in the development of the main characters. On the other hand, some of the minor characters have not been developed as they might be. . . ." His evaluation continued along in this vein. The paper was returned the next class meeting along with this comment by the professor: "This is the best evaluation of this novel I have ever read."

Students have been exposed to so many poorly designed essay items that the confident writer tends to think of them as something to "fake my way through by impressing the teacher with how well I write." Less confident writers simply want to avoid them.

Poor Intrascorer and Interscorer Reliabilities   Essay items, *as they are typically designed,* tend to have poor intrascorer and interscorer reliabilities. Hundreds of studies have been conducted that support the conclusions from some classic works about essay items (Chase, 1978):

> The passing or failing of forty percent (of students) depends, not on what they know, but on *who* reads the papers. . . . The passing of about ten percent . . . on *when* the papers are read.   (Ashburn, 1938, pp. 1–3)

> . . . a C paper may be graded B if it is read after an illiterate theme, but if it follows an A paper . . . it seems to be of D caliber.   (Stalnaker, 1936, p. 41)

> Scorer unreliability tends to increase when one attempts to capitalize on the essay test's unique characteristics—flexibility and freedom of choice. This factor, no doubt, accounts for the great disparity in the reader [scorer] reliability values reported in the literature; the disparity ranges from as low as .32 to as

high as .98. It is not difficult to obtain high scorer reliability if essay questions are narrow and carefully structured.   (Stanley & Hopkins, 1972, p. 199)

SPECIFYING THE TASK

Detail   You no doubt noticed that the sample essay item opening the section on Designing Essay Items is not typical of the essay items found in schools. For one thing, the task is described in greater detail than in typical items (e.g., "Explain the formula for the area of a rectangle"). Lack of detail in presenting the item's task is a principal reason essay items are reputed to measure only writing skills rather than intended objectives.

With the help of an assertive student, one teacher improves an essay item in the following example.

The following is included among Mr. Turpin's objectives for a unit on the human circulatory system:

Explains the mechanism by which blood is moved through the heart (*Cognitive: conceptualization*)

Mr. Turpin has not learned to maintain item pools, but out of concern for this objective, he writes as item 12 on the test

12.   Discuss the passage of blood through the heart.

Vanessa, one of Mr. Turpin's eleventh-graders, thinks as she reaches item 12 on the test, "Discuss with whom? It takes two to have a discussion! What does he want me to write? How about 'I'm really happy blood passes through my heart or else I'd be dead'? That might make Turpin laugh but not give me a grade. Get serious; you're running out of time! Okay, I'll give him a paragraph on the importance of the heart's function."

The next day as Mr. Turpin returns the test papers, he comments to the class, "I'm very disappointed in the answers I got for item 12. Three of you wrote way too much. Jamie gave me four pages and apparently didn't have time to finish the test. But most of you didn't even tell why blood moves through the heart."

ROSS: You only gave me 2 out of 10 points on that one and I did write *why* blood moves through the heart!

MR. TURPIN: Read your answer to the class.

ROSS: Blood passes through the heart so that the oxygen-poor blood is replaced with oxygen-rich blood.

JAMIE: That's all you wrote?

ROSS: I gave the reason why blood passes through the heart.

MR. TURPIN: But that's not what I meant. You were supposed to write a lot more and describe how blood passes through the heart.

VANESSA: But the test just says "discuss." It doesn't say anything about describing how or why blood passes through the heart. I'll bet every one of us did what the test asked. We all discussed the passage of the blood through the heart.

MR. TURPIN: But some discussed it very well in a nice one-page essay; others just wrote a sentence.

VANESSA: You can't blame them. Whole books are written to describe how blood passes through the heart. How much detail did you want us to put?

Mr. Turpin begins to realize that item 12 did not clearly define the task. After some thought, he changes the item so that it reads as follows:

With the aid of a diagram, explain the mechanics of how venous blood while in the heart is transported through the human heart and to the lungs. Make sure you indicate the direction and locations of the venous blood while in the heart. Note how action of the heart maintains the flow. Write, not including the diagram, from 1 to 1.5 pages.

Describe, compare, contrast, explain, and *summarize* are just a few of the terms that provide students with a better idea of the intended task than does *discuss*.

Length   As Mr. Turpin discovered, students need guidelines for how much to write. Phrases like "in the space provided below" and "from one to two pages" help define the task. They also help you control the length of the papers you will have to read.

Target Audience   The essay item beginning at the bottom of page 116 directs students to write the essay as if it were to be read by a fifth-grade friend. This tactic of identifying target readers for essays further defines the task for students. After all, the teacher who will actually read students' essays doesn't need an explanation of why $A = l \times w$. Identifying an audience for a particular piece of writing helps students adjust their writing to the level expected by the teacher.

ENHANCING INTRASCORER AND INTERSCORER RELIABILITIES

The intrascorer and interscorer reliability problems associated with essay items are solved by having *detailed scoring keys* that are faithfully followed. In the previous example, Mr. Turpin improved his item. However, unless he devises easy-to-follow parameters for scoring the item *before* administering the improved item, he will fail to score the item consistently.

Here are two possible scoring keys for Mr. Turpin's improved item. The first will make the item *analytically scored;* the second, *globally scored.*

Scoring key: (8 points possible) Points distributed as follows:

+1 for each of the following the student indicates in the essay: (1) venous blood enters through the superior and inferior venae cavae; (2) venous blood gathers in the right atrium; (3) proper role of the valves in the right side of the heart; (4) venous blood gathers in the right ventrical; (5) venous blood exits the heart through the pulmonary arteries; (6) the heart's pumping motion; (7) how the heart's pumping motion causes the venous blood to flow.

+1 if the essay does not indicate venous blood anywhere that it does not actually reside.

(*Note:* The scoring should not be influenced by whether or not the student accurately labels the parts mentioned in the key. Only the ideas play a role in the scoring of this item.)

Scoring key: (5 points possible to be based on the degree to which the essay displays an understanding of (1) the mechanics of how the heart causes venous blood to circulate through the heart and (2) the path that venous blood takes through the heart). The following rating scale is to be used:

+5 for understanding well above the average of the class
+4 if slightly above this average
+3 if about this average
+2 if slightly below this average
+1 if well below this average

Which scoring method for essay items will tend to have superior intrascorer and interscorer reliabilities? Analytical scoring is usually more reliable. However, if well-defined rating scales are used, globally scored items can have satisfactory intrascorer and interscorer reliabilities.

DESIGNING ORAL DISCOURSE ITEMS

An item that presents a task to which the student is to respond by giving a talk or speech that is more complex than a simple recitation is an oral discourse item. For example,

Task presented to the students:

(Presented by audiotape recording) "I made up this story to test your understanding of the Constitution. One day Johnny was walking down one of our city's streets when two police officers stopped him. One said, 'We saw what you did and you're under arrest. You'll have to come with us to the police station.' Johnny asked, 'What did I do wrong?' The officer replied, 'You know, and you'll stay in jail until you admit your crime to a judge.' Johnny protested, 'That would violate my constitutional rights!' The officer asked, 'And why would it violate your constitutional rights?' That's the end of my story. Now, your job is to wait until you hear a bell on this recording. When you hear the bell, take out this tape and replace it with the blank one with your name on it. It's on the table.

Then put this machine on record and speak into the mike as you answer the police officer's question for Johnny. How is the officer threatening to violate Johnny's constitutional rights? You have exactly four minutes to record your answer after the bell rings. Ring-ring!"

Scoring key: (5 points possible) +1 for each of the following about the recorded oration: (1) reference to the Bill of Rights, (2) reference to the Fifth Amendment, (3) indication that it's illegal to hold Johnny without informing him of the reason, (4) indication that it's illegal to require Johnny to testify against himself, and (5) nothing erroneous is included.

The same ideas for selecting and designing essay items apply to oral discourse items, with one exception and one addition:

1. Whereas essay items tax students' writing skills, oral discourse items tax their speaking skills.
2. To facilitate scoring and item review with students, responses to oral discourse items should be recorded on audio or video tape.

DESIGNING PRODUCT-RATING ITEMS

A product-rating item directs students to complete a production task and provides a scheme for judging the quality of that work. Product-rating items are similar to essay and oral-discourse items except that the product is not necessarily a written composition or a speech. Here are four examples.

1. *Task presented to the students:*
   First-graders are instructed to prepare a visual display that will illustrate something about one of the following topics: air resistance, air pressure, vacuums, or air flow. They are also given such details as size and due date.
   Scoring key: From an examination of the display, the teacher's ratings are recorded with Likert scales by placing either SA, A, NO, D, or SD for each of the following statements:
   a. A point about the chosen topic is illustrated.
   b. The work suggests some creative thinking by the student.
   c. The work could not have been completed in less than an hour.
   d. It should capture the attention of other students.
2. *Task presented to the students:*
   Students in wood-working class are scheduled to submit the stools they produced for evaluation.
   Scoring key: (10 points possible) The points are distributed according to five rating scales:
   a. +2 if the product is a stool that generally fits the guidelines; +1 if a stool is submitted with major deviations from the guidelines; 0 if no stool is submitted.

b. +2 if the stool can clearly support a 300-pound person; +1 if the stool can clearly support a 150-pound person; otherwise 0.

c. +2 if the stool stands level; +1 if the stool nearly stands level, but rocks; 0 if the stool tips over easily.

d. +2 if all exposed wood surfaces (discounting nails and glue) are smooth and free of rough spots; +1 if there are some rough spots detectable by feel only, but none is detectable by sight; 0 if rough spots can be seen.

e. +2 if glue or nails are not detectable by feel; +1 if glue or nails are detectable by feel but not sight; 0 if glue or nails are detectable by sight.

3. *Task presented to the students:*
Students are directed to type accurately as many lines from Exercise 3-7 of their typing manual as they can in a five-minute timed session. They are told that punctuation and spacing should be accurate, but they need not worry about style and format.
Scoring key: Compute the number of words per minute less the number of errors according to the Yvonne formula.

4. *Task presented to the students:*
The student is directed to apply a pressure bandage to a partner as if it were first aid for a lateral sprain of the left ankle. The partner's left foot is bare and the rolled pressure bandage is handed to the student.
Scoring key: The teacher examines the finished wrap with reference to the following checkpoints:

_____ **a.** inside-out weave	_____ **d.** allows for adequate
_____ **b.** smooth and stable	circulation
_____ **c.** tight enough	

Concerns and suggestions similar to those raised for other item formats should be taken into account when selecting or designing product-rating items. The major work in designing a product-rating item is to develop a scoring key that can be reliably followed.

DESIGNING PERFORMANCE-OBSERVATION ITEMS

With a performance observation, the scorer (e.g., the teacher) observes students as they respond to the task. The students' methods for responding are scored rather than the end results or products. For example,

1. *Task presented to the students:*
The student is seated at a desk with a flat top and supplied with kindergarten writing paper and a pencil and shown a card with a capital O. The teacher says, "This is a capital O." The picture is removed and the teacher says, "Make a capital O on your paper."

Scoring key: Check one blank in each category:

a. Positioning of paper:
    left of 11 o'clock———————   11–12 o'clock———————
    12 o'clock———————   12–1 o'clock———————
    right of 1 o'clock———————   position unstable———————

b. Hand used:
    left———————   right———————   both———————

c. Wrist position:
    straight———————   hooked———————   unstable———————

d. Method of grasping pencil:
    standard and satisfactory———————
    not standard but satisfactory———————
    Describe: ————————————————————————————
    ————————————————————————————————————

e. Direction of printing:
    clockwise———————   counterclockwise———————
    both or other———————
    Explain: ————————————————————————————
    ————————————————————————————————————

f. Continuity of printing:
    nonstop motion———————   pauses———————
    other———————
    Explain: ————————————————————————————
    ————————————————————————————————————

2. *Task presented to the students:*
    The student, stationed in front of a barbell with only a light weight that would offer little resistance, is directed to demonstrate one two-arm press.
    Scoring key: (11 points possible) +1 for each blank checked on the following form:
    ——————— feet properly positioned under the bar throughout the entire lift
    ——————— proper grip and hand spread
    ——————— back straight throughout
    ——————— head facing forward throughout
    ——————— clean initiated with knees flexed
    ——————— clean initiated with elbows extended
    ——————— clean properly executed
    ——————— pauses with bar just above the chest
    ——————— executes press properly
    ——————— returns bar to position just above chest and pauses
    ——————— gently returns bar to floor, flexing knees on the way down

3. *Task presented to the students:*
    The student (who in this case is in a teacher preparation course) is directed to conduct a ten-minute mini-lesson to a group of 12 fifth-graders. The plan for the lesson has been previously approved for this purpose and the lesson was scheduled several days in advance. The lesson is videotaped.

Scoring key: The videotape is reviewed and Flanders' (1970) Interaction Analysis scores are recorded (i.e., percent of teacher talk, percent of pupil talk, number of high level questions, etc.).

Some of the ideas for other types of items apply to the selection and design of performance-observation items. Here are more to consider.

DIAGNOSTIC VALUE

Performance-observation items are particularly valuable for providing data for formative evaluations. The scoring keys for all three of the previous items yield information on *what* students are doing right and wrong in their performances, not simply on the overall quality of the performance. The form of teaching known as *coaching* depends heavily on feedback from performance-observation items. Think of how you go about coaching a student to do something (e.g., pass a basketball, read music, or write in cursive). Coaching requires you to analyze performances so that correct steps can be reinforced and errors corrected.

MINIMIZING OBSERVERS' INFLUENCES ON PERFORMANCES

In some situations, particular care must be taken to design the item so that the observer does not intrude on the performance. The introduction of an observer, especially one who is busy with a rating scale or checklist, can be quite distracting. The performance of the student who conducts a mini-lesson in item 3 is likely to be affected by the knowledge that the lesson will be observed. However, in most elementary, middle, and secondary schools, students are used to performing under the watchful eyes of teachers. Thus, as long as the observer only observes and resists the temptation to coach, there is only a minimal influence on the performance.

USE OF RECORDING DEVICES

You gain at least three advantages by using recording devices (e.g., video cameras) for performance-observation items:

1. You do not have to score the live performance, allowing you to supervise the administration of the items.
2. Performances can be examined in greater detail and more reliably when they can be played back.
3. Students can review their own performances.

PRACTICAL SCORING FORMS

As with essay and product-rating items, scoring keys need to be carefully designed for the items to have satisfactory intrascorer and interscorer reliabilities. The following is an example of a scoring form devised to facilitate adherence to a scoring key. It was designed to be used during kindergarten "sharing" presentations.

Check one blank in each category:

1. Identifies the topic, idea, or object to be shared.
   clearly in the opening _____
   clearly, but not in the opening _____
   in the opening, but not clearly _____
   somewhat, but neither clearly nor in the opening _____
   not at all _____
2. Comments or demonstrations relate to the topic.
   entirely _____
   the majority do _____
   yes, but not most _____
   not applicable because the topic was never clearly identified _____
3. Maintained eye contact with class.
   most of the time, looking toward all areas _____
   most of the time, but ignored some areas _____
   part of the time, but not most of the time _____
   not at all _____
4. Speech was easily audible.
   to all in the class _____
   only to some _____
   to none _____
5. Speech was easily intelligible.
   to all in the class _____
   only to some _____
   to none _____

DESIGNING INTERVIEW ITEMS

An *interview item* is an item that is administered to one student at a time so that

1. A sequence of questions or directives are orally (sometimes complemented by visual aids) presented to the student.
2. The student orally responds to each question or directive as it is presented, usually with the opportunity to elaborate.
3. Subsequent questions or directives may be influenced by responses the student makes to prior questions or directives.
4. The scoring key is such that the interviewer (a) takes notes or marks a scorer's form as the student completes each response (either during the interview or while listening to a recording) and (b) compiles the scores or results from the item after the interview.

Here is an account of a teacher administering an interview item:

Mr. Sanchez and Lenora sit at a table located away from the other fifth-graders who are working on a written assignment.

MR. SANCHEZ: Lenora, I am going to ask you some questions about math. I could ask you about using math when you cook or when you travel or when you shop or when you play sports. Which one do you want me to ask you about?

LENORA: What are the choices?

MR. SANCHEZ: Cooking, traveling, shopping, or sports.

LENORA: Traveling.

Mr. Sanchez looks into a file and pulls out a document labeled "Traveling."

MR. SANCHEZ: These questions will be about traveling. Please remember that I am trying to find out what math you would use to solve certain problems. I will ask you questions, but I won't be telling whether or not I agree with your answers until later when we go over the test. Do you understand?

LENORA: Yes, sir.

MR. SANCHEZ: We'll put this on tape so you can play it back and study it later. I will be making some notes as we go—but don't worry about that.

LENORA: Okay.

He turns on a tape recorder.

MR. SANCHEZ: Here is the first one. Suppose that you were going to take a trip from here to St. Louis, and you wanted to know how long it would take to get there by car. Do you know how long it would take?

LENORA: No.

MR. SANCHEZ: How would you find out?

LENORA: I'd ask my Mom.

MR. SANCHEZ: But what would you do if your Mom told you to try to figure it out for yourself.

LENORA: Get a map.

Out of Lenora's view, he marks +1 in a square on his scorer's sheet as he continues.

MR. SANCHEZ: And what would you learn from the map?

LENORA: How far St. Louis is.

He marks +1 in a second square.

MR. SANCHEZ: Then would you know how much time the trip will take?

LENORA: Yes.

He marks 0 in the third square.

MR. SANCHEZ: Suppose you found out St. Louis is 200 miles away. What else would you need to know?

LENORA: How fast my car could go.

MR. SANCHEZ: Is your car going to be driven its fastest?

LENORA: No.

MR. SANCHEZ: Then what *do* you need to know?

LENORA: I don't know.

MR. SANCHEZ: Take a moment to think. Then give me your best guess.

LENORA: How fast I would go.

He marks +1 in the fourth square.

MR. SANCHEZ: Let's suppose you average 50 miles for every hour you travel in your car. Now, how would you figure the time the trip would take?

LENORA: I'd multiply 50 and 200.

Mr. Sanchez marks +0 in the fifth square. He then *branches* to a sequence of *easier* questions he had prepared for students whose responses up to this point merited a 0 in the fifth square. Had Lenora correctly responded to the last question, he would have branched to a sequence of more difficult questions.

Here are some ideas for you to consider when selecting or designing interview items.

CLARIFYING

Two weaknesses tend to plague short-answer, multiple-choice, essay, and oral discourse items: (1) ambiguously presented tasks and (2) dependency on students' language arts skills. A major feature of the interview format is that it readily allows for clarification and elaboration of expressions by both the interviewer when presenting a task and the student when responding. In the example, Mr. Sanchez could reword directions when he sensed Lenora didn't understand them and ask her to explain answers when her intent was not clear to him.

BRANCHING AND PROBING

An interview item's sequence of questions or directives can be either *linear* or *branching*. With a linear sequence, the student's response to one question or directive cannot influence subsequent questions or directives. With a branching sequence (e.g., the one used by Mr. Sanchez), predetermined optional lines of questions or directives are selected based on the student's performance in prior stages of the interview.

Branching sequences allow the teacher to probe for specific information about the student's level of achievement. As indicated in Chapter 3, easy items measure lower levels of achievement and hard items measure advanced levels. Branching allows the interviewer to adjust the difficulty as dictated by the student's performance. In the example, it would have been a frustrating waste of time for Mr. Sanchez to present Lenora with even more difficult tasks after she had failed on earlier ones.

Interview items with branching sequences should be designed so that

1. Students who perform very well on initial tasks are subsequently presented with increasingly difficult tasks until they begin to falter and their levels of achievement can be assessed.
2. Students who perform poorly on initial tasks are subsequently presented with increasingly easy tasks until they begin to succeed and their levels of achievement can be assessed.

MINIMIZING THE INTERVIEWER'S INFLUENCE

As a teacher your job is to help your students achieve learning objectives. Normally, you try to reinforce correct responses and discourage incorrect ones. It is natural for you to coach students as they struggle with a task. But to administer an interview item properly, you temporarily forgo these normal and natural teaching behaviors so that students' responses reflect their levels of achievement rather than your influence during the interviews. For interview items, you are advised to

1. Remind students from the outset that the purpose of the interviews is to gather information on their achievement, and consequently, they can expect you not to be your usual "helpful self."
2. Position yourself during the interview so that you and the student can see one another but she or he cannot tell what you're marking on the scorer's sheet.
3. Avoid making comments, gestures, facial expressions, or sounds that the student might interpret as agreement or disagreement with responses.
4. Avoid deviations from the interviewer's script as written when the item was designed.

USE OF RECORDING DEVICES

Having a record of the interview on tape allows you to (1) detect details that might have been initially missed, (2) check on interscorer and intrascorer reliabilities, and (3) allow students to review the results. Thus, it is advisable to tape interviews, except in sensitive situations when the presence of the recorder may provoke anxiety.

POOR USABILITY

The principal drawback of interview items is serious enough to prevent most teachers from using them extensively. For obvious reasons, interview items have poor usability.

INTERVIEWS AS FOLLOW-UPS TO OTHER TYPES OF ITEMS

Interview items can be quite valuable in following up more usable but less probing items from tests. For example,

Ms. Curry is baffled by some of the answers her sixth-graders gave on a math test. To help her diagnose the problem, she administers an interview item to a small sample of the students that is designed to get them to think aloud as they work some of the problems from the test.

COMPUTER-ADMINISTERED TESTS

The recent proliferation of microcomputers in classrooms affords teachers access to a convenient tool for administering tests, providing that the tests are made up of items (e.g., multiple choice, short answer, and essay) that visually present tasks to which students respond with written or drawn expressions. Software packages are readily available that allow you to tell the computer (1) how to lay out the test according to the test blueprint, (2) which items to copy onto the test from your item pool files, (3) how to present the items to the students and in what sequence, (4) how to react to students' responses to items (e.g., by saving the text they type for essay items or tallying the number of points according to multiple-choice item scoring keys) and (5) what to include in a report of the results. Information on such software is available from the same sources as software for maintaining item pools (i.e., computer software catalogues, computer retail stores, computer magazines, professional journals for teachers, and school district resource and media centers for teachers).

Of course, some tests (e.g., those with performance-observation items) do not lend themselves to computer administration. But when appropriate, computer-administered tests can have some distinct advantages:

1. Computerized tests are individually administered without the necessity of the teacher's presence for every administration. Not all students need to be tested at the same time, thus facilitating individualized testing for varying achievement levels.

2. With computers, items can be presented in branching sequences without resorting to interview items, which are so time-consuming. For example,

Mr. Little used a software package to help create a multiple-choice test with the following features:

1. Items 1–5 are *moderately* difficult. If the student scores five out of five on those items, items 6–10 are *hard*. A score of less than three on items 1–5 causes items 6–10 to be *easy*. Scores of three or four trigger *moderate* items for 6–10.

2. A perfect score of five on items 6–10 causes items 11–15 to be a little harder than items 6–10. A score less than three causes items 11–15 to be a little easier than 6–10. A score of three or four causes items 11–15 to be as difficult as 6–10.

3. The process is repeated for items 16–20, 21–25, and so forth until the student has remained on the same level of difficulty for ten items.

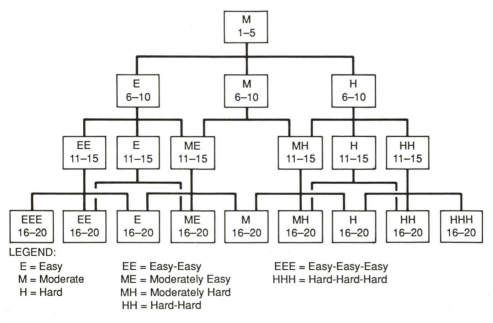

LEGEND:
E = Easy   EE = Easy-Easy   EEE = Easy-Easy-Easy
M = Moderate   ME = Moderately Easy   HHH = Hard-Hard-Hard
H = Hard   MH = Moderately Hard
                    HH = Hard-Hard

NOTE:
Fewer than 3 out of 5 correct answers triggers the next five items to be chosen from the next column to the left; 3 or 4 correct answers triggers the next five items to be chosen from the same column; 5 correct answers triggers the next five items to be chosen from the next column to the right.

FIGURE 4.2   Branching Item Sequences for Mr. Little's First 20 Items

    4. The test results are reported as the level of the last ten items on the test. A nine-point scale is used for this purpose, with 1 representing the easiest items on the test and 9 the hardest.
The branches of item sequences are diagrammed in Figure 4.2.

3. Having students enter their responses to essay and short-answer items on computers allows them to take advantage of the features of word-processing programs, thus facilitating editing and removing the emphasis on handwriting. Note that you will find it much easier to read computer-printed copy than handwritten copy.

SELF-ASSESSMENT OF YOUR ACHIEVEMENT OF CHAPTER 4'S OBJECTIVES

I.   For each of the following multiple-choice items, select the one response that best answers the question or correctly completes the statement:

   A.   Which one of the following types of items is most likely to have high interscorer reliability?
      1. performance observation
      2. essay
      3. matching
      4. product rating

   B.   Which one of the following item formats is the most advantageous for measuring objectives requiring students to recall rather than recognize information?
      1. short answer
      2. matching
      3. true/false
      4. multiple answer multiple choice

   C.   Which one of the following would be more likely to enhance the usability of a measurement?
      1. Use a table of specifications.
      2. Select matching items instead of true/false items from existing item pools.
      3. Select essay items instead of short-answer items from existing item pools.
      4. Select multiple-choice items instead of short-answer items from existing item pools.

   D.   Interview items with branching sequences have which one of the following advantages over those with linear sequences?
      1. During the administration, opportunities exist for students to clarify the intent of their expressions.
      2. As it is administered, the item can be geared to individual achievement levels.

     3. Higher interscorer reliability is possible.

     4. The interviewer is able to reword questions or directives.

E. Compared to conventionally administered essay items, computer-administered essay items are _____.

     1. more clearly worded

     2. capable of providing more diagnostic data

     3. easier to score

     4. not as vulnerable to cheating

F. Which one of the following types of items is most appropriate for measuring creative behavior?

     1. product rating

     2. true/false

     3. multiple answer multiple choice

     4. matching

G. Analytically scored essay items tend to _____ than globally scored essay items.

     1. provide richer diagnostic data

     2. be more usable

     3. use rating scales more

     4. have lower intrascorer reliability

H. According to advice given by this textbook, which one of the following is the best way to control for the guessing factor when designing multiple-choice tests?

     1. Use a reputable correction-for-guessing formula.

     2. Decrease the number of alternatives per item.

     3. Increase the number of items.

     4. Use weighted instead of dichotomously scored items.

I. Which one of the following is a way of increasing the difficulty of a multiple-choice item without contaminating its relevance?

     1. Redesign the item so that it pertains to a higher-level behavioral construct.

     2. Change the alternatives to make them more similar.

     3. Reduce the amount of information in the directions.

     4. Replace pairs of parallel alternatives with nonparallel ones.

J. Which one of the following item formats would be *least* appropriate for measuring an objective with a knowledge-of-a-process behavioral construct?

     1. multiple choice

     2. performance observation

     3. product rating

     4. essay

K. Which one of the following types of items would be the *least* desirable for a one-item test?

     1. matching

     2. true/false

     3. essay

     4. product rating

Compare your choices to the following key: A–3, B–1, C–4, D–2, E–3, F–1, G–1, H–3, I–2, J–4, K–2.

II. Critique each of the following items and identify the item design principles that are violated:

A. *Task presented to the students:*

Matching:

1. William James	a. Deductive logic
2. ontology	b. The theory of what is valuable
3. epistemology	c. Naturalism
4. Aristotle	d. Neorealism
5. Francis Bacon	e. The scientific method
6. axiology	f. Modern pragmatism
7. aesthetics	g. The theory of how to acquire knowledge
8. Rousseau	h. The theory of what is real
9. Thomas Aquinas	i. The theory of beauty

Scoring key: (9 points possible) +1 for each of the following: 1–f, 2–h, 3–g, 4–a, 5–e, 6–b, 7–i, 8–c, 9–d.

B. *Task presented to the students:*
Explain the value of the Constitution.

C. *Task presented to the students:*
Thomas Jefferson was _____ .
  1. opposed to the Bill of Rights
  2. born in New York
  3. killed in the Revolutionary War
  4. the chief author of the Declaration of Independence
  Scoring key: +1 for 4 only; otherwise 0.

D. *Task presented to the students:*
You are bitten by a rattlesnake. You should _____ .
  1. capture the snake and bring it to the hospital
  2. keep quiet and reduce your circulation
  3. go directly to the hospital
  4. cut an "X" over the wound and suck out the poison
  5. find a quiet place to lie down and die
  Scoring key: +1 for 3 only; otherwise 0.

Discuss with someone your critiques and his or hers.

III. Retrieve the set of objectives you listed for Exercise IV in Chapter 1. For each objective, develop two items and enter them in the item pool file you set up for Exercise III of Chapter 3's self-assessment. As you develop each item, note what you did for each of the five critical steps listed on pages 82–83. After you've developed each item, review the ideas from this chapter for that type of item. Determine which, if any, of the principles for designing items you violated. Improve the item if you can. Exchange your work on this exercise with someone else and critique one another's items.

Items for Cognitive Objectives

GOAL OF CHAPTER 5

Chapter 5 focuses on attributes of items that make them relevant to cognitive objectives at each of the following levels: (1) simple knowledge, (2) knowledge of a process, (3) comprehension of a communication, (4) conceptualization, and (5) application. More specifically, Chapter 5 will help you to

1. Design items at each of the five cognitive levels (*Cognitive: application*)
2. Given an item that's relevant to a content familiar to you, determine for which, if any, of the five cognitive levels the item has construct validity (*Cognitive: conceptualization*)

SIMPLE-KNOWLEDGE ITEMS

STIMULUS-RESPONSE

Reread the section entitled Simple Knowledge on page 9. Note that students achieve a simple-knowledge objective by *remembering* the desired response (e.g., area = length × width) to a particular stimulus (e.g., formula for the area of a rectangle). Thus, a simple-knowledge item asks students to show that, upon exposure to the stimulus, they remember the formula, image, sound, word, symbol, name, date, definition, principle, location, or other content the objective specifies.

When designing an item for a simple-knowledge objective, maintain the same stimulus-response relationship that is defined by the objective. For example, design an item that is relevant to the following objective taken from a middle school science curriculum guide:

So that the student will be able to read scientific material, he or she will recall the meanings of the following terms: *hypothesis, empirical observation,* and *experiment.*

Compare your item to the following one, included in the curriculum guide as a sample test item for the stated objective:

A generalization that appears to be true from direct observation is a(n) _____ .

Hypothesis is the correct response according to the answer key.

The objective is concerned with students' being able to know word meanings as they read about science. Thus, it is important for the students to *respond* with a definition upon seeing the word *hypothesis*, not respond with *hypothesis* upon seeing a definition. The curriculum guide's sample item reverses the objective's stimulus with its response. The objective's stimulus-response relationship remains intact with the following item:

Task presented to the students:
What does *hypothesis* mean? _____

_____

Scoring key: (4 points possible) +1 for each of the following: (1) a generalization, (2) unproven, and (3) based on direct observation or experience; +1 if nothing false is included.

Some might favor the curriculum guide's sample item over this item because the former depends less on students' writing skills and is easier to score. However, thinking of a particular word in response to a definition is a different cognitive task than that implied by the objective. To illustrate this difference, answer the following question:

What is the word that means *having an abundance of riches*?

Even though you'll remember the definition of this word when you read it, you may not think of the word upon reading its definition. The word is *affluent*, but you may have answered the question with *wealthy, opulent, rich,* or some other synonym. How many times have you been unable to remember someone's name, although you readily remember who she or he is upon hearing the name?

Regarding the example of the science curriculum guide, an easy-to-score item that maintains the objective's stimulus-response relation without taxing students' writing skills is possible. With a multiple-choice format, the stem could contain the word and the alternatives could be definitions. Such a multiple-choice item would present students with the task of identifying the definition rather than recalling it. Compared to the short-answer format, that is a disadvantage for this particular objective.

AVOIDING RESPONSES BEYOND SIMPLE KNOWLEDGE

Students' responses to simple-knowledge items should depend only on how well they remember information. Items are not relevant to simple-knowledge objectives whenever students use reasoning or higher-order cognitive processes to determine responses. But because an item is designed to measure simple-knowledge behavior does not guarantee that students will respond at the simple-knowledge level. For example,

---

To measure her first-graders' recall of addition facts, Ms. Blair administers a five-minute test made up of 12 items similar to the following:

$7 + 4 =$ _____

When Casey confronts this item, he uses his fingers to count to himself, "eight, nine, ten, eleven." He scores 12 out of 12 on the test.

Casey used knowledge-of-a-process cognitive behavior to respond to Ms. Blair's test items. To prevent a recurrence of this response, Ms. Blair should redesign the test so that students do not have time to work through a process. Possibilities include (1) increasing the number of items and reducing the administration time or (2) rapidly displaying items, one at a time, on flash cards, pausing only long enough for students to respond on answer sheets.

In the following example, a student responds to what was supposed to be a simple knowledge-level item with reasoning because of ambiguous wording.

In a health unit on nutrition, Ms. Brewer emphasizes that the consumption of tea interferes with the body's ability to use iron. To learn whether his students remember this fact, he includes the following true/false item on the unit test:

Task presented to the students:
T   F   Drinking tea provides iron for the body.
Scoring key: +1 for F only; otherwise 0.

Maxine remembers that tea interferes with the body's use of iron as she reads the statement. However, she moves beyond the simple-knowledge level as she thinks, "Tea is not the way to get iron into the body. But the statement says, 'drinking tea provides iron.' Tea is mixed with water and most water contains traces of iron. So actually, drinking tea does provide iron. The answer is T."

Mr. Brewer might argue that if Maxine had paid attention in class she would know what he meant by that true/false statement and she would have answered F. However, a simple-knowledge item doesn't and shouldn't contain a warning label for students "not to reason on this one." The problem is best avoided by wording items so that there is little or no room for misinterpretations.

KNOWLEDGE-OF-A-PROCESS ITEMS

STIMULUS-RESPONSE-RESPONSE- . . . -RESPONSE

Reread the section on Knowledge of a Process on pages 9–10. Students achieve a knowledge-of-a-process objective by remembering how to carry out a procedure or use a method. Thus, a knowledge-of-a-process item asks students to show that they know the first step, second step, third step, and so forth in the process specified by the objective.

Because a knowledge-of-a-process objective is concerned with students' remembering a *sequence* of responses, not only a single response, each response in the sequence serves as a stimulus to the next response. Thus, the accuracy of subsequent steps in the process depends on the accuracy of previous steps in the process. Because of this phenomenon, the design of a knowledge-of-a-process item should differ considerably from the design of a simple-knowledge item.

EMPHASIS ON THE PROCESS, NOT THE OUTCOME

Develop your own scoring key for the test shown in Figure 5.1, and then score Shannon's paper as it appears there. Consider Shannon's actual case:

Mr. Hancock administered a test to Shannon and his other fourth-graders to measure their achievement of the following objective:

Computes the product of any two-digit whole number by a one-digit whole number
  (*Cognitive: knowledge of a process*)

Shannon's completed test appears in Figure 5.1. Figure 5.2 shows the same test paper after Mr. Hancock scored it and returned it to Shannon.

Name *Shannon Roach*

Multiplication Test

1.
```
   32
 × 4
 128
```

2. ²37
```
  × 4
  208
```

3. 3 54
```
   × 8
   642
```

4. ¹ 17
```
  × 2
  44
```

5.
```
   80
 × 9
 720
```

6. 4 69
```
   × 5
   505
```

7. 3 16
```
  × 5
  200
```

8. ¹ 54
```
  × 3
  182
```

9. 6 29
```
   × 7
   563
```

FIGURE 5.1   Shannon's Test Paper

What do you think Mr. Hancock learned from the test about Shannon's achievement of the objective? What do you think Shannon learned from seeing the returned paper?

Apparently, Mr. Hancock scored the items with a key similar to this one for item 2:

Task presented to the students:
```
   37
 ×  4
```
Scoring key: +11 percent for 148, otherwise 0.

However, does the objective imply that Shannon should know that 148 is

Name *Shannon Roach*

22% = F

Multiplication Test

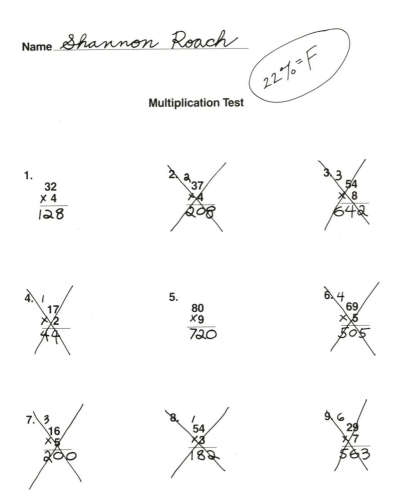

FIGURE 5.2   Shannon's Paper with Mr. Hancock's Marks

the product of 37 times 4? No, the objective implies that Shannon should know a process for finding the product of 37 times 4. The objective is concerned not with students' knowing answers but with knowing how to find answers.

For Shannon to obtain 148, the correct response to item 2 on Mr. Hancock's test, she would have to execute steps similar to the following:

1. Recognizes that the task is to multiply
2. Recognizes that the multiplicand is a two-digit number, and thus memory of multiplication facts alone will not be adequate
3. Checks to see if the numerals are aligned for the algorithm
4. Remembers first to multiply 7 by 4
5. Remembers that $7 \times 4 = 28$

6. Writes 8 as follows:

$$
\begin{array}{r}
37 \\
\times \ 4 \\
\hline
8
\end{array}
$$

7. Carries the 2:

$$
\begin{array}{r}
^2 37 \\
\times \ 4 \\
\hline
8
\end{array}
$$

8. Remembers to multiply 3 by 4
9. Remembers that $3 \times 4 = 12$
10. Remembers to add the carried 2 to the 12
11. Computes $2 + 12 = 14$
12. Writes the 14 to the left of the 8:

$$
\begin{array}{r}
^2 37 \\
\times \ 4 \\
\hline
148
\end{array}
$$

Once again, examine Shannon's answers in Figure 5.1. How many of the 12 steps just listed did she seem to remember? She actually remembered almost all the steps, but she consistently executed step 10 before step 8.

Imagine that instead of Mr. Hancock, Shannon's fourth-grade teacher is Ms. Tankersley. Shannon's experiences would have been quite different:

Ms. Tankersley administers a four-item test to her fourth-graders to help assess how well they've achieved the following objective:

Computes the product of any two-digit whole number by a one-digit whole number
(*Cognitive: knowledge of a process*)

The following is the second item on the test:

Task presented to the students:

$$
\begin{array}{r}
37 \\
\times \ 4 \\
\hline
\end{array}
$$

Scoring key: (7 points possible) +1 for each of the following that is detectable from the response: (1) multiplied 7 and 4, (2) placed the one's digit of the partial product (should be 8) as the unit's place in the answer, (3) carried the ten's digit (should be 2), (4) multiplied 4 and 3, (5) added the carried digit to that partial product (should be $2 + 12$), (6) put the result in its proper place (should be 14), and (7) answered 148.

The day following the test, Ms. Tankersley returns the scored papers. Shannon's paper, as it was returned to her, appears in Figure 5.3.

Name _Shannon Roach_

Shannon,
You have done almost every step right.
But, you are making one mistake on the
regrouping problems. Please come and talk
to me about what you are doing.
                              — Ms Tankersley

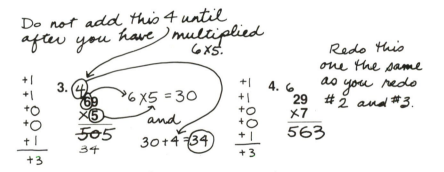

FIGURE 5.3 Shannon's Paper with Ms. Tankersley's Marks

The results of Ms. Tankersley's version of Shannon's test indicate exactly what Shannon needs to learn to correct her errors.

KNOWLEDGE, AFFECTIVE, AND PSYCHOMOTOR COMPONENTS OF THE PROCESS

Students' abilities to carry out a process (e.g., forming manuscript letters, diagramming a sentence, computing with a mathematical formula, performing cardiopulmonary resuscitation, bench-pressing a barbell, reciting the alphabet, and typing a letter) often depend not only on their knowledge of the process but also on some affective and psychomotor behaviors. To teach students to perform such a process, you must be concerned with the cognitive knowledge, affective, and psychomotor aspects of the process. Consider the following example:

Task presented to the students:
   The student is given a pencil and lined paper and told to make a capital letter A.

   Scoring key: Using a 5-point check sheet, watch student proceed.

   _____ If a legible A is made
   _____ Used exactly 3 strokes
   _____ Strokes were made in proper sequence:

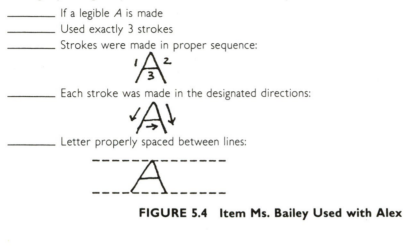

   _____ Each stroke was made in the designated directions:

   _____ Letter properly spaced between lines:

FIGURE 5.4   Item Ms. Bailey Used with Alex

To measure five-year-old Alex's achievement of the following objective, Ms. Bailey administers the item in Figure 5.4:

Follows the steps described in the Groves-Haimowitz handwriting manual to write an uppercase A (*Cognitive: knowledge of a process*)

Alex's response to the item appears in Figure 5.5.

FIGURE 5.5   Alex's Response to Item from Figure 5.4

If Alex's response isn't a very accurate representation of an *A,* it is possible, however, that he *knows* the steps in the process but lacks the psychomotor skills to put that knowledge into effect. Another possibility is that Alex *can* write better *A*'s but is unwilling to put forth the effort (i.e., he has failed to achieve a requisite affective objective).

To make a formative evaluation that will help her decide how to teach Alex, Ms. Bailey should measure the psychomotor and affective objectives separately from the knowledge-of-a-process objective.

COMPREHENSION-OF-A-COMMUNICATION ITEMS

DERIVING MEANINGS FROM EXPRESSIONS

Reread the section on Comprehension of a Communication on pages 10–11. Note the two types of comprehension-of-a-process objectives:

1. The content of some objectives specifies a particular expression (e.g., the First Amendment to the Constitution, quadratic formula, or classroom rules for conduct) for students to translate or interpret. An item relevant to this type of objective asks students to show the meaning they have derived from the expression specified by the objective.
2. The content of other objectives specifies a particular communication mode (e.g., reading a compound sentence, listening to a debate, or reading signed English) from which students can make meaningful translations or interpretations. An item relevant to this type of objective asks students to show the meaning of a message expressed in the mode specified by the objective.

ITEM RESPONSE MODE

The principal concern of comprehension-of-a-communication objectives is for students to derive meaning from given expressions. In other words, these objectives focus on students' receptions of expressions, not their formulations of expressions. How they exhibit what they understand from expressions is normally not specified by the objective. However, comprehension-of-a-communication items must be designed to provide students with a means of exhibiting that understanding. Consider the following objective and item to measure it.

Objective:
Explains the general provisions in the Bill of Rights (*Cognitive: comprehension of a communication*)
Task presented to the students:
Write a paragraph explaining the parts of the Bill of Rights that have anything to do with allowing people to communicate with one another. Use your own words. Don't quote directly from the Bill of Rights.
Scoring key: Note: Score only if the response is limited to one paragraph with no quotes as directed; otherwise have the students redo the item. (8 points possible) +1 for each of the following "freedoms" whose relevance

to communications among people is brought out: (1) religion, (2) speech, (3) press, and (4) assembly; +1 for relevant protections that are brought out from each of the following amendments: (1) Fifth, (2) Ninth, and (3) Tenth; +1 for including nothing false.

This item appears quite relevant to the objective, *providing* that students have the requisite writing skills. Items should use only response modes (i.e., how the item requires students to express themselves) in which students are competent. For students who lack the necessary writing skills for the essay item, an oral discourse item or a *group* of multiple-choice items may serve as a suitable substitute.

NOVELTY

Comprehension of a communication is an intellectual-level behavioral construct; thus it involves reasoning and judgment that takes the learner beyond what is simply remembered. Unlike knowledge-level items, comprehension-of-a-communication items present students with tasks that are not identical to tasks they've previously encountered. There should be some aspect to the task presented by the item that is novel to the students.

An item relevant to an objective *specifying a particular expression* should require students to translate or interpret the expression in some way that they've never before encountered. For example,

Objective:
Explains the general provisions in the Bill of Rights (*Cognitive: comprehension of a communication*)
Task presented to the students:
(Multiple-choice) The First Amendment to the Constitution states, "Congress shall make no law . . . abridging the freedom of speech." This means that the federal government _____ .
   A. declares that people have the right to express their ideas
   B. may not take away people's right to express their ideas
   C. must provide a way for its citizens to express their ideas
   D. may not bridge gaps between speeches and other forms of free expression
Scoring key: +1 for B only; otherwise 0.

This item measures the comprehension-of-a-communication objective as long as students select B only because of their understanding of the First Amendment, not because they remember having read or heard the exact words of the alternative. In order to be relevant to the stated objective, the items should give students their *initial* exposure to that interpretation expressed in those words.

An item relevant to an objective *specifying a particular communication mode* should require students to translate or interpret an expression that they've

FIGURE 5.6 The Administration of an Item for a Comprehension-of-a-Communication Objective

not previously encountered. Of course, the expression must use the familiar communication mode that is specified by the objective. For example,

Objective:
From watching a hearing-impaired person expressing two or more thought units in American signed English, translates the thoughts into conventional spoken English (*Cognitive: comprehension of a communication*)

Task presented to the students:
(Written directions are accompanied by a videotaped presentation—see Figure 5.6.) When the number for this item appears on the TV monitor, translate the sign language of the person on the screen. After the signing is completed, select the best interpretation that is given below and circle the letter of your choice:

   A. Stated that only one job is still available.
   B. Asked if he should continue to seek a job.
   C. Stated that a few jobs are still available.
   D. Stated that a particular job is still available.
   E. Asked if any jobs are still available.

Scoring key: +1 for D only; otherwise 0.

For this item to be relevant to the stated objective, it should give students their first experience in translating exactly what is expressed on the screen.

Note that the item does not ask students to select a direct word-for-word translation. Comprehension of a communication involves determining meanings of whole expressions, not simply decoding single symbols, words, or other units of expressions.

CONCEPTUALIZATION ITEMS

CONCEPTS AND RELATIONSHIPS

Reread the section on Conceptualization on page 11. Note that the content of a conceptualization objective is either a concept or a relationship.

Concepts   Two lists, labeled A and B, appear in Table 5.1. What do the entries in Column A have in common? What do the entries in Column B have in common? How do the entries in Column A differ from those in Column B?

Column A is a list of specifics; Column B lists abstractions or generalities, referred to as *concepts*.

All Column B's entries (e.g., a city) refer to things in general. Each is a *concept*, that is, a category for specifics that share certain common attributes. *A city* could refer to any one of thousands of communities that have the attributes (e.g., a formal government) of a city. Baton Rouge (from Column A) is an *example* of a city, but it's not just any city. It has characteristics (e.g., it is the capital of Louisiana and is located near the Mississippi River) that are not common to all cities.

Examine Table 5.2; it gives examples for each of the concepts listed in Table 5.1.

Note that different examples of the same concept share all the attributes of the concept but are distinguishable because of other characteristics. For example, both Baton Rouge and East Berlin have all the attributes of a city (e.g., a community of people with a formal government), but they are different because of their other characteristics (e.g., Baton Rouge is located in North

TABLE 5.1   How Do the Two Lists Differ?

A	B
U.S. Constitution	a city
the book you are now reading	U.S. goverment documents
49	verbs
Baton Rouge, Louisiana	a book
Mexico City, Mexico	deceased people
81 miles	people
Abraham Lincoln	words
the word *go*	a real number
The Old Man and the Sea	distances
Martin Luther King	

TABLE 5.2   Examples of Concepts from Table 5.1

a city	words
Baton Rouge, Louisiana	go
East Berlin, East Germany	people
Logan, Utah	throw
Mexico City, Mexico	zebra
U.S. government documents	a real number
Congressional Record for 1949	−50
U.S. Constitution	0
verbs	.33
go	49
throw	306
a book	distances
The Old Man and the Sea	81 miles
the book you are now reading	.33 centimeters
deceased people	1.98 inches
Martin Luther King	
Abraham Lincoln	
people	
Abraham Lincoln	
Martin Luther King	
you	

America, East Berlin in Europe). *The characteristics of an example of a concept that are not attributes of the concept are known as* psychological noise.

Look at Table 5.2 again. What is some of the psychological noise associated with the examples of the concept *words*? The word *zebra* has five letters, two vowels, starts with z, and is a noun. But all words don't have to have five letters, two vowels, start with z, and be a noun. Thus, for the concept *word*, characteristics like the number of letters, number of vowels, starting letter, and type of word are considered psychological noise.

Relationships   Two lists, labeled C and D, appear in Table 5.3. What do the entries in Column C have in common? What do the entries in Column D have in common? How do the entries in Column C differ from those in Column D?

Column C's entries are either concepts or examples of concepts. Column D's entries are *statements*. Each statement expresses an association between two or more concepts or examples of concepts. These associations are referred to as *relationships*. Comprising a major share of curricula content at all school levels from prekindergarten through college, relationships include facts, hypotheses, theorems, laws, principles, formulas, generalizations, axioms, and rules.

GROUPING EXAMPLES

An item relevant to a conceptualization objective that specifies a concept for content presents students with the task of discriminating among examples and nonexamples of the concept. For example,

TABLE 5.3   How Do These Two Lists Differ?

C	D
U.S. Constitution	The U.S. Constitution provides a plan for governing the nation.
306 + 49	Abraham Lincoln was president in 1861.
weightlifting, rest, and nutrition	306 + 49 > .33
books	Adequate rest and nutrition are essential to an effective weightlifting program.
the person who was president in 1861	People are mammals.

One of the first units Mr. Quarters teaches his kindergarten students includes the following mathematical objective:

Groups sets according to their numbers of elements (*Cognitive: conceptualization*)

The following item is included in Mr. Quarters' item pool for that objective:

Task presented to the students:
(One-to-one interview format) The illustration in Figure 5.7 is shown to the student, who is asked, "Which group is different from the others?" After the student makes the selection, he or she is asked, "Why is that group different?" After the explanation, the student is asked, "How is that group (pointing to the student's first choice) like one of the others?" After the student chooses, he or she is asked, "How are those two groups alike?" After that explanation, the student is asked about the two groups that he or she has yet to indicate are alike: "Are these two groups alike in any way?" If the answer is yes, the student is asked, "How are they alike?" If the answer is no, no further questions are asked.

Scoring key: The following chart is marked during the interview:
First grouping according to (check one)

———————— number   ———————— shape
———————— color   ———————— location

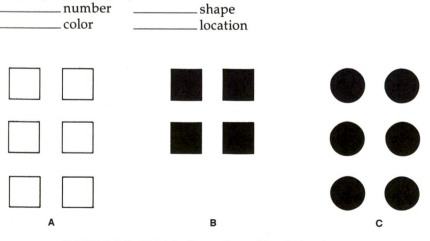

A   B   C

FIGURE 5.7   Which Group Does Not Belong?

Second grouping according to (check one)
_____ number   _____ shape
_____ color   _____ location
Third grouping according to (check one)
_____ number   _____ shape
_____ color   _____ location
+1 if number is checked for one of the three groupings.

For students who do not score +1 on this item because they do not associate group A with C in number, Mr. Quarters moves to an easier item. The easier item is identical to the previous one except the student is given two tries instead of three and the illustration in Figure 5.8 is used.

For the concept of *number*, color and shape serve as *psychological noise* in Mr. Quarters' first item. To obtain an easier item, he supplanted Figure 5.7 with Figure 5.8. Note that color does not vary in Figure 5.8. Thus, Mr. Quarters manipulated the psychological noise in his examples to control the difficulty level of a conceptualization item. With one less variable (i.e., color) to distract students, Mr. Quarters' students find similarities and differences in the number of elements easier to detect in the second item.

To measure more advanced achievement levels of a conceptualization objective, items use examples with high levels of psychological noise. Lower levels of achievement of conceptualization objectives are measured with items requiring students to discriminate among examples with little interference from psychological noise.

Here is an example of an objective and a relevant item for a high school or college psychology class.

Objective:
Distinguishes between examples of Pavlov's classical conditioning and
   other influences on behavior patterns (*Cognitive: conceptualization*)

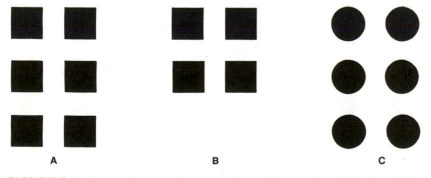

     A   **B**   **C**

FIGURE 5.8   Examples and Nonexamples with Low Psychological Noise

Task presented to the students:

(Multiple answer multiple choice) Circle the letter in front of each of the following that tells of a situation in which a subject is displaying a response to *classical conditioning* (None, one, or more than one letter may be circled):

A. A cat salivates whenever it tastes food.

B. A man hears the sound of a bell from a radio program and recalls the day of his wedding.

C. A man coughs involuntarily when he sees the image of a cigarette in a movie.

D. A dog sits up and begs whenever it is hungry and sees a person holding a bowl.

E. A dog was mistreated by a woman, who would often say, "Bad dog!" and hit him. Now the dog flinches every time he hears someone speak.

F. Every time a pupil talked out of turn in a classroom, the teacher required the pupil to stand and face a corner of the room for an hour. The pupil no longer talks out of turn in that classroom.

Scoring key: (6 points possible) +1 for each one of the following circled: C and E; +1 for each of the others *not* circled.

Notice the role played by psychological noise in the item. Classical conditioning, as you may remember from your study of psychology, is associated with Ivan Pavlov's experiments with dogs being conditioned to salivate at the sound of a bell (Myers, 1986). But with respect to the concept of classical conditioning, dogs, bells, and salivation are psychological noise, not attributes. Nonexamples of classical conditioning that include this psychological noise are selected as alternatives for the item to distract students who remember facts about classical conditioning but do not truly conceptualize it.

EXPLAINING WHY

An item relevant to a conceptualization objective that specifies a relationship for content presents students with the task of explaining why the relationship exists. Here, for example, is an objective from a sixth-grade math unit and an item designed to measure it.

Objective:

Explains why the area of a rectangle equals the product of its length and width (*Cognitive: conceptualization*)

Task presented to the students:

Illustrate with one or more pictures why $A = l \times w$, where $A =$ the area of a rectangle, $l =$ its length, and $w =$ its width. Write one paragraph that helps illustrate why the formula works.

Scoring key: (7 points possible) Points distributed as follows:

+1 for drawing a rectangle

+1 for highlighting the units for the length along one edge

+1 for highlighting the units for the width along an adjacent edge

+1 for representing the area as the number of unit squares in the rectangle's interior

+1 for alluding to how adding *l* to itself *w* times or *w* to itself *l* times yields the same results as counting the unit squares in the rectangle's interior

+1 for not including anything false

+1 for not including anything irrelevant

Of course, the item would lack construct validity for the conceptualization objective if students simply reproduced an explanation from memory. Conceptualization items, like all intellectual-level items, confront students with tasks that cannot be accomplished without reasoning beyond what is remembered.

APPLICATION ITEMS

DECIDING HOW TO SOLVE PROBLEMS

Reread the following sections that include explanations and examples pertinent to the design of application items: (1) Application on pages 11–12, (2) Measurement Relevance on pages 27–29, and (3) Item Difficulty on pages 53–54.

An application item presents students with a problem and the task of deducing whether or not a particular relationship (e.g., a principle or formula) is useful in solving that problem. Here is an example of an objective and an item designed to measure it.

Objective:

From observing the symptoms of a person in distress and from considering the availability and accessibility of other means of help, determines whether or not CPR (cardiopulmonary resuscitation) should be initiated (*Cognitive: application*)

Task presented to the students:

On a hot summer day, you see a middle-aged jogger grab his chest, stagger for several meters, and fall to the sidewalk. You find him motionless, pupils dilated, pulse rapid, and skin very dry. Assume that no one else is available to help and you have no immediate means of transporting the victim. In a one-half page essay, (1) indicate if and when you should use CPR on this man and (2) explain the reasons for your decision.

Scoring key: (4 points possible) Score 0 if immediate use of CPR is suggested. Otherwise, distribute 4 points as follows:

+1 if CPR is *not* suggested for initial aid

+1 if rapid pulse is given as a reason for withholding CPR

+1 for any other tenable reason for withholding CPR (e.g., victim is displaying signs of heat stroke)

+1 for an implicit or explicit indication that symptoms that warrant the use of CPR (e.g., lack of respiration) would be considered

AVOIDING "GIVE-AWAY" WORDS

Sometimes knowledge-level items are mistaken for application items.

For years, Ms. Saunders has taught her first-graders how to count, add, and subtract. Recently, however, she's discovered that many of her students learn these processes but are unable to apply them to real-life problems. Thus, she redesigns her math units to include application objectives. For a subtraction unit she includes the following:

Distinguishes between problems that can be efficiently solved by using subtraction and those that cannot (*Cognitive: application*)

Her item pool for this objective includes the following:

Task presented to the students:
(Oral directions, written responses) Students respond on an answer sheet with blanks numbered 1 to 4. The teacher presents the task orally to the group as follows: "I'm going to give you four problems. Some of them can be solved by addition. Some can be solved by subtraction. And then there are some for which you don't need to add or subtract. Your job is to write down a plus sign for those that are addition problems, a minus sign for the subtraction problems, and a big *N* if you wouldn't use either addition or subtraction. Put your pencil on blank number one as I read the first one:

1. Dustin has some money and Casey has some money. They agree to add their money together and buy a transformer from the toy store. How much money can they spend for a transformer?

Mark a plus, minus, or *N* for number one. Put your pencil on blank number two as I read the second one:

2. Sally has 15 books on her shelf; she takes away 4 and gives them to Amanda. How many books are left on the shelf?

Mark a plus, minus, or *N* for number two. Put your pencil on blank number three as I read the third one:

3. Brandon started reading a book from page 1. He just finished page 16. How many pages has he read?

Mark a plus, minus, or *N* for number three. Put your pencil on blank number four as I read the fourth one:

4. Sybil had 19 stickers in a box before she took away 7 to decorate her door. How many stickers are left in her box?

Scoring key: (4 points possible) +1 for each of the following: minus for 2 and 4, plus for 1, and *N* for 3.

Several students who Ms. Saunders believes have not achieved the objective perform very well on this item when she includes it on a test. To help her resolve the inconsistency between her belief about the students' achievement and the test results, she interviews some of the students, asking them to explain how they derived their answers. One student provided this explanation:

"It was easy! It's plus for one, 'cause they agreed to *add* their money. It's minus for two and four since they say *take away*. *Take away* means minus. You told us that a long time ago."

Ms. Saunders realizes that the students were simply remembering word associations. To rectify this weakness, she modifies the item so that the directions remain unchanged, but the four problems are reworded and the scoring adjusted as follows:

1. Dustin has some money and Casey has some money. They agree to buy one transformer and share it. How much money can they spend for a transformer?
2. Sally has 15 books on her shelf, she takes away 4 and gives them to Amanda. How many books did Sally give Amanda?
3. Brandon started reading a 20-page book from page 1. He is now on page 16. How many pages must he read to finish the book?
4. Sybil had 19 stickers in a box before she used 7 to decorate her door. How many stickers are still in her box?

Scoring key: (4 points possible) +1 for each of the following: minus for 3 and 4, plus for 1, and *N* for 2.

Note the use of *takes away* in the wording of a *nonexample* of a subtraction problem.

MIXING RELATIONSHIPS

Even before she modified the item, Ms. Saunders realized that measuring achievement of an application objective necessitated confronting students with two types of problems: (1) those with solutions that utilize the relationship specified by the objective and (2) those with solutions that do not. That is why her item included both subtraction and nonsubtraction problems. If only problems that use the objective's content are included, students do not have to decide whether or not to use the relationship. Ability to decide when and when not to use relationships is the essence of application-level achievement.

BEYOND APPLICATION ITEMS

Reread the section "Cognition beyond Application" on page 12. Objectives specifying cognitive behavioral constructs that are even more sophisticated than application focus on analytical and creative thinking. Although such objectives are extremely important, they are not generally emphasized in most school curricula.

A comprehensive treatise on designing items beyond the application level is not within the scope of this book. However, the following two examples of objectives accompanied by relevant items may serve to stimulate your thinking about measuring cognition beyond application.

1. *Objective:*
   From examining a bioecological system, identifies components of that system and the relationships among those components that are necessary to the maintenance of the system (*Cognitive: beyond application*)
   Task presented to the students:
   A 1,000-square-mile grassy plain was inhabited by a healthy, stable population of wolves and a variety of smaller animals including rabbits, birds, rodents, snakes, and insects. This self-sustaining plain existed for thousands of years. People then began to hunt and kill the wolves that inhabited the area. Ten years after men and women began killing the wolves, dust storms started to plague the plain and erosion changed its face considerably. Before this time, no dust storms or erosion had occurred.

   There are, of course, many possible theories for the onset of the dust storms and erosion. Describe in a half-page essay one possible scenario of events that could explain a link between the erosion, dust storms, and hunting of wolves. Be as specific as space permits.
   Scoring key: (6 points possible) +1 for establishing a plausible connection between the hunting and the erosion; +1, up to +5, for each relevant event that would lead to that connection.

2. *Objective:*
   Incorporates light sources in the design and production of realistic sketches of live models (*Cognitive: beyond application*)
   Task presented to the students:
   The student has the necessary supplies and a live model. The following directions are given: "Make a shaded line drawing of the model. The model will hold the pose for 20 minutes. Make the drawing as realistic as possible. Pace yourself so that you take nearly 20 minutes to complete the work. There will be a one-minute break after the first 10 minutes."
   Scoring key: +1 if the drawing indicates a light source and its effect on the form. The illustration in Figure 5.9 provides an example for the scorer.

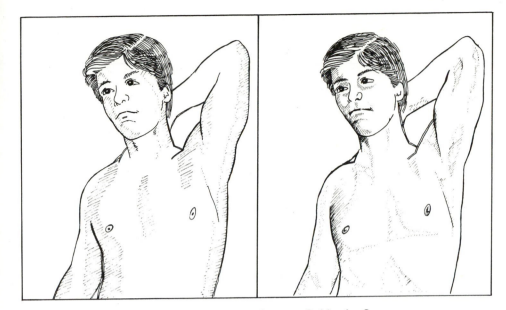

FIGURE 5.9   Sample Drawings to Guide the Scorer

SELF-ASSESSMENT OF YOUR ACHIEVEMENT OF CHAPTER 5'S OBJECTIVES

In Exercise III of Chapter 3's self-assessment section you established an item pool file. You entered items into that file for Exercise III of Chapter 4's self-assessment. The following exercises for Chapter 5 refer to your item pool file.

    I.   Select one of the items from your file that you designed to be relevant to a simple-knowledge objective. If there is no pool for a simple-knowledge objective in your file, write one in the realm of your teaching specialty and develop an item that is relevant to it. Now answer the following questions about your item:

        A. Is the stimulus-response relationship of the objective maintained by the item?

        B. Is there a danger that students who have not achieved the objective could correctly respond to the item by applying a cognitive process beyond simple knowledge?

        C. Is there ambiguity in the item's wording that might lead a student who has achieved the objective to use reasoning to obtain an incorrect response?

    Refine the item unless the answers to the questions are yes for A and no for both B and C.

II. Select one of the items from your file that you designed to be relevant to a knowledge-of-a-process objective. If there is no pool for a knowledge-of-a-process objective in your file, write one in the realm of your teaching specialty and develop an item that is relevant to it. Now answer the following questions about your item:

   A. Is the item designed so that from observing students' responses, you will be able to detect the steps of the process that they remembered?

   B. Does your scoring key focus on knowledge of individual steps in the process rather than on the final outcome?

Refine the item unless the answer to both questions is yes. Also, if you haven't already done so, develop a means for measuring the affective and psychomotor aspects of the process separately from the stated knowledge-of-a-process objective.

III. Select one of the items from your file that you designed to be relevant to a comprehension-of-a-communication objective that specifies a particular expression for students to translate or interpret. If there is no pool for such an objective in your file, write one and develop an item that is relevant to it. Now answer the following questions about your item:

   A. Is the item response mode clearly within the skill level of your students?

   B. Will students who have not achieved the objective be able to respond correctly to the item simply because they remember an interpretation or translation they've previously made or to which they've been exposed?

Refine the item unless the answer is yes for A and no for B.

IV. Select one of the items from your file that you designed to be relevant to a comprehension-of-a-communication objective that specifies a particular communication mode from which students are to make a translation or interpretation. If there is no pool for such an objective in your file, write that type of objective and develop an item that is relevant to it. Now answer the following questions about your item:

   A. Is the item response mode clearly within the skill level of your students?

   B. Will students who have not achieved the objective be able to respond correctly to the item simply because they were familiar with the content of the communication before being exposed to the item?

Refine the item unless the answer is yes for A and no for B.

V. Select one of the items from your file that you designed to be relevant to a conceptualization objective that specifies a concept for its content. If there is no pool for such an objective in your file, write that type of objective and develop an item that is relevant to it. Now answer the following questions about your item:

    A. Does the item present students with the task of discrimination between examples and nonexamples of the concept?

    B. Are the examples and nonexamples novel to the students?

    C. Was the item designed so that the level of psychological noise in the examples and nonexamples was manipulated to achieve the desired degree of item difficulty?

Refine the item unless the answer to all three questions is yes.

  VI. Select one of the items from your file that you designed to be relevant to a conceptualization objective that specifies a relationship for its content. If there is no pool for such an objective in your file, write that type of objective and develop an item that is relevant to it. Now, answer the following questions about your item:

    A. Does the item present students with a task that correlates with how well they can explain why the relationship exists?

    B. Would students who have not achieved the objective be able to respond correctly to the item by remembering an explanation they had previously given or to which they had been exposed?

    C. Is the item's response mode clearly within your students' skill levels?

Refine the item unless the answer to A and C is yes and the answer to B is no.

  VII. Select one of the items from your file that you designed to be relevant to an application objective. If there is no pool for an application objective in your file, write one and develop an item that is relevant to it. Now answer the following questions about your item:

    A. Does the item confront students with a problem and the task of deciding whether or not the relationship from the objective's content is relevant to the solution of the problem?

    B. Is there a danger that students who have not achieved the objective could correctly respond to the item because they remember associations between key words and the relationship?

    C. Does the item require students to discriminate between problems with solutions that use the relationship and those that do not?

Refine the item unless the answers to the questions are yes for A and C and no for B.

CHAPTER 6

Items for Affective Objectives

GOAL OF CHAPTER 6

Chapter 6 focuses on attributes of items that cause them to be relevant to affective objectives at each of two levels: (1) appreciation and (2) willingness to act. More specifically, Chapter 6 will help you to

1. Design items at each of the two affective levels (*Cognitive: application*)
2. Given an item that's relevant to a content familiar to you, determine for which, if any, of the two affective levels the item has construct validity (*Cognitive: conceptualization*)

APPRECIATION ITEMS

PREFERENCES, OPINIONS, DESIRES, AND VALUES

Reread the section Appreciation-Level Affective Behavior on page 13. When you teach a cognitive or psychomotor objective, you are attempting to help students to *be able* to do something. When you teach an appreciation objective, you are attempting to influence their *preferences for, opinions about,* or *desires for* something. The "something," of course, is specified by the objective's content.

To affect preferences, opinions, and desires is to teach values. Questions about the appropriateness of teaching values in public schools have been debated in philosophical arenas for years (Kohlberg, 1987). The scope of this book does not allow inclusion of that debate. However, attention to measuring student achievement of affective objectives is included because

1. You may choose to teach units that include affective objectives. For example, on pages 16–19 the goals for seven units, from kindergarten

through high school level, are defined by sets of objectives. Each of four of those units includes at least one affective objective.

2. Often, students must display certain affective behaviors (e.g., a desire to learn to read) before they are ready to achieve particular cognitive or psychomotor objectives. Consequently, you may need to make formative evaluations about students' attitudes to help you plan how to help students achieve a cognitive or psychomotor objective.

IS APPRECIATION MEASURABLE?

An item is relevant to achievement of a cognitive or psychomotor objective when students who have achieved the objective can perform the task presented by the item with a higher success rate than those who have not achieved the objective. On the other hand, appreciation objectives are not concerned with students' being able to do anything. Achievement of an appreciation objective is the acquisition of a particular attitude.

Since you cannot distinguish between students who have achieved an appreciation objective and those that haven't because of what they *can* do, how is it possible for an item to present a task that's relevant to an appreciation objective? To help yourself answer this question, consider the following objective:

Wants to maintain a healthy diet (*Affective: appreciation*)

List the names of four or five people you believe have achieved this objective to a high degree. Make a second list of people who you believe have much lower levels of achievement. Keep in mind that because the objective specifies "appreciation," not "willingness to act," your group of achievers may include persons who don't actually try to follow a healthy diet but only wish they would. Some achievers may be at the willingness-to-act level and, thus, try to follow a healthy diet but don't know how.

For each person in your group of high achievers, list one or two observations you made that affected your decision. Do the same for each person in your group of low achievers.

Your two lists may be somewhat similar to the following.

OBSERVATIONS INDICATING HIGH ACHIEVEMENT

SANDRA: Frequently mentioned that she ought to diet. Once, before eating junk food, said, "I really shouldn't eat this."

KAY: Often inquired about what she should eat to maintain good health. Read magazine articles on nutrition.

EDDIE: Frequently mentioned that he has to start watching what he eats. Asked, "I haven't had much energy lately; I wonder if it's my diet?"

OTIS: Told someone who was eating junk food, "That stuff'll kill you!" Once said, "People ought to drink more water."

OBSERVATIONS INDICATING LOW ACHIEVEMENT

PHIL: Once said, "I don't worry about cholesterol. When you die, you die!" Said, "Eating is for pleasure. If God didn't want us to eat sugar and fat, then he wouldn't have given them to us."

MARION: Never reads or talks about nutrition.

JIM: Said, "Listening to the health nuts makes me think if it tastes good, it's bad, and if it tastes bad, it's good! I don't care what they say; I eat the way I want."

MAVIS: Said, "You don't need to worry about what you eat as long as you exercise."

PRESENTING CHOICES

Because you are able to associate observable behaviors with objective achievement and others with a lack of achievement, it is possible for you to design items that are relevant to the objective. The trick is to confront students with situations in which they have a choice of behaving either like a person who has achieved the objective or like one who has not.

1. *Task presented to the students:*
   Do you think people should avoid some foods (even if they taste good) and eat others (even if they taste bad)? Check one: _____ Yes _____ No
   Scoring key: +1 for yes only; otherwise 0.

2. *Task presented to the students:*
   Sugar-Fizz is a new candy that is being sold in grocery stores. Here are some facts about Sugar-Fizz:
   (1) It is not poisonous.
   (2) It is not known to cause any fatal diseases.
   (3) It has no nutritional value.
   (4) There is some evidence that it sometimes lowers the body's resistance to some infections.
   Johnny is a 14-year-old, has no health problem, has never tasted Sugar-Fizz, and has heard it tastes delicious. What should Johnny do? Check only one answer:
   _____ **a.** Eat it whenever he wants but stop if he gets sick.
   _____ **b.** Try it, but not often.
   _____ **c.** Never even try Sugar-Fizz.
   _____ **d.** Eat it whenever he wants it.
   Scoring key: (3 points possible) +3 for either b or c only; +1 for a only; 0 for d.

THE DIRECT APPROACH

The first of the two items just listed is quite direct. To test whether or not students appreciate something, just ask them. The direct approach is best for situations in which students are confident that they risk nothing by answering honestly. Fortunately, you may want to measure your students' achievement of affective objectives only for formative, not summative, evaluations. Unfortunately, many students have been conditioned to think that teachers evaluate only to grade. Consequently, you will need to make a concerted effort to teach them when it is "safe" to provide honest answers to affective items.

THE INDIRECT APPROACH

In the following example, the teacher uses an indirect approach to measure achievement of an appreciation objective.

Objective I of Ms. Parino's second-grade citizenship unit is

Wants classmates to succeed in their efforts to learn (*Affective: appreciation*)

Ms. Parino considers using the direct approach with an item that simply asks, "Do you want your classmates to learn how to do the math we cover in class?" However, she feels such an item won't work for two reasons: (1) The question is ambiguous and would be interpreted differently by different students. (2) Students would try to say what they think she wants them to say.

Consequently, she uses an indirect approach to item design and enters the following into the item pool for Objective I:

Task presented to the students:
The student is given an audio tape player containing a cassette on which the directions for the item are recorded. The student is instructed to circle either *Yes* or *No* by each letter on the following answer sheet:

A.	Yes	No
B.	Yes	No
C.	Yes	No
D.	Yes	No
E.	Yes	No
F.	Yes	No
G.	Yes	No

Following is the script on the cassette: "Things can happen that make us feel happy and sad at the same time. But some things make us only happy or only sad. I'm going to ask you to pretend something and ask you some questions about why you feel happy or sad about what you pretended. [pause] Pretend you are playing third base during a gym class softball game. The other team is batting and their batter strikes out. Does seeing the batter strike out make you feel happy because it will help your team win? Answer by circling *Yes* or *No* next to A on your answer sheet. [pause] Does seeing the batter strike out make you feel sad because it will help their team win? Circle *Yes* or *No* next to B. [pause] Does seeing the batter strike out make you happy because the pitcher for your team did well? Circle *Yes* or *No* next to C. [pause] Does seeing the batter strike out make you feel happy because it will make the other team feel sad? Circle *Yes* or *No* next to D. [pause] Does seeing the batter strike out make you feel sad because the batter will feel sad? Circle *Yes* or *No* next to E. [pause] Does seeing the batter strike out make you feel said because the game will soon be over? Circle *Yes* or *No* next to F. [pause] Does seeing the batter strike out make you feel happy because the batter will feel sad? Circle *Yes* or *No* next to G."

Scoring key: (2 points possible) If the student circled *Yes* for A and No for B, continue scoring the item. Otherwise, do not score the item because it appears the student did not understand the directions. Score +1 for each of the following that is marked *Yes* only: C and E. Score −1 for each of the following that is marked *Yes* only: D and G.

Ms. Parino realizes that this item alone cannot provide much of an indication of students' standings with respect to the objective. However, she thinks that if she draws on a wide variety of situations (e.g., softball, math, and the science project) to design and administer several similar items, patterns might emerge from the responses that will indicate progress toward the objective.

WILLINGNESS-TO-ACT ITEMS

CHOOSING BEHAVIORS

Reread the section on Willingness-to-Act-Level Affective Behavior on page 13. Students achieve a willingness-to-act objective by choosing to behave in accordance with a value specified by the objective's content. Although they may lack certain cognitive or psychomotor skills actually to effect the behavior, students achieve the willingness-to-act objective by *trying*. Here's an example:

Chris' teacher includes the following objective for his class:

Attempts to follow a healthy diet (*Affective: willingness to act*)

Chris is convinced of the value of a good diet and eats what he thinks is good for him. However, having yet to achieve some of the cognitive objectives of his teacher's health unit, Chris mistakenly believes that since fat is stored energy, he will gain energy by eating a lot of animal fats. In his enthusiasm for maintaining a healthy diet, Chris makes a concerted effort to consume large quantities of animal fats.

Because he *acted* on his beliefs about nutritious diets, Chris achieved the objective listed in the example.

Is Willingness to Act Measurable?

Since willingness-to-act objectives require students to take some sort of observable action, not only to embrace unseen values, these objectives are usually easier to measure than appreciation objectives.

Willingness-to-act items are designed like appreciation items. For example,

---

Mr. Clemente is embarking on a new school year as a junior high social studies teacher. He plans to use a number of learning activities in which students work with partners on projects. Because one of his long-range goals is for students to increase their interest in reading about social studies topics, he wants to plan some of the projects so that the more enthusiastic readers are teamed with students who dislike reading. He hopes some of the enthusiastic students' interest in reading will rub off on the others.

To implement his plan, he needs to assess his students' interest in reading so he'll know whom to team together. Mr. Clemente is not concerned with identifying the more skilled readers but rather those who enjoy and advocate reading. Thus, he wants to devise items relevant to the following objective:

Chooses to read and expresses the merits of reading to others (*Affective: willingness to act*)

To begin devising items, he thinks about persons (not necessarily students) whom he considers avid readers and reading advocates. He also thinks of some he believes dislike reading. Asking himself what he has observed about these people to so classify them, he develops the following lists of observable behaviors characterizing the two groups:

OBSERVATIONS INDICATING HIGH ACHIEVEMENT

1. Speak about literary works they have read, are reading, or plan to read
2. When confronted with problems, refer to reading material as solution sources
3. Frequent libraries, book stores, and magazine stands
4. Recommend reading selections to their friends
5. Often seen reading

OBSERVATIONS INDICATING LOW ACHIEVEMENT

1. Complain about the length of readings assigned in school
2. When confronted with problems, seek solution sources that do not require reading

3. When given the option of going to the library or some other comparable place, do not go to the library
4. While spending time in a waiting room (e.g., in a physician's office) do not pick up available reading materials

Mr. Clemente builds several items from these lists.

Observing Behaviors

Items can place students in a situation in which they have the choice of behaving either as if they are willing to act regarding the objective's content or as if they are unwilling. Mr. Clemente, for example, developed the following item for the objective in the previous example:

Task presented to the students:
The student is directed to wait outside the guidance counselor's office where a variety of books and magazines are prominently displayed.
Scoring key: An unobtrusive observer in the waiting room uses a watch and makes notes to record the number of minutes the student spent
   A. Waiting for the counselor
   B. Looking at, thumbing through, or holding magazines or books but not actually reading
   C. Appearing to be reading
Score for the item =

$$2\left(\frac{\text{number of minutes for C}}{\text{number of minutes for A}}\right) + \frac{\text{number of minutes for B}}{\text{number of minutes for A}}$$

The difficulty of this item can be manipulated by varying the interest levels of the reading matter available in the guidance counselor's waiting area. For an easy item, sports, music, video, and teenage magazines would be available. For a hard item, only low-interest reading material would be available.

Inferring Behaviors

Willingness-to-act items (e.g., the previous one) that depend on direct observation of behaviors often lack usability. Thus, items must often be designed that can be incorporated into a usable questionnaire. Instead of directly observing the behaviors specified by the objectives, you can ask the students how they would behave or have behaved in some relevant situations. Below is a multiple-choice item relevant to the objective given in the previous example.

Task presented to the students:

Suppose you find out that next week you will be meeting a visitor from Mexico. You would like to know more about life in Mexico before visiting with this person. Which one of the following would you *most* likely do? Circle one and only one:

A. Watch the travel channel on television in hopes that you would see a program about Mexico.

B. Read about Mexico in an atlas.

C. Look up Mexico in an encyclopedia.

D. Phone a travel agent and ask her or him about life in Mexico.

E. Go to the library and ask the reference librarian what he or she knows about Mexico.

F. Wait for the visitor from Mexico to arrive and ask her or him.

G. Go to the library and look up some references in the card catalogue.

Scoring key: +1 for any one of the following: B, C, or G; otherwise 0.

Items (e.g., the previous one) for willingness-to-act objectives that do not depend on direct observations are of little value unless they are used with other, similar items that present a variety of situations. As with appreciation items with an indirect approach, a number of items are needed to identify patterns that indicate students' attitudes.

The difficulty of these items can be manipulated by varying the attractiveness of the alternatives. Students, for example, are more likely to select a reading activity over a movie if it's a movie they consider boring rather than exciting.

SELF-ASSESSMENT OF YOUR ACHIEVEMENT OF CHAPTER 6'S OBJECTIVES

In Exercise III of Chapter 3's self-assessment, you established an item pool file. You entered items into that file for Exercise III of Chapter 4's self-assessment. The following exercises for Chapter 6 refer to your item pool file.

    I.   Select one of the items from your file that you designed to be relevant to an appreciation objective. If there is no pool for an appreciation objective in your file, write one in the realm of your teaching specialty and develop an item that is relevant to it. Now answer the following question about your item:

> Does the task presented by the item place students in a situation that requires them to select either a response that is indicative of people who embrace the value specified by the objective or a response that is indicative of people who do not hold the value?

Refine the item unless the answer to the question is yes.

  II.   Select one of the items from your file that you designed to be relevant to a willingness-to-act objective. If there is no pool for this objective in your file, write one in the realm of your teaching specialty and develop an item that is relevant to it. Now answer the following question about your item:

> Does the task presented by the item place students in a situation that requires them to select either a response that is indicative of people who would act in accordance with the value specified by the objective or a response that is indicative of people who would not choose to act in that manner?

Refine the item unless the answer to the question is yes.

CHAPTER 7

Items for Psychomotor Objectives

GOAL OF CHAPTER 7

Chapter 7 focuses on attributes of items that cause them to be relevant to psychomotor objectives at each of two levels: (1) voluntary muscle capability and (2) ability to perform a specific skill. More specifically, Chapter 6 will help you to

1. Design items at each of the two psychomotor levels (*Cognitive: application*)
2. Given an item that's relevant to a content familiar to you, determine for which, if any, of the two psychomotor levels the item has construct validity (*Cognitive: conceptualization*)

VOLUNTARY-MUSCLE-CAPABILITY ITEMS

ENDURANCE, STRENGTH, FLEXIBILITY, AGILITY, AND SPEED

Reread the section on Voluntary Muscle Capability on page 14.

Typically, voluntary muscle capability can be measured more precisely than other types of behavioral constructs. A voluntary-muscle-capability item requires students to use the type of capability (i.e., endurance, strength, flexibility, agility, or speed) with the muscle groups specified by the objective.

Measuring Endurance If the objective's capability is endurance, items should provide a means for observing either (1) the number of continuous repetitions a muscle group can execute a particular task or (2) the amount of time during which the muscle group works. Here, for example, is an objective and an item designed to measure it.

Objective:
Increases endurance of the abdominal muscles (*Psychomotor: voluntary muscle capability*)
Task presented to the students:
The student is directed to perform as many nonstop bent-leg sit-ups, using the technique learned in class, as possible.
Scoring key: The number of completed sit-ups is counted.

Measuring Strength   If the objective's capability is strength, items should provide a way to observe the amount of weight moved a particular distance by the muscle group. Here, for example, is an objective and an item designed to measure it.

Objective:
Increase the strength of the quadricep muscles (*Pychomotor: voluntary muscle capability*)
Task presented to the students:
After appropriate warm-up, the student is directed to execute a left leg extension lift on a leg-lift bench. The weight attempted is determined as follows:
   The weight is set markedly below the student's maximum for the lift. The lift is attempted with gradually increasing weight (e.g., in 2-kilogram increments) until the student is unable to perform the lift. Adequate recuperation occurs between attempts.
The item may be administered over several days.
Scoring key: The maximum weight the student lifts is recorded.

Measuring Flexibility   If the objective's capability is flexibility, items should provide a means for observing the angle at which a muscle group extends or flexes a joint. Here, for example, is an objective and an item designed to measure it.

Objective:
Increases flexibility of the lower back muscles (*Psychomotor: voluntary muscle capability*)
Task presented to the students:
After appropriate warm-up exercises, the student is directed to (1) sit on the floor with knees extended 180 degrees and hands clasped beneath lower thighs and (2) bring the head as far down between the knees as possible and hold it there until receiving directions to relax.
Scoring key: The inside angle at the waist is measured and recorded (see Figure 7.1).

Measuring Agility   If the objective's capability is agility, items should provide a means for observing the amount of time it takes muscle groups to respond to

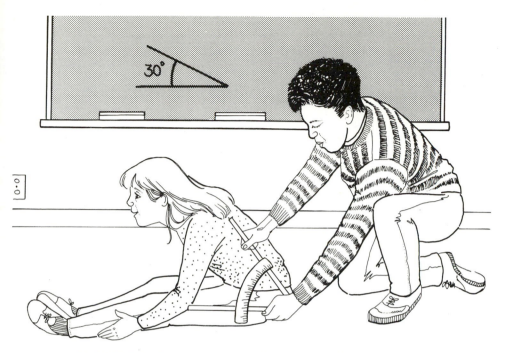

FIGURE 7.1   Measuring Flexibility of Lower Back Muscles

a particular stimulus in a prescribed manner. Here, for example, is an objective and an item designed to measure it.

> *Objective:*
> Increases eye-to-hand reaction (*Pyschomotor: voluntary muscle capability*)
> *Task presented to the students:*
> The student sits at a panel with (1) three push-buttons (from left to right, one green, one blue, and one red) and (2) a display of three lightbulbs (from left to right, one red, one green, and one blue). The student is directed to immediately push the button that matches the color of the light that flashes. The lights flash one at a time in a randomly determined sequence. A light comes on as soon as any button has been pushed by the student.
> *Scoring key:* The total number of correct buttons pushed in a one-minute span is recorded (see Figure 7.2).

Measuring Speed   If the objective's capability is speed, items should provide a means for observing the time it takes muscle groups to perform a specified amount of work. Here, for example, is an objective and an item designed to measure it.

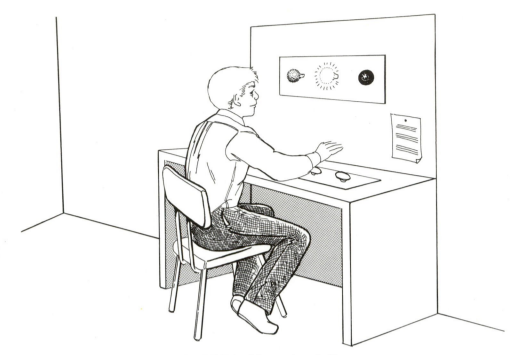

FIGURE 7.2 Measuring Agility

Objective:
Increases speed at which hamstrings flex and quadriceps extend the knees
(*Psychomotor: voluntary muscle capability*)
Task presented to the students:
Student lies face down, flat on a wrestling mat. He or she is then directed
to execute rapidly the following movement as many times as possible in
a 30-second span:
While only moving the lower part of the left leg, bring the left heel into
contact with the buttocks and then return to the original position.
Scoring key: The number of movements completed in the 30-second span is
recorded (see Figure 7.3).

ISOLATING THE MUSCLE GROUP

Designing items relevant to voluntary-muscle-capability objectives requires at
least a rudimentary working knowledge of anatomy and kinesiology. You, for
example, are hardly in a position to design an item for measuring the strength
of the muscles of the upper back unless you understand what movements the
upper back muscles affect. An understanding of anatomy and kinesiology is thus
essential to design items that truly isolate the muscle groups specified by the
objective.

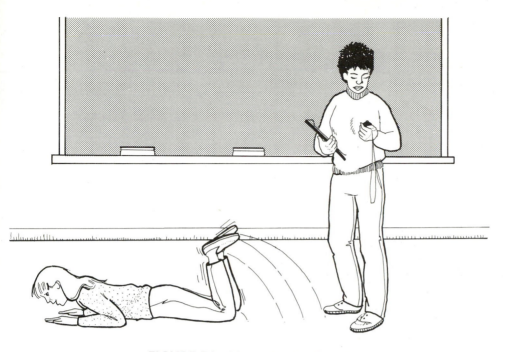

FIGURE 7.3 Measuring Leg Speed

Measures of chest muscle strength, for example, will be influenced by upper arm strength. Item designers with a more sophisticated understanding of anatomy and kinesiology are better able to isolate the muscles specified by the objective (e.g., to minimize the role of the upper arms in items relevant to chest strength). Similar problems exist for cognitive and affective measures. It takes a sophisticated understanding of both behavioral constructs and content, for example, to minimize the role of knowledge-level behaviors when designing application items.

TAXING KNOWLEDGE OF A PROCESS

Items relevant to a voluntary-muscle-capability require students to attempt some sort of work that involves a process (e.g., executing a leg lift or pushing buttons in response to a colored light). Students' performances on these items will be influenced by how well they know the steps in the process (i.e., a cognitive skill). For example,

To test students' chest strength, Mr. Ascione records the maximum weight that each bench-presses. Using excellent technique, bringing the bar up evenly in a concentrated thrust, Devon benches 160 pounds for his record. Barely managing to balance the bar without dropping it, Richard obtains a record of 110 pounds. However, after some knowledge-of-a-process instruction on technique and several days of practice, Richard's record improves to 185. Devon never benches more than 165.

The processes students are required to use for voluntary-muscle-capability items should be taught and practiced before the items are administered for summative or formative evaluations.

FLUCTUATING PHYSICAL CONDITIONS

Students' performances on voluntary-muscle-capability items are influenced by variable physical conditions (e.g., fatigue, warm-up, and food in the stomach). To keep such fluctuating factors from contaminating measurement reliability, repeated administrations of the items should occur under comparable conditions (e.g., when students have had similar amounts of rest and warm-up).

EQUIPMENT AND ENVIRONMENT

The type and condition of equipment used in voluntary-muscle-capability items can affect students' performances. Even room temperature and time of day can have a major impact. Thus, comparable equipment and testing conditions should be similar for all administrations of the same item.

REPEATABLE MEASUREMENTS

Unlike many cognitive and affective items, voluntary-muscle-capability items can be administered repeatedly to the same students without contaminating measurement validity. That is, test security is not a concern for psychomotor tests as it is for most cognitive and affective tests. A student's performance on a psychomotor item cannot be enhanced by her or his prior knowledge of the item.

CAUTION

The design and administration of a voluntary-muscle-capability item should include safeguards against injuries and accidents. For example, unless bent-leg sit-ups are properly executed, there is a danger of back injuries. Again, a knowledge of anatomy and kinesiology, as well as an understanding of the safe operation of equipment, is critical.

ABILITY-TO-PERFORM-A-SPECIFIC-SKILL ITEMS

EXECUTION

Reread the following sections that include explanations and examples pertinent to the design of ability-to-perform-a-specific-skill items: (1) Ability to Perform a Specific Skill on page 14 and (2) Knowledge, Affective, and Psychomotor Components of the Process on pages 143 through 145.

The item on page 144 testing five-year-old Alex's ability to print an uppercase *A* is designed for a knowledge-of-a-process objective. To diagnose why Alex might have performed poorly on that item, it is necessary to measure the following objective:

> Manipulates a pencil well enough to follow the steps for printing an uppercase *A*. (*Psychomotor: ability to perform a specific skill*)

Here is one example of an item designed to be relevant to that objective.

Task presented to the students:
The student is given three pencils, one that marks red, another that marks blue, and one that marks green. As the student observes, the teacher puts two colored dots on lined paper (as shown below) and directs the student to draw a straight red line from the blue dot to the red dot:

• (blue)

(red) •

If the student succeeds in drawing a straight line segment, touching but not starting or finishing significantly away from either dot, the item continues; otherwise, the item is terminated. The teacher then puts a green dot as follows and directs the student to draw a straight blue line from the blue dot to the green dot:

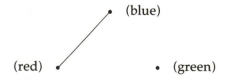

If this is successful, the student is told to draw a straight green line from the *middle* of the red line to the *middle* of the blue line. The teacher points to those points as he or she says "middle" but immediately removes his or her finger before the student begins.

Scoring key: The following are checked as satisfactorily completed:
_____ red line   _____ blue line   _____ green line
Any unsatisfactory lines should be commented on and the error explained.

FOCUS ON STEPS IN THE PROCESS

Ability-to-perform-a-specific-skill objectives are concerned with how well students can execute the steps in a process, much like knowledge-of-a-process objectives are concerned with how well they can remember the steps in a process. Thus, the same principles for focusing knowledge-of-a-process items on the steps in processes instead of final outcomes are applicable to the design of ability-to-perform-a-specific-skill objectives.

Ability-to-perform-a-specific-skill items almost exclusively use a performance-observation format. As suggested in the section on Designing Performance-Observation Items in Chapter 4, it is advisable to incorporate the use of videotaping in their design. Here is an example of an objective and an item designed to measure it.

Objective:
Properly executes a back dive from a 3-meter spring board (*Psychomotor: ability to perform a specific skill*)
Task presented to the students:
The student is directed to perform a back dive from a 3-meter springboard. The dive is videotaped.
Scoring key: The observer views the videotape repeatedly to complete the following ranking scale:
A. Rank the parts of the dive first, second, and third from strongest to weakest:
_____ takeoff   _____ turn   _____ entry
B. Rank the parts of the *takeoff* from strongest to weakest:
_____ body position   _____ height   _____ angle
C. Rank the parts of the *turn* from stronger to weaker:
_____ body position   _____ timing for entering the turn
D. Rank the parts of the *entry* from strongest to weakest:
_____ timing for stopping turn   _____ body position
_____ angle

SIMILARITIES TO VOLUNTARY-MUSCLE-CAPABILITY ITEMS

As with voluntary-muscle-capability items, the following should be kept in mind when designing ability-to-perform-a-specific-skill items:

1. Students' performances on the items are affected by their achievement of knowledge-of-a-process and willingness-to-act objectives.
2. Performances will be affected by fluctuating physical conditions, type and condition of equipment, and environmental factors.
3. Items are repeatable without fear of contamination to validity. In fact, for an ability-to-perform-a-specific-skill objective, students attempt the same tasks presented by relevant items that they practice for lessons designed to help them achieve the objective.

SELF-ASSESSMENT OF YOUR ACHIEVEMENT OF CHAPTER 7'S OBJECTIVES

In Exercise III of Chapter 3's self-assessment, you established an item pool file. You entered items into that file for Exercise III of Chapter 4's self-assessment. The following exercises for Chapter 7 refer to your item pool file.

    I.   Select one of the items from your file that you designed to be relevant to an voluntary-muscle-capability objective. If there is no pool for that objective in your file, write one and develop an item that is relevant to it. Now answer the following questions about your item:

        A.   Does the item focus on the capability (i.e., endurance, strength, flexibility, agility, or speed) of the muscle groups specified by the objective?

        B.   Does the item's design control for the influences of (1) knowledge-of-a-process achievement, (2) fluctuating physical conditions, and (3) variations in equipment and environment?

        C.   Are there provisions for minimizing the risk of injuries?

Refine the item unless the answer to all questions is yes.

    II.   Select one of the items from your file that you designed to be relevant to an ability-to-perform-a-specific-skill objective. If there is no pool for this objective in your file, write one and develop an item that is relevant to it. Now answer the following questions about your item:

        A.   Does the item focus on the steps in the process rather than the final outcome?

        B.   Does the item's design control for the influences of (1) knowledge-of-a-process achievement, (2) fluctuating physical conditions, and (3) variations in equipment and environment?

        C.   Are there provisions for minimizing the risk of injuries?

Refine the item unless the answer to all questions is yes.

Interpreting Standardized Test Scores

GOAL OF CHAPTER 8

Chapter 8 focuses on the meanings of scores from standardized tests that are administered in school-wide assessment programs. More specifically, Chapter 8 will help you to

1. Describe some of the common uses and misuses of standardized tests in schools (*Cognitive: simple knowledge*)
2. Give the results of a standardized test in the form of commonly used derived scores (e.g., percentiles, NCE scores, and stanines) and explain the meaning of those results (*Cognitive: comprehension of a communication*)
3. State the definitions of the following: *aptitude test, norm group, standardized test norms, derived scores, percentile, NCE score, grade equivalent, scaled score, stanine,* and *standard score*

DISTRICT-WIDE TESTING PROGRAMS

STANDARDIZED TESTS IN SCHOOL

Reread the section on Commonly Used Measurements of Achievement on pages 26–27. Most school districts have some sort of program for periodically administering standardized tests in all their schools. A typical program includes a popular achievement test battery complemented by aptitude tests and single-subject achievement tests.

Aptitude Tests   Whereas achievement tests are used in evaluating what students have learned, *aptitude* tests are used to *predict* how well they will learn if given the opportunity.

The administration and interpretation of standardized aptitude tests, along with interest inventories and personality assessments, usually fall within the domain of guidance counselors, special education diagnosticians, or school psychologists. Some aptitude tests are individually administered (e.g., the Stanford-Binet and the Wechsler Scales); others are group-administered (e.g., the Cognitive Abilities Test and the Otis-Lennon School Ability Test).

Single-Subject Achievement Tests Standardized achievement tests are available for a number of individual subjects. The more popular ones are either in reading (e.g., the Gates-MacGinitie Reading Tests and the Stanford Diagnostic Reading Test) or in mathematics (e.g., the Modern Math Understanding Test or the Stanford Diagnostic Mathematics Test).

Achievement Test Batteries A standardized achievement test battery is a package of subtests that are (1) designed to be relevant to different content areas, (2) field-tested (or normed) on the same population, and (3) coordinated for efficient administration over a period of one to three days. The main events of most district-wide testing programs are the administrations once or twice a year of an achievement test battery.

Levels Most achievement tests, whether a single test or a subtest in a battery, are organized into *levels*. Lower levels of the test are administered to younger students, higher levels to older ones. The Comprehensive Tests of Basic Skills (CTBS) for example, has four levels: Level 1 for grades 2.5–4, Level 2 for grades 4–6, Level 3 for grades 6–8, and Level 4 for grades 8–12 (Mitchell, 1985). Each level has nine subtests (reading vocabulary, reading comprehension, language mechanics, language expression, language spelling, math computation, math concepts, math applications, and study skills).

Sources of Information on Standardized Tests For information on and assessments of particular standardized tests, you are advised to seek the following sources from the reference section of a college library or a teacher resource center:

Mitchell, J. V., Jr. (Ed.). (1983). *Tests in Print III*. Lincoln: University of Nebraska Press.
———. (1985) *The ninth mental measurements yearbook*. Lincoln: University of Nebraska Press.

A Typical Story

The following example is representative of the history of many district-wide standardized testing programs.

The Alkena County School District contains 36 elementary, nine middle, three junior high, eight high, one vocational, and two special schools. Before 1972, the district had no policy regarding the use of standardized tests in schools. Some individual schools found room in their budgets for rather extensive standardized testing programs; others did not. Consequently, practices among the schools varied considerably. For example,

1. Grove Street Elementary School pretested grades 2, 4, and 6 in September and posttested those grades in May with the Key Math Diagnostic Arithmetic Test and Woodcock Reading Mastery Test.
2. Clayhills Middle School did not administer standardized tests.
3. Barber Elementary School administered the Otis-Lennon School Ability Test (OLSAT) in August to place students in either a "remedial," "average," or "accelerated" track. Scores from a February administration of the Metropolitan Achievement Tests to all grades was used in concert with August *OLSAT* scores to label students as "underachievers," "expected achievers," and "overachievers" for reading, mathematics, language, science, social studies, and study skills.
4. Aloyisius High School administered the Iowa Test of Educational Development in April to all "college-bound" eleventh-graders.

In response to complaints about inefficiency and a lack of accountability, the Alkena District, in 1972, established an evaluation department that would be responsible for designing and implementing a uniform district-wide standardized testing program. To save money, the school board declared a moratorium on standardized testing until the new program was in place.

The evaluation department impaneled a committee of teachers, school administrators, and measurement specialists to (1) set the goals of the program, (2) review available standardized tests and test batteries, (3) select the tests that would provide the most cost-effective means for realizing the goals, and (4) design a plan for administering and using the test results.

It took the committee three months to establish the goals. Some members wanted to use standardized test results to (1) provide end-of-the-year pass/fail cutoff scores for each student, (2) compare students' progress in one subject to that in other subjects, (3) provide data for decisions about retention of and merit pay for teachers, (4) place students in "homogeneous" groups or tracks, and (5) rank schools. Other members argued that standardized tests are not capable of providing valid data for those purposes. The following goals were ultimately accepted:

1. Periodically provide data on student achievement to which teachers could compare the results from their own teacher-made tests (The intent is for teachers to reconsider evaluations based on test results that are dramatically inconsistent with the standardized test results.)
2. Make data available for research and evaluation studies that address questions about how to improve the district's curricula, programs, and schools
3. Fulfill the need to have standardized test data for developing school-improvement grant proposals and for evaluations of existing grant projects

By a split vote, the committee agreed that standardized tests would not be used for purposes other than these three goals.

In light of their goals, the committee reviewed nearly a hundred publishers' catalogues; examined sample copies of tests; interviewed sales representatives from different test publishers; and studied excerpts from *Tests in Print*, the *Mental Measurement Yearbook*, and measurement and evaluation textbooks. Unanimously, the members decided

1. That any one of four of the 14 available standardized achievement test batteries could meet the needs of the district's program as well as any other
2. That the district office would enter into competitive negotiations with the publishers of those four test batteries to contract for one of the batteries to be administered in grades K through 12 in September and April of each school year
3. That no group-administered aptitude test would be used in the district but that a program for individually administered standardized aptitude tests for special needs should be coordinated by the district office
4. That a second committee (including guidance counselors, school psychologists, special education teachers and diagnosticians, and representatives from this original committee) would be formed to plan the individually administered aptitude testing program

In 1974, the program was fully implemented. The original achievement battery was replaced in 1979 when a contract was negotiated with a different publisher. For the most part, the program has been considered a success. Data have been used in several research and evaluation studies that affected school operations. District schools have been awarded several curriculum development grants as a result of needs assessments utilizing the data from the standardized tests. Most teachers have used the tests as an outside check on their students' achievement. Whenever standardized test results are incongruent with their own test results, these teachers try to explain the discrepancies (e.g., with interviews).

However, in recent years, the three goals established by the committee of 1972 seem to be forgotten. Average test results for individual schools are being publicized in newspapers and on television. Administrators are beginning to pressure teachers to raise scores. Some teachers have begun to "teach to the tests." Because of the "big event" atmosphere of the administration of the standardized achievement test battery and because results appear on computer printouts (see Figure 8.1), many parents mistakenly think the tests measure their children's intelligence.

The Alkena County School Board is considering a proposal that would

1. Permit elementary students to pass to the next grade only if their reading and math scores on the May-administered achievement test battery represented a "gain of at least six months" over their grade equivalent scores from the September-administered test
2. Tie merit pay raises for teachers to the scores their students receive on the standardized achievement test battery

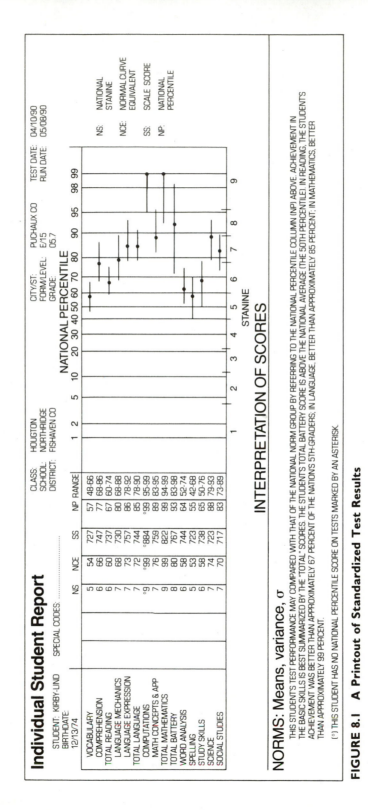

Individual Student Report

SPECIAL CODES: ....

STUDENT: KIRBY-LIND
BIRTHDATE: 12/13/74

CLASS: HOUGTON
SCHOOL: NORTHRIDGE
DISTRICT: FISHAVEN CO

CITY/ST: PUCHAUX CO
FORM/LEVEL: E/15
GRADE: 05.7

TEST DATE: 04/10/90
RUN DATE: 05/08/90

NS: NATIONAL STANINE
NCE: NORMAL CURVE EQUIVALENT
SS: SCALE SCORE
NP: NATIONAL PERCENTILE

	NS	NCE	SS	NP	RANGE
VOCABULARY	5	54	727	57	48-66
COMPREHENSION	6	66	747	77	68-86
TOTAL READING	6	60	737	67	60-74
LANGUAGE MECHANICS	7	68	730	80	68-88
LANGUAGE EXPRESSION	7	73	757	86	78-92
TOTAL LANGUAGE	7	72	744	85	78-90
COMPUTATIONS	°9	°99	°884	°99	95-99
MATH CONCEPTS & APP	7	76	759	89	83-95
TOTAL MATHEMATICS	9	99	822	99	94-99
TOTAL BATTERY	8	80	767	93	83-98
WORD ANALYSIS	6	58	744	64	52-74
SPELLING	5	53	723	55	42-68
STUDY SKILLS	6	58	738	65	50-76
SCIENCE	7	74	723	88	79-93
SOCIAL STUDIES	7	70	717	83	73-89

NATIONAL PERCENTILE

STANINE

INTERPRETATION OF SCORES

NORMS: Means, variance, σ

THIS STUDENT'S TEST PERFORMANCE MAY COMPARED WITH THAT OF THE NATIONAL NORM GROUP BY REFERRING TO THE NATIONAL PERCENTILE COLUMN (NP) ABOVE. ACHIEVEMENT IN THE BASIC SKILLS IS BEST SUMMARIZED BY THE "TOTAL" SCORES. THE STUDENT'S TOTAL BATTERY SCORE IS ABOVE THE NATIONAL AVERAGE (THE 50TH PERCENTILE). IN READING, THE STUDENT'S ACHIEVEMENT WAS BETTER THAN APPROXIMATELY 67 PERCENT OF THE NATION'S 5TH-GRADERS; IN LANGUAGE, BETTER THAN APPROXIMATELY 85 PERCENT; IN MATHEMATICS, BETTER THAN APPROXIMATELY 99 PERCENT.

(°) THIS STUDENT HAS NO NATIONAL PERCENTILE SCORE ON TESTS MARKED BY AN ASTERISK.

FIGURE 8.1 A Printout of Standardized Test Results

Uses and Misuses of Standardized Tests in Schools

The three goals established by Alkena County's committee in 1972 are certainly important and they can be accomplished with a standardized achievement testing program. It is unfortunate that the committee's ideas faded over time. Too often, people attribute untenable capabilities to standardized tests and use them inappropriately. Please keep the following in mind:

1. Standardized tests are relevant to skills that are far more general than the goals of any one curriculum. Rarely do they have construct validity for cognitive objectives beyond comprehension of a communication. Thus, standardized tests should not be the principal data source for evaluations of student achievement.

2. The validity of standardized tests are based on correlational statistics that deem the tests more appropriate for evaluations that pertain to *groups* rather than to individuals. Thus, they should be used primarily in the assessment of the average achievement or aptitude of a group (e.g., all fifth-graders in a district or class) rather than for making decisions about individual students (e.g., to determine whether or not an individual student passes or fails a grade or subject).

3. Achievement and aptitude test scores are affected by some degree of error (i.e., they are not perfectly valid). Thus, it is inadvisable to use any one test (standardized or not) as the sole measure for any evaluation.

4. The dangers of basing judgments of teachers' effectiveness on their students' standardized achievement test scores are well documented throughout the educational literature (Cangelosi, 1986). Some of the drawbacks of this practice are these:
    a. Student achievement is affected by many factors (e.g., students' aptitudes and prior experiences) that teachers cannot control).
    b. The validities of standardized tests are questionable for the goals of most school curricula.
    c. Teachers are encouraged to limit their lessons to what appears on the standardized tests. This focus has been shown to occur even in cases where there is a poor match between the test items and the objectives of the curriculum.

5. It is a popular myth among laypersons that standardized tests somehow measure "real intellectual ability or achievement" that teacher-produced tests cannot measure. Because standardized test scores appear mystifying and the tests themselves look more impressive than teacher-produced tests, people assume standardized tests are far more powerful than they actually are.

6. Like most educational and psychological tests, standardized tests provide gross, not precise, data. Consequently, the scores of two students suggest that their achievement levels might be different *only* if their scores are *markedly* different.

7. Standardized test results are often reported in scores (e.g., percentiles and grade equivalents) that lack the properties of familiar cardinal numbers.

Consequently, arithmetic operations may distort the meaning of the scores. For example, the difference between a percentile of 50 and a percentile of 40 represents a smaller difference in test performances than does the difference between a percentile of 10 and a percentile of 5. Grade equivalent scores from standardized tests are particularly misused by the misapplication of arithmetic.

8. Comparisons between scores from different standardized tests or from different subtests of the same standardized test battery are often misleading and should be avoided. The problem is inherent in the method by which the tests are standardized.

STANDARDIZING TESTS

NORM GROUPS

The first step in standardizing a test is to field-test it on a representative sample of the population for which the test is designed. The sample is referred to as the test's *norm group*. The scores of the students in the norm group become the standards to which the results of subsequent administrations of the test are compared.

National The more popular standardized tests that enjoy a nationwide market are *nationally normed*. In other words, the norm groups for these tests are samples that were drawn from geographical regions widely spread across the United States. Typically, demographic information about a standardized test's national norm group is provided by the test's *user's manual*. Figure 8.2 gives an example of an excerpt from a user's manual.

Whenever your students take a standardized test, their scores will be compared to those from the norm group. Thus, information about the norm group is relevant to your interpretations of your students' performances.

Local Your students' performance on a standardized test can be compared to the scores of a *local norm group* if a sample of previous scores from your geographic region is available. Scores from the more popular standardized tests can be reported in comparison to both national and local norm groups.

Just how "local" a local norm group is varies considerably, depending on who gathered the sample, what test is used, and the size of the school district purchasing the test. The local norm group for a rural school district in Wyoming might include students across the western one-third of the country. For a large urban school district, the norm group may be drawn from within the district itself.

VALIDATION

Part of the standardization process includes a study of the test's validity. Reliability coefficients are computed from the norm group's scores and reported

Standardization   This edition of the PIT is a revision of the edition published in 1951. The 1982 edition differs from the previous version in that it contains more up-to-date content and illustrations. For standardization purposes, the PIT was administered in October of 1981 to a sample of approximately 11,000 pupils in 63 school systems. An attempt was made to use school systems so that their geographic and socio-economic characteristics were comparable to the country as a whole. Pertinent descriptive data of the norm group that was ultimately tested are given below:

1. Regional Distribution of Norm Group

Region	States	Number of Schools	Number of Pupils
Northeast	Pa., Mass., N.Y., N.J.	128	5,950
South	La., Tex., S.C.	16	980
Central	Wis., Minn., Mo.	52	1,623
Pacific	California	78	2,052

2. Population of Community in Which Pupils Live:

Population	Number of Pupils
Above 100,000	645
25,001–100,000	4,712
10,000–25,000	2,241
Less than 10,000	3,005

3. Aptitude Test Scores:

IQ	Number of Pupils
Above 140	81
120–139	2,748
100–119	4,267
80–99	2,333
60–79	983
Below 60	191

FIGURE 8.2   Excerpt about a Norm Group from a Standardized Test User's Manual

in the user's manual. Figure 8.3 provides an example of a reliability report from a user's manual.

Besides reliability coefficients, further evidence of relevance is usually obtained by (1) correlating the results of the test with those from other tests and (2) impaneling subject-matter and teaching specialists to judge the content and behavioral constructs of the items.

TEST NORMS

Average Norm Group Score   The average of the norm group's scores for each level of the test is the standard to which your students' scores are compared. For example,

Reliability   Reliability is defined as the consistency or precision of a test. Reliability data are provided in table 6 for the tests normed on beginning 8th grade pupils in the norm group. Two measures of reliability are presented for each subtest: one is based on odd-even scores corrected by Spearman-Brown Formula (r_{11}), and the other is based on Kuder-Richardson Formula 20 (r_{kr20}).

Standard Errors of Measurements were determined using the Kuder-Richardson reliability coefficients. Standard Errors of Measurement are given in table 6 in terms of raw scores but they can be found in terms of scaled scores and grades equivalents in the "Score Interpretation Section" of this manual.

The Standard Errors of Measurement in table 6 provides information regarding the degree to which chance fluctuations can be expected in test scores. For example, the Vocabulary Skills subtest Standard Errors of Measurement is 3.1 raw score points, which means that one might expect chance fluctuations within 3.1 points of an obtained score about two thirds of the time. If a pupil scores 35, one could say with about 68 percent certainty that the true score is between 31.9 and 38.1

Table 6
Reliability Coefficients and Standard Errors of Measurement

Test	Number of Items	r_{11}	r_{kr20}	Std. Error Measure.
Vocabulary Skills	50	.94	.93	3.1
Reading Comprehension	68	.96	.93	3.3
Math Computations	45	.94	.93	2.5
Math Application	24	.89	.88	2.8
Math Concepts	30	.83	.83	3.4
Social Science	62	.94	.92	3.6
Listening Skills	45	.76	.76	5.2

FIGURE 8.3   Excerpt about Reliabilities from a Standardized Test User's Manual

In October, Mr. Adkins' fifth-grade class is given Level 3 of a standardized achievement test battery. The maximum possible score for the listening comprehension subtest is 39. The average Level 3 national norm group score for October administrations is 20.4. For the local norm group it is 22.7.

According to the report on the listening comprehension subtest Mr. Adkins received in December, 7 of his students performed below the national norm, 4 near the norm, and 17 above the norm. Compared to the local norm, 9 scores are below, 2 near, and 17 above.

The raw scores (i.e., the number of points out of the 39 possible) for Mr. Adkins' class appear in Table 8.1.

The Variability of Norm Group Scores   According to Table 8.1 and to the report Mr. Adkins received, the test performances of his 17 students with scores of 25 or higher are rated above the national norm. The next 4 scores, between 17 and 24, are near the national norm; the 7 scores below 17 are below the national norm. But how much greater than the norm group's average (in this case, 20.4) must a score be to be rated "above average"? How much less than the average must a score be to be rated "below the norm"?

For standardized tests the answers to these questions depend on the

TABLE 8.1   Raw Scores for Mr. Adkins' Class from a Standardized Listening Comprehension Test

Student	Raw Score	
Bryce	39	
Deanna	37	
Mary Frances	35	
Amalya	33	
Otis	33	
Anna	33	
Roe	31	
Karen	28	
Eva	28	Above both national and local norm groups' averages
Tom	27	
Sue	27	
Elaine	26	
Lee	26	
Phil	26	
Nancy	26	
Desiree	25	
Wiona	25	
Sua	24	Near local norm group's average
Ahem	21	
George	20	Near national norm group's average
Bernie	17	
Maxine	16	
Judy	16	
Ron	16	Below local norm group's average
Ruth	13	Below national norm group's average
Kirt	10	
Robin	10	
Blaine	8	

National norm group average = 20.4.
Local norm group average = 22.7.

degree of *variability* of the norm group's scores. Table 8.2 has two sets of scores. The scores in the left column are highly variable; those in the right column are more homogeneous. The more variable scores deviate farther from their average than the less variable scores.

To be significant, a difference between a raw score and the norm group average must be greater for standardized tests with highly variable norm group scores than for those with less variable norm group scores.

Norm Group Standard Deviation   The statistic referred to as the standard deviation is used to measure the variability of norm group scores. Roughly speaking, the *standard deviation* for a set of scores is approximately the average difference between the group's scores and the average of the scores. So whether or not a raw score is considered far enough above or below the norm group average to escape the "near the norm" rating depends on two factors: (1) the size of the standard deviation and (2) the type of *derived score* that is used in the standardized test report.

TABLE 8.2 Two Sets of Scores That Differ
in Variability

More Variable Scores	Less Variable Scores
44	51
80	67
13	65
27	51
65	58
50	62
19	55
71	66
9	62
9	59
43	54

Derived Scores Standardized tests typically report each student's performance on a subtest in terms of scores that have been *derived* from three sources: (1) the student's *raw score*, (2) the *average* of the norm group's scores, and (3) the *standard deviation* of the norm group's scores. Figure 8.4 is an example of such a report.

The grade equivalent, percentile, and stanine scores from Figure 8.4 are examples of derived scores. Each indicates how the student's raw score on each subtest compares to the norms established by the subtest averages and standard deviations from the norm group's scores.

COMMONLY REPORTED DERIVED SCORES

STANINES

There are nine possible stanine scores (1, 2, 3, 4, 5, 6, 7, 8, 9) derived by the following rules from the norm group average and standard deviation:

1. Raw scores less than 1.75 standard deviations below the average are assigned the stanine score 1.
2. Raw scores between 1.75 and 1.25 standard deviations below the average are assigned the stanine score 2.
3. Raw scores between 1.25 and .75 standard deviations below the average are assigned the stanine score 3.
4. Raw scores between .75 and .25 standard deviations below the average are assigned the stanine score 4.
5. Raw scores between .25 standard deviations below the average and .25 standard deviations above the average are assigned the stanine score 5.

Pupil Profile for Charlie Loy	Reading	Math	Social Studies	Science	Study Skills
Grade equivalent	5.1	6.3	4.8	5.7	5.3
Percentile	29	62	27	48	42
Stanine	4	6	4	5	5
Raw score	28	17	36	31	42

FIGURE 8.4   Charlie Loy's Standardized Test Results

6. Raw scores between .25 and .75 standard deviations above the average are assigned the stanine score 6.
7. Raw scores between .75 and 1.25 standard deviations above the average are assigned the stanine score 7.
8. Raw scores between 1.25 and 1.75 standard deviations above the average are assigned the stanine score 8.
9. Raw scores greater than 1.75 standard deviations above the average are assigned the stanine score 9.

What would Bill's stanine be if his raw score is 22 on a standardized test with a norm group average of 40 and a standard deviation of 12? Bill's raw score is 18 below the average, and 18 is 1.5 standard deviations ($18/12 = 1.5$). Thus, 22 falls 1.5 standard deviations below the average, which is between 1.75 and 1.25 standard deviations below the mean. Thus, Bill's stanine score is 2, and his test performance is somewhat below the norm.

Interpret Charlie's five stanine scores from Figure 8.4. According to the report, Charlie's performance is near the averages of the norm group on all five subtests.

The beauty of stanines is that they do not suggest that standardized test scores are precise (which, of course, they are not). Scores are located in gross intervals. Two scores should be at least two stanines apart before they may be considered significantly different. That is why Charlie's scores, from Figure 8.4, are considered near the norm for all subtests. Each of his stanines is no more than 1 from 5.

PERCENTILES

The percentile score associated with a particular raw score is the percentage of norm group scores that are less than the raw score. Interpret the five percentiles from Charlie's standardized test report in Figure 8.4. Charlie's raw score in reading is greater than 29 percent of the raw scores obtained by the norm group. Seventy-one percent of the norm group scores are higher than Charlie's. Charlie's test performance in math is greater than 62 percent and less than 38 percent of those from the norm group.

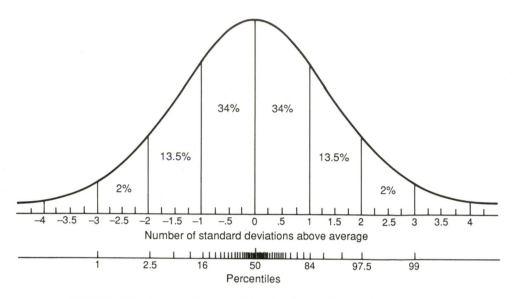

FIGURE 8.5   Percentiles in a Distribution of Norm-Group Scores

Percentiles are ranks and as such should not be added, subtracted, multiplied, or divided. Examine Figure 8.5. Note that the intervals for percentiles are more closely spaced near the average of the norm group than they are at either extreme. Consequently, a greater difference in test performance is reflected between percentiles of 80 and 85 than between 40 and 60. But in arithmetic, 60 − 40 > 85 − 80. *Arithmetic should not be used with percentiles.*

NCE SCORES

Percentiles are the most commonly reported type of standardized test score. But if *gains* or *differences* between scores are to be considered, the use of percentiles is inappropriate since percentiles shouldn't be subtracted. In response to this problem, *normal curve equivalent* (NCE) scores were invented.

NCE scores are numbers from 1 to 99 fabricated from percentiles. Unlike percentiles, NCEs are drawn from a scale of equally spaced intervals and, thus, can be added and subtracted. Conceptually, NCEs were created by taking a percentile scale (i.e., the top scale in Figure 8.6) and repositioning the benchmarks so that they are equidistant from one another (i.e., creating the bottom scale in Figure 8.6.

The only time you need bother with NCE scores is if, for some reason (e.g., computing gain scores or testing the difference between two averages), you need to use arithmetic with percentile scores. For such cases, if the NCE scores are not reported, convert the percentiles by using a conversion table from either a standardized test user's manual or a book of statistical tables. Do the arithmetic with the students' NCEs, not with their percentiles.

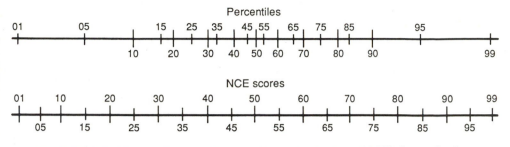

FIGURE 8.6   Percentile and Normal Curve Equivalent (NCE) Score Scales

GRADE EQUIVALENTS

One of the more misused derived scores is the *grade equivalent score*. Figure 8.4 shows a math grade equivalent of 6.3 for Charlie. Many persons mistakenly take this score to mean that Charlie's mathematics achievement is that of an average student who had just completed the third month of sixth grade. Such an interpretation is in error. Charlie's 6.3 grade equivalent score in math is properly interpreted as follows:

> Charlie's raw score on the math subtest of this *particular* standardized test is approximately equal to the average of the raw scores obtained by the norm group members who had just completed the third month of the sixth grade when they took the test.

That is a mouthful! It would be easier to say simply, "Charlie scored at the sixth year, third month grade," which, unfortunately, is what many teachers would be inclined to say. This interpretation is misleading. The score doesn't indicate that Charlie can do sixth-grade, third-month, math, nor does it indicate that he can't do ninth-grade math. At best, the 6.3 indicates that Charlie did about as well on the specific skills measured by this test as the average for norm group members who had just completed the third month of the sixth grade.

The grade equivalent associated with a raw score represents the grade level of norm group students with an average approximately equal to that raw score. Because standardized tests aren't field-tested at every month of every grade level, test publishers use mathematical interpolation and extrapolation to estimate average raw scores for each possible grade equivalent score (i.e., K.0 . . . , 2.1, 2.2, 2.3 . . . , 2.8, 3.0, 3.1 . . . , 12.8).

Like percentiles, grade equivalents are only ranks and, thus, cannot be added, subtracted, multiplied, or divided. Unfortunately, many people do not realize this and use grade equivalents to assess student gains. Reporting student gains in terms of "months" from differences in posttest and pretest grade equivalent scores seems to be a popular pastime of the naive.

SCALED SCORES

Scaled scores are fabricated from grade equivalents in a fashion similar to the way NCEs are fabricated from percentiles. The user's manuals for the more widely used standardized tests provide conversion tables for grade equivalent to scaled scores. Scaled scores are three-digit numbers derived by mathematical methods far more sophisticated than any of the other popular derived scores. Unlike other forms of standardized test scores, they may be used in conjunction with arithmetic operations to compare performances between different levels of the same test.

OTHER DERIVED STANDARDIZED TEST SCORES

Scores for standardized achievement tests that are used in schools typically report results as percentiles, grade equivalents, stanines, and raw scores. NCE and scaled score conversions are often provided in user's manuals. However, other types of derived scores, especially for aptitude tests, have also been invented. These include T-scores, z-scores, deviation IQ scores, mental ages, GRE scores, and CEEB scores, among many others. All these scores are simply different ways of indicating how raw scores compare to norm group averages. They should be defined in user's manuals.

SELF-ASSESSMENT OF YOUR ACHIEVEMENT OF CHAPTER 8'S OBJECTIVES

I. For each of the following multiple-choice items, select the one response that best answers the question or correctly completes the statement:
   A. If a test is standardized, then it _____ .
       1. has been field-tested
       2. is valid
       3. is expensive
       4. is an aptitude measure.
   B. By definition aptitude tests are _____ .
       1. standardized
       2. a type of IQ test
       3. designed for predicting
       4. not designed for adults
   C. Suppose a student takes two different levels of the same test on successive days. Which one of the following will the student most likely discover about the two levels of the test?
       1. They relate to different subject matters (e.g., one math, the other history).
       2. They measure exactly the same objectives but with different items.

    3. One is harder than the other.

    4. They do not differ.

D. Standardized achievement tests are best suited for providing data for_____ .

    1. evaluations of group learning

    2. determining which students have achieved and which have not

    3. diagnosing individual differences

    4. evaluating learning capabilities

E. Compared to a typical nonstandardized teacher-produced test, standardized achievement tests are usually_____ .

    1. less comprehensive

    2. more focused

    3. more relevant

    4. less focused

F. Sue's report from a standardized test battery included the following:

Subject	National percentile	Local percentile
Science	37	44

Which one of the following can be concluded from those data?

    1. The national level of the science test is harder.

    2. Sue performed better on the locally normed test than she did on the nationally normed one.

    3. Sue's "true score" lies between 37 and 44.

    4. The national norm group performed better on the test than the local norm group.

G. Peter and Roxanne obtain raw scores on a standardized test of 16 and 21, respectively. Which one of the following values for the norm group standard deviation will provide the best opportunity for Roxanne's score to be significantly greater than Peter's?

    1. 5.6   2. 9.3   3. 19.7   4. 23.3

H. Waylon's stanine score of 7 from a standardized achievement test was affected by his raw score as well as the_____ .

    1. average of the other raw scores in Waylon's class

    2. average of the norm group and the standard deviation of the scores from Waylon's class

    3. average of the norm group and the variability of the norm group's scores

    4. average and standard deviation of the scores obtained by Waylon's peers throughout the country

I. Freddy obtains a stanine score of 6 on a standardized achievement test. Which one of the following is an accurate conclusion?

    1. Freddy scored near the average of those in the norm group who were in the first month of the sixth grade when they took the test.

    2. Freddy's raw score is slightly above the nationwide average for the test.

    3. Freddy's raw score is slightly above the average of the scores from the norm group.

    4. Freddy's score indicates that he is achieving slightly better than others in his grade level.

J. Miriam's percentile score on a standardized test is 58. Which one of the following is an accurate conclusion?

    1. Miriam answered 58 percent of the items correctly.

    2. Fifty-eight percent of Miriam's classmates obtained a raw score less than hers.

    3. Miriam's raw score is 58 percent higher than the average norm group raw score.

    4. Miriam scored higher than 58 percent of those in the norm group.

K. Gloria's stanine score on a standardized test is 2. Which one of the following is an accurate conclusion about Gloria's raw score?

    1. It is two standard deviations above the mean of the norm group.

    2. It is significantly lower than the average score in the norm group.

    3. It is significantly lower than it should be.

    4. It is two standard deviations below the average of the norm group.

L. Which one of the following types of derived scores can be appropriately used for computing posttest-pretest gain scores?

    1. stanines

    2. scaled scores

    3. percentiles

    4. grade equivalents

Compare your choices to the following key: A–1, B–3, C–3, D–1, E–4, F–4, G–1, H–3, I–3, J–4, K–2, L–2.

II. Write a paragraph pointing out how Ms. Blanding misused standardized test results in the following example:

Mona took a standardized test battery at the end of the third, fourth, and fifth grades. Her language arts subtest grade equivalent scores are as follows:

Mona's Teacher	Mona's Grade Level	Mona's Grade Level Equivalent Score
Mr. Swink	3.8	2.4
Mr. Kitson	4.8	4.1
Ms. Ortego	5.8	4.6

Ms. Blanding, the school's principal, showed these scores to Ms. Ortego and said, "Mona was only able to make *five months' progress* in nine months of work in your class, whereas she had been able to *advance* one year and six months under Mr. Kitson's tutelage."

Exchange your work on this exercise with someone and critique one another's papers.

Grading and Reporting Student Achievement

GOAL OF CHAPTER 9

Chapter 9 focuses on the problems and methods of communicating evaluations of student achievements to students, their parents, and appropriate professionals. More specifically, Chapter 9 will help you to

1. Explain the position presented here regarding the communication of teachers' evaluations of student achievements (*Cognitive: comprehension of a communication*)
2. Describe at least two commonly used types of student achievement reports (*Cognitive: simple knowledge*)
3. Describe the following methods for converting test scores to grades and explain the relative advantages and disadvantages of each: traditional percentage, competency checks, classical curve grading, visual inspection, and compromise (*Cognitive: conceptualization*)
4. Select the most appropriate method for determining and reporting grades for your own teaching (*Cognitive: application*)

WHO SHOULD KNOW ABOUT A STUDENT'S ACHIEVEMENT

VIOLATIONS OF PROFESSIONAL TRUST

What, if anything, bothers you about the behaviors of the teachers in the following three episodes?

In a parent–teacher conference with Jan's father, Mr. Spivey says, "Jan is one of my very best fourth-graders. I only wish some of her friends, like Riley Dykes and Patricia Wotumso, could show me half of what Jan does on their tests!"

Walt Brousseaux, a high school science teacher, meets one of his friends, Clio Clark, in a grocery store.

MR. BROUSSEAUX: Well, hello, Clio! I haven't seen you in some time. What's going on?

MS. CLARK: Hello yourself, Walt. Good to see you! I'm gathering stuff for dinner tonight. My daughter, Lavina, is bringing her new boyfriend over.

MR. BROUSSEAUX: That's exciting!

MS. CLARK: She just broke up with Timmy Dantin and now she's got this new guy, Wellington something.

MR. BROUSSEAUX: I'll bet it's Wellington Staples! Super guy! He was in my chemistry class; made all A's. Lavina's making a good move. I also had that Dantin kid in my class; barely passed!

Ms. Smith, a high school mathematics teacher, receives a phone call from a local bank where one of her students has applied for a job. Although the student did not authorize her to provide a reference, she relates the student's math grades to the bank representative over the phone.

Trust between a teacher and student is an important ingredient for a classroom climate that is conducive to learning. Some teachers violate that trust by communicating their evaluations of student achievements to people who lack either the need or the authorization to be privileged to those evaluations.

PRIVILEGED INFORMATION

Obviously, there are times when you, as a teacher, should communicate evaluations of student achievement to others. For example, teachers are expected to provide grades on reports for parents and for school files. Who should be privileged to these evaluations? *Classroom Management Strategies: Gaining and Maintaining Students' Cooperation* (Cangelosi, 1988) suggests the following in response to that question:

1. In most cases, the *student* needs to know his or her own status regarding achievement of learning goals and evaluations of personal behaviors.

2. The student's *guardians* often need to be aware of their child's level of achievement and behaviors for two reasons:
   a. Guardians who understand just what their children are and are not accomplishing in school are able to serve as partners to teachers to help their children cooperate and achieve.
   b. Guardians are legally responsible for their children's welfare. They do, after all, delegate and entrust some of their responsibilities to teachers. They should know how the school is affecting their children.
3. *Professional personnel* (e.g., a guidance counselor or another of the student's teachers) who have instructional responsibilities for that student sometimes need to know about the student's achievement and behaviors so that they are in a better position to help that student.
4. *Professional personnel* (e.g., the principal, subject area supervisor, or curriculum director) whose judgments affect the curricula and conduct of the school sometimes need to be aware of an individual student's achievements or behaviors so that they will be in an advantageous position to make school-level decisions.
5. Because a school often acts as an agency that qualifies students for occupations, as students at other institutions, or for other privileges (e.g., scholarships), it may sometimes be necessary for a *representative of an institution* to which a student has applied to have knowledge of that student's achievements and behaviors. However, school personnel should seriously consider following a policy in which they release information on an individual student's achievements or behaviors to such representatives only with that student's and guardians' authorization.

COMMUNICATING EVALUATIONS

FORMATIVE

Traditionally, students and their parents or guardians expect to be informed about teachers' summative evaluations. "How well did I do?" "Did Preston fail?" "What grade did I make?" "Did Shirley learn what she was supposed to?" These are the types of questions teachers are used to hearing from students and parents, more often than "When will Jimmy begin using regrouping in subtraction?" "How much more time do you think we need before we can understand enough about cell division?" "When do you think Fran will be ready to read this book?"

You are advised to break from this tradition and begin conditioning students, parents, and others to whom you communicate evaluations to realize that

1. Your evaluations are not concerned only with successes and failures.
2. Formative evaluations help you plan and institute lessons that help students achieve appropriate objectives.

Besides the informal means (e.g., chance meetings with parents) that are commonly used to communicate formative evaluations, planned formal procedures for keeping students and parents informed on *what* students are achieving should be instituted. Here are two examples:

Mr. Delaney teaches 32 fourth-graders and has little time to confer with each student's parents on a frequent basis. But by routinely phoning parents with whom he does not ordinarily meet at school (e.g., at P.T.A. meetings), at the rate of six per week, he speaks with a parent of each student once every three weeks. It usually takes two conversations before a parent realizes that Mr. Delaney's intentions are to keep the parent informed about *what* the child is doing in school and not to report that the child is in trouble.

Ms. Durant teaches five sections of ninth-grade general science. Periodically, she writes a form letter for her students' parents about the goals and activities of the classes. At the bottom of each letter, she writes a note about the individual student's work. The following is an example:

Mrs. & Mr. Belinski:
Tess really seems interested in the experiment with rotting logs mentioned in the letter above. Her display of interest convinced me that I should assign more tasks where she must collect data from natural, outdoor settings. I believe Tess understands how different organisms depend on each other in an ecological system. But I don't think she understands some of the chemical interactions that take place within organisms as well as she needs to. Possibly, she has yet to complete all the readings that were assigned from pages 137–192 in her general science text. I would like to use her interest in the out-of-doors to motivate her study of science.

SUMMATIVE

Schools provide a formal structure for communicating teachers' summative evaluations of student achievements with periodic reports (usually containing grades) for students, their parents, and permanent records.

PERIODIC REPORTS

CLEARLY DEFINED PURPOSE

What is the purpose of the periodic reports, commonly known as "report cards," that are recorded and given to students and parents in virtually every type of school? Here is a sampling of answers given by teachers, students, parents, and school administrators.

TEACHERS

"To let students and their parents know how well they've learned what they were supposed to learn."
"Grades should motivate students to learn and reward those that try."

STUDENTS

"Tell parents how their kids are doing."
"To show who's smart and who's dumb."

PARENTS

"For the records, to show who should strive for the more ambitious goals, like college."
"Let us know how our kids are doing."

SCHOOL ADMINISTRATORS

"You have to have grades and reports; it's part of the accountability system."
"To provide a means for students, parents, teachers, and administrators to gauge progress."

Those comments suggest rather varied agendas for one simple grade report. The purposes—to communicate evaluations of achievement level, motivate learning, reflect progress, and "weed out" according to potential—are more than grade reports are capable of accomplishing.

If the purpose involves either *motivation* or *progress*, then grading would have to be individualized. Mindy, for example, would have to be given a higher grade than Allison if Figure 9.1 accurately reflects their entry and exit achievement levels. Otherwise, Mindy would not be motivated, realizing that she's unlikely to "catch" Allison. If progress is to be communicated, the posttest-pretest gain is more relevant than the posttest score.

In any case, grades and reports cannot be meaningful unless their purpose is clear. Clearly, they cannot serve multiple purposes unless either (1) multiple grades (e.g., for progress, achievement level, potential, and effort) per subject replace the traditional one grade per subject or (2) written narratives replace traditional letter grades.

Even if multiple grades per subject (e.g., see Figure 9.2) or narratives are used, people will still ask one basic question: What is the student's achievement level? With this in mind, the remainder of this chapter is presented under the

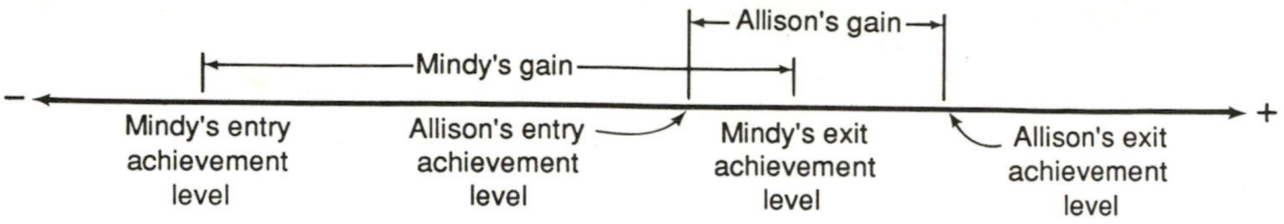

FIGURE 9.1 Which Student Displays Greater Achievement?

Grade Level Five's Six-Week Report

Student's Name Amanda Ricelosi   Report No. 4

Teacher Completing Report Mr. Christopher James

Reporting Period for 1/24 to 3/6

Key to Symbols:

A—Far Better than Adequate.   D—Nearly Adequate.
B—Better than Adequate.   F—Not Nearly Adequate.
C—Adequate.   NG—No Grade Given.

Reading Vocabulary: Rating

Level of Achievement	D
Rate of Progress	C

Speaking Vocabulary:

Level of Achievement	B
Rate of Progress	A

Spelling:

Level of Achievement	D
Rate of Progress	D

Reading Comprehension:

Level of Achievement	B
Rate of Progress	D

Listening Comprehension:

Level of Achievement	C
Rate of Progress	D

Ability to Communicate in Writing:

Level of Achievement	C
Rate of Progress	C

FIGURE 9.2 Report Form with Multiple Grades per Subject

assumption that the sole purpose of grades and reports is to communicate teachers' summative evaluations of student achievement levels.

REPORT FORMATS

Hundreds of different report formats are used in schools. Figure 9.3 reflects one of the more common types used in elementary schools. Figure 9.4 shows a typical one for middle, junior, and high schools.

COMPLEMENTING REPORTS WITH
PARENT-TEACHER CONFERENCES

Parents and students alike are more likely to understand your evaluations if grade reports are clarified and explained in well-planned face-to-face conferences. However, if conferences, now commonplace even in high schools, are not well organized and if all parties do not understand their purpose, the meetings can degenerate into exhausting, time-consuming social encounters. Consider the following suggestions before embarking on your next grade report conference:

1. Prepare in advance by writing out a meeting agenda that specifies
   a. The purpose of the meeting (e.g., to communicate what the student has achieved regarding certain learning goals during the previous nine-week period)
   b. A sequence of topics to be discussed (e.g., specifics from a report card and plans for the next nine weeks)
   c. A beginning and ending time for the conference
2. Except for special situations, plan for the student to attend and participate in the conference. Healthy open attitudes are more likely to emerge when every involved party participates.
3. Hold the conference where distractions are minimal and there is little chance that outsiders (e.g., other parents, students, and teachers) will overhear the conversation. Make arrangements to use a private office or small conference room where neither a phone nor a public address system will be a disturbance.
4. Provide the parent(s) and student with a written agenda. Focus on the planned topics by directing their attention to items on the report or the agenda.
5. Concentrate your remarks on evaluations of the student's achievement of specific goals. Avoid character or personality judgments, for example, "Willie is a well-behaved child" or "Tommy is lazy." Instead say things such as "Willie begins his work promptly" or "Tommy often seems unwilling to work on school tasks for more than five minutes at a time." Similarly, avoid making gross judgments such as "Craig is very smart" or "Viola is a slow learner." Express, instead, your judgments about specific goal achievements,

Edith Bowen Laboratory School
College of Education
Utah State University
Student Education Program
1985–1986

Name _Allison Cangelosi_
Teacher _Ilone Long_
Grade 1 (2) 3 4 5
Reporting Period 1 (2) Final
Date of Reporting Period _1/31/86_
Promoted to Grade

A check shows that school work is adversely affected by frequent absences and tardiness.
Attendance [ ] Punctuality [ ]

Action to be taken by: (signatures)
Student _Allison_
Educator _Ilone D. Long_
Parent _Jim Cangelosi_
Dr. Ted R. Williams, Director

Achievement Level: Excellent | Satisfactory | Effort needed

READING (Grades 1,2,3 / Grades 4&5)
- Recognizes differences in sounds
- Word attack skills
- Vocabulary development
- Reads with understanding
- Enjoys reading
- Vocabulary
- Comprehension
- Independent reading

LANGUAGE
- Expresses ideas orally
- Expresses ideas in written work
- Understands language concepts

SPELLING
- Applies spelling skills
- Spells assigned words correctly

HANDWRITING
- Style (form)
- Spacing
- Size (uniformity)
- Slant
- Applies handwriting skills

ART
- Participation

MUSIC
- Participation

PHYSICAL EDUCATION
- Participation
- Sportsmanship

MATHEMATICS
- Understands concepts
- Computational skills
- Problem solving

SCIENCE AND HEALTH
- Understands concepts
- Has scientific inquisitiveness

SOCIAL STUDIES
- Participates in class
- Knowledge of subject matter

WORK STUDY SKILLS
- Follows directions
- Works independently
- Works well in a group
- Listens attentively
- Uses time effectively
- Takes care of materials

SOCIAL GROWTH
- Observes school rules
- Respects authority
- Respects rights of others
- Developing self control
- Accepts responsibility
- Has positive attitude toward work

FIGURE 9.3 Example of a Report Card from an Elementary School

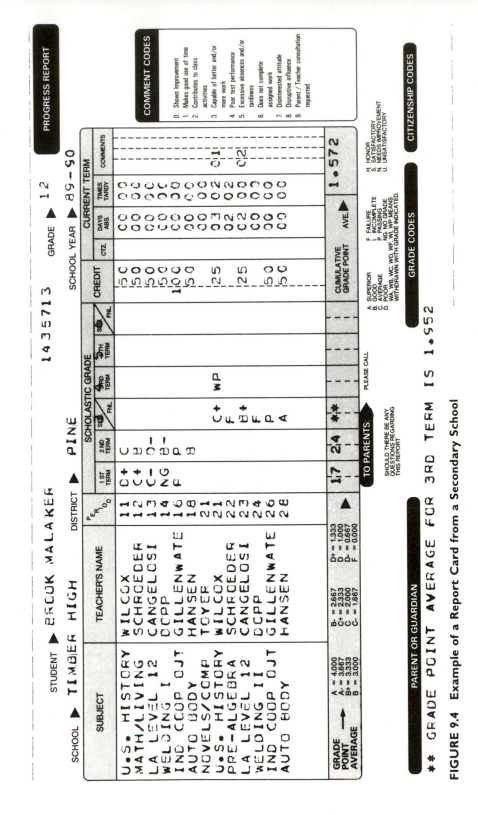

FIGURE 9.4 Example of a Report Card from a Secondary School

such as "Craig understands the basics of cell division" or "When Viola is reading, she has difficulty distinguishing opinions from facts."

6. Although the main purpose of the conference is for you to explain and clarify information that is supposed to be communicated through the report card, plan to utilize some portion of the allotted time for you to learn from the parents things that will help you to work more effectively with their child.

DETERMINING TEST GRADES

SCORING AND GRADING

Scoring a student's test is a step in a measurement process by which the rules of the items' *scoring keys* are followed and the items' points are totaled, yielding a test score. The test is *graded* by assigning a *qualitative value* to the test score. Grades (e.g., A, B, C, D, or F; satisfactory or unsatisfactory; and excellent, good, fair, or unacceptable) on reports are typically based on test grades.

There are many methods for converting test scores to grades. Two norm-referenced methods, two criterion-referenced methods, and a method that combines features from both are described in the remainder of this section.

CRITERION-REFERENCED GRADING

The Traditional Percentage Method Reread the section on Criterion-referenced Methods on pages 72–73.

For laypersons and teachers who are uninitiated in measurement and evaluation principles, the most familiar method for converting test scores to grades is the traditional percentage method. The "percentage," of course, refers to the percentage of correct responses on tests. However, who displays greater achievement, a student who scores 95 percent on an easy test or one who scores 40 percent on a hard test? Consider the following example.

Mr. Nelson, a high school history teacher, uses the following criteria for percentage grading:

94%–100% for an A
86%– 93% for a B
78%– 85% for a C
70%– 77% for a D
 0%– 69% for an F

The students and their parents are pleased with such a seemingly "objective" scheme. They think they understand exactly what it takes to make a certain grade in Mr. Nelson's class.

On his first test of the semester, over half the students correctly responded to no more than 77 percent of the items. Mr. Nelson holds fast to his "standards" and gives the majority of the students D's and F's. However, either consciously or not, he constructs the next test so that it is much easier than the first. The grade distribution for the second test is more in line with what he had anticipated for the first test. Mr. Nelson commends the class for their efforts, commenting that they must have studied harder for the second test.

Because of Mr. Nelson's so-called "standards," his tests must generally be constructed so that the average percentage score is in the 78 percent to 85 percent range because he thinks of C as being the average. This requirement leads him to make tests so easy that he never tests the higher-achieving students at their levels. If he includes enough hard items to measure high-achievement levels, too many students would "fail." Since the more capable students don't find his tests challenging, they don't bother even to approach the level they are capable of achieving.

To illustrate the second major weakness of traditional percentage grading, here is another entry in Mr. Nelson's grading story.

Mr. Nelson administers a test consisting of 25 four-point items. Joyce, Albin, and Winthrop score 93, 86, and 84, respectively. Thus,

Joyce receives a B by answering 23.25 items correctly (since 93/4 = 23.25). Albin also receives a B for being correct on 21.5 items (86/4 = 21.5). But Winthrop receives a C for correctly answering only one-half item less than Albin (84/4 = 21). (See Figure 9.5.)

Competency Checks   Tests used for criterion-referenced evaluations are sometimes designed to produce a score per student for each objective rather than only one score for goal attainment. Such a test, for example, might have four clusters of five items each, each cluster relevant to a particular objective. A criterion, such as "four out of five," is set to define "achievement" of each objective. The test's scores for each student indicate which objectives were "passed."

The criteria (e.g., four out of five or two out of three items correct in a cluster), the number of objectives measured, and the number of items per objective vary. The idea is to identify which objectives were met according

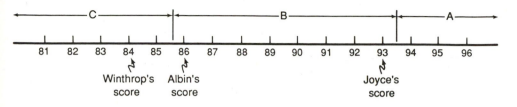

FIGURE 9.5 Comparison of Three Grades Determined by the Traditional Percentage Method

to the criterion for each. Scores from this type of test are usually converted to grades by one of two methods:

1. A checklist indicates which objectives, skills, or competencies the student "passed."
2. Grades are defined as the percentage of objectives the student "passed." For example, the achievement of a student passing between 80 percent to 100 percent of the objectives is graded "competent," 60 percent to 80 percent merits "marginally competent," and 0 percent to 60 percent is labeled "incompetent."

NORM-REFERENCED GRADING

Classical Curve Grading   Classical curve grading has been somewhat popular in postsecondary schools since the 1930s. This method, which assumes that grades should reflect how the scores compare to the average of all scores from the test, is tenable only for extremely large test groups (e.g., 500 or more). If the distribution of scores follows a bell-shaped, normal curve, the following criteria are used with this method:

> The highest 7 percent of the scores are given A's.
> B's are assigned to 24 percent of the scores.
> The middle 38 percent receive C's.
> D's are assigned to 24 percent of the scores.
> The lowest 7 percent of the scores are given F's.

The Visual Inspection Method   One of the more commonly suggested methods for assigning letter grades to test scores is the *visual inspection* method (Smith & Adams, 1972). The method includes the following steps:

1. Draw a number line that encompasses the range of the test scores. For example, if the lowest test score is 5 and the highest is 44, the number line given in Figure 9.6 would suffice.
2. Graph the frequency distribution of the test scores onto the line. Figure 9.7 is an example of such a graph.
3. Identify gaps or significant breaks in the distribution.

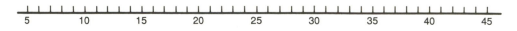

FIGURE 9.6   Number Line for Use with Visual Inspection Grading

4. Assign a letter grade to each cluster of scores appearing between gaps. If, for example, C is defined as average, the cluster containing the middle score might be given the grade C. Or you may choose to sample some of the test papers from a particular cluster and decide the grade for that cluster based on the quality of the sample. In this method, every score within the same cluster is given the same grade. Figure 9.8 depicts one possible assignment of grades to scores from Figure 9.7.

THE COMPROMISE METHOD

A Conflict between Theory and Practice   Teachers who are introduced to the visual inspection method readily recognize the following advantages it has over the traditional percentage method:

1. Tests can include appropriate proportions of easy, moderate, and hard items without fear that too many students will receive low grades. The difficulty of the test can be factored into the grading scheme.
2. Scores that are not markedly different from one another are not given different grades; the error of the measurement is recognized.

However, teachers tend to reject the visual inspection method because

1. Establishing criteria for A, B, C, D, and F *after* a test has been administered does not seem to be as objective as having predetermined cutoff scores (e.g., 70% for passing), which students can be aware of before taking the test.
2. Norm-referenced methods encourage an unhealthy competition among students for grades more than do criterion-referenced methods.

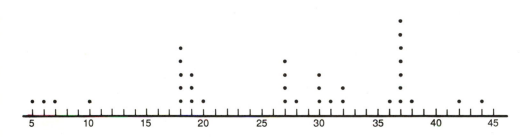

FIGURE 9.7   Sample Score Distribution

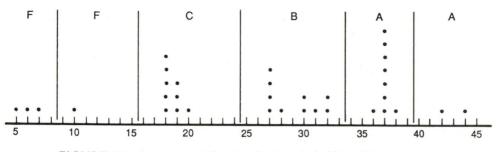

FIGURE 9.8   Example of Grades Assigned via Visual Inspection

3. Test scores don't always fall into convenient clusters with significantly large enough gaps to distinguish between different grades according to the visual inspection method. The distribution of Figure 9.9 is possible.

A Resolution   The method suggested here realizes the principal advantages of the visual inspection method while obviating the three weaknesses mentioned above. This method is a *compromise* between the traditional percentage and the visual inspection methods and is implemented as follows:

1. As with traditional percentage grading, establish cutoff scores for each letter grade before the administration of the test. However, there are two differences:

   a. To allow for the use of a test that includes hard and moderate, as well as easy, items, the percentage of points that a student must score to obtain a certain grade is set unconventionally low. Figure 9.10, for example, presents possible criteria for a test designed to produce an average score of 40 out of a possible 80.

   b. The cutoff score for each letter grade is established with the understanding that there be a buffer or "grey" zone between each letter grade category. In Figure 9.11, for example, to be assigned a *definite* B, a score would have to be at least three points above a possible B cutoff score of 50 and no greater than three points below an A cutoff score of 70. For those familiar with the *standard error of measurement* (SEM), a SEM would be an ideal way to determine the length of this buffer zone (Cangelosi, 1982, pp. 292–300).

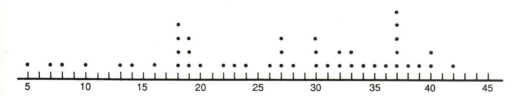

FIGURE 9.9   Inconvenient Sample Score Distribution for Use with Visual Inspection Grading

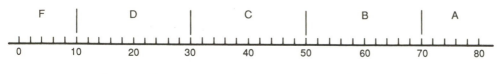

FIGURE 9.10   Sample Letter Grade Cutoff Scores

However, simply "backing off" several points in both directions around each cutoff point is sufficient.

2. Assign in-between grades to scores that fall within cutoff score intervals. For example, a score of 51 might convert to a grade of B or C. Final determination of whether the higher or lower grade prevails in any of these in-between cases depends on data collected from other sources (e.g., an abbreviated retest or an interview that requires the student to elaborate on her or his responses). You also have the option of simply letting the grade for that test remain in limbo between two letter grades and then factoring the in-between grade into your final determination of the specific report card grade.

Point and Counterpoint   The compromise method is likely to be criticized for two reasons:

1. Some teachers are uncomfortable with scores falling within the buffer zones. There *should* be clear lines of demarcation between grades.
2. Unconventionally difficult tests, replete with moderate and hard items, may lead to greater frustration since the students will miss more items than on more commonly used, easier tests.

There *should* be clear lines of demarcation between letter grades, and it isn't always convenient for a score to fall within a buffer zone. However, the state of the art of measuring student achievement is not advanced to the point that definite lines of demarcation, discriminating between levels of achievement, are tenable. The educational community needs to recognize this fact.

Regarding the second criticism, there are some distinct pedagogical disadvantages to using unconventionally difficult tests. However, once students become accustomed to struggling with challenging test items, a teacher can utilize such tests as tools to help students achieve higher-level cognitive (e.g., application level) learning objectives (Bloom, Madaus, & Hastings, 1981).

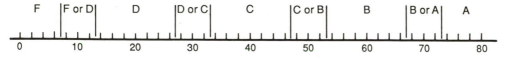

FIGURE 9.11   Sample Letter Grade Cutoff Scores with Grey In-between Scores

DETERMINING TERM GRADES

The Averaging Method

Ultimately, test grades from a grading period need to be compiled into a single report grade. Teachers who grade tests by the traditional percentage method often determine term grades for reports by simply averaging the percentages for each student's tests and then using the same grade scale (e.g., as the one from the Mr. Nelson example) to convert the average percentage to a letter grade. For example,

Mr. Nelson records a C in history for Rembert's term grade because on the four summative tests she took during the term, she scored 100 percent, 81 percent, 87 percent, and 53 percent. Mr. Nelson figures, "100 + 81 + 87 + 53 = 321; 321/4 = 80.25, which converts to a C since C's fall between 78 percent and 85 percent."

The Weighting Method

The teacher in the following example uses the *weighting* method because she (1) thinks of test scores as only gross indicators of achievement and believes that minor differences (e.g., between 80 percent and 83 percent) in scores shouldn't affect grades and (2) wants grades on more important tests to have greater weight than grades from less important tests.

Ms. Goldberg administered four summative tests during a school term to her science class. She designed the tests so that some of the objectives that were covered on a test were covered again (in addition to new objectives) on subsequent tests. She did this to (1) maintain some continuity between units, (2) encourage students to review past content, and (3) provide students with opportunities to be retested over previous content.

Because she wants the subsequent tests to retest some of the previous objectives and because she wants the term grade to be a greater reflection of student achievements near the end of the term rather than the beginning, she figures term grades with the following rules:

1. An A counts 4 points, B's 3, C's 2, D's 1, and F's 0. In-between grades (e.g., C or D from the *compromise method*) count as an average (e.g., 1.5 for C or D).
2. Grades from the first test count their face values (i.e., 4 for A, 3 for B, etc.). But the value for grades on the second test is multiplied by 2 (8 for A, 6 for B, etc.), grade values for the third test are multiplied by 3 (12 for A, 9 for B, etc.), and grades for the fourth test are multiplied by 4 (16 for A, 12 for B, etc.).

3. An average for the four *weighted* values is figured for each student by dividing the sum of the weighted values by 10. The number 10 is used because the first test counted once, the second twice, the third three times, and the fourth four times $(1 + 2 + 3 + 4 = 10)$.

4. If the weighted average is 3.5 or greater the term grade is A; between 2.5 and 3.5, B; 1.5 to 2.5, C; 0.5 to 1.5, D; and less than 0.5, F.

Ellie's test grades on the four tests were D, B, C, and C, respectively. Ms. Goldberg gave Ellie a C for her science term grade because $1 + (3 \times 2) + (2 \times 3) + (2 \times 4) = 21$, and $21/10 = 2.1$.

SELF-ASSESSMENT OF YOUR ACHIEVEMENT OF CHAPTER 9'S OBJECTIVES

I. For each of the following situations, write one or two sentences describing how you would respond, assuming that you act in accordance with the position stated in the section Who Should Know About a Student's Achievement in this chapter:

A. You are a high school math teacher. A parent of a middle school student asks you to provide the names of your "best math students" so he can find one to tutor his child.

B. The student president of one of your school's service clubs asks you to nominate your ten best students for membership.

C. One of your good friends asks you about Herman, a student in your class: "I heard he's not very bright; is that true?"

D. Lisa and Laurie are two of your students. Lisa's mother asks you, "How's Lisa doing in comparison to Laurie?"

E. Donald and Ronald are two twins in your class. Their father asks you, "Which one is doing better?"

F. Ms. Joost, a history teacher, is sitting in the cafeteria with some students when Mr. Honneycut, a physical education teacher, loudly asks her, "Mavis is having trouble remembering soccer rules; does she have trouble remembering facts in your class?"

G. A college asks you to send a letter of recommendation for one of your former students who has applied for admission.

Exchange your work on this exercise with someone and discuss the responses.

II. Write two or three paragraphs comparing the traditional percentage method for converting grades to scores to the visual inspection method. Point out the relative advantages and disadvantages of each. Exchange your work on this exercise with someone and discuss differences in your two essays.

III. Retrieve the test blueprint you developed in response to Exercise II for Chapter 3's self-assessment. Rethink your method for determining cutoff scores for that test and decide how you would convert scores from that test to grades. Write a paragraph explaining your rationale. Ask someone to critique your work on this exercise and offer to critique that person's work.

EPILOGUE

Teaching: A Complex Art

To be a truly effective teacher who helps students achieve worthwhile goals, you must solve problems and make decisions far more complex than those faced in other professions. As a teacher, you are expected to do the following for a *group* of students who vary considerably in personality, aptitude, attitude, background, preparation, and interests.

1. Develop curricula that are relevant to students' needs by (a) establishing and sequencing learning goals, (b) defining each goal by a set of learning objectives, and (c) designing learning activities or lessons for each of those objectives.
2. Organize a learning environment or classroom that enhances the efficiency of lessons and the management of students.
3. Prepare for each lesson (e.g., acquiring learning materials).
4. Conduct each lesson, keeping students engaged in the learning activities.
5. Supervise students between, as well as during, lessons.
6. Make and report summative evaluations of student achievement.

Inextricably involved with all these teaching responsibilities are the *formative evaluations* you are making almost continuously. For such a complex art with so many professional practitioners (nearly 2,300,000 full-time teachers of grade K–12 students in the United States alone (Lanier & Little, 1986)), it is not surprising that some aspects of teaching are not universally practiced in expert fashion. Evaluating student achievement appears to be an area that needs attention (Stiggins, 1988).

ALL TEACHERS EVALUATE STUDENT ACHIEVEMENT ONE WAY OR ANOTHER

Whether or not they follow the principles suggested by this or any other text on evaluating student achievement, teachers simply cannot avoid making both formative and summative evaluations. As reported by Stiggins, Conklin, and Bridgeford (1986, pp 10–11), numerous research reports (e.g., Clark and Peterson, 1986; Shalveson & Stern, 1981; Yinger, 1977) suggest that

. . . teachers make an interactive decision on average every two minutes. To understand the measurement implications of this pace and its importance for learners, consider that in half of these decisions teachers have antecedent thoughts based on concerns about the learner, including comparisons of behavior, knowledge, and so forth, with expectations or standards. . . . In this context, the teacher must either assess very rapidly with validity and reliability, or rely on an existing reservoir of valid, reliable information. Surely, this is an assessment and information-processing task unparalleled in other professions.

AN EVALUATION PLAN THAT WORKS FOR YOU

Since evaluating student achievement plays an unavoidable major role in teaching, you are faced with the following critical question: How do you manage to incorporate sound measurement and evaluation practices into an already overloaded schedule of complex teaching responsibilities?

Is it really practical for you to

1. Clarify each learning goal with a set of objectives that specify content and behavioral constructs (as explained in Chapter 1)
2. Be concerned with the measurement relevance, reliability, and usability (i.e., cost-effectiveness) of each test you use in evaluating student achievement (as explained in Chapter 2)
3. Follow the seven-step systematic approach to designing and selecting achievement tests (as explained in Chapter 3)
4. For each learning objective, design test items that are relevant to the specified content and behavioral construct and are free from some of the common contaminates, for example measuring test-taking skills (as explained in Chapters 4 through 7)
5. Accurately interpret the results of standardized achievement tests, avoiding pressures to overuse them (as explained in Chapter 8)
6. Use grades and reports only to apprise authorized persons (e.g., students and their parents) of your evaluations of students' achievements (as explained in Chapter 9)

By engaging in these six practices, you will actually streamline the manner in which you meet your teaching responsibilities (e.g., developing curricula, planning lessons, managing behavior, organizing the classroom, and conducting learning activities) for two reasons:

1. Your decisions (e.g., those regarding students' needs and lesson plans) will be based on more accurate information.
2. You will have set into motion a system for evaluating student achievement that will increase in efficiency with use (e.g., expanding item pools).

You will need to work out a system for practicing sound evaluation principles that fits your particular personality, teaching situation, and resources. I hope that the work you have done in conjunction with this textbook has helped you to organize your thinking about how to evaluate student achievement. However, the quality of the measurements you design and select depends on your creative and critical thinking abilities. By following the principles presented here, you enable your creative mind to answer puzzling questions about what your students have learned and are learning.

Glossary

ABILITY-TO-PERFORM-A-SPECIFIC-SKILL-LEVEL OBJECTIVE A psychomotor objective requiring students to utilize voluntary muscle capabilities in executing a specified physical process.

ACHIEVEMENT TEST A measurement designed to be an indicator of student progress relative to a specified learning goal.

AFFECTIVE OBJECTIVE A learning objective specifying that students are to develop a particular attitude or feeling toward the objective's content (e.g., a belief in something or a willingness to work on something).

ANALYTICALLY SCORED ITEM A weighted item with a scoring key associating each point of the maximum possible score with a particular feature of students' responses.

APPLICATION OBJECTIVE An intellectual-level cognitive objective requiring students to use deductive reasoning to decide how to solve a specified type of problem.

APPRECIATION-LEVEL OBJECTIVE An affective objective requiring students to believe that a content specified in the objective has value.

APTITUDE TEST A measurement designed to predict how well students will achieve learning goals if they are given appropriate learning opportunities.

BEHAVIORAL CONSTRUCT OF A LEARNING OBJECTIVE The cognitive, affective, or psychomotor level of learning that students display by achieving the objective.

BRANCHING INTERVIEW SEQUENCE Plan for presenting tasks in an interview item so that predetermined optional lines of questions or directives are based on the student's performance in prior stages of the interview.

COGNITION-BEYOND-APPLICATION OBJECTIVE An intellectual-level cognitive objective requiring students to display cognitive behaviors that are more advanced than the application level (e.g., analysis, synthesis, or evaluation) (Bloom, 1984).

COGNITIVE OBJECTIVE A learning objective specifying that students are to develop the ability to perform some particular mental task with the objective's content (e.g., remember a fact or deduce a method for solving a problem).

COMPLETION ITEM A short-answer item that requires students to fill in the missing parts of an incomplete statement.

COMPREHENSION-OF-A-COMMUNICATION OBJECTIVE An intellectual-level cognitive objective requiring students to determine the explicit or implicit meaning of a message.

CONCEPT   An abstraction or category of specifics that share certain common attributes. For example, each of the following is a concept: (1) furniture, (2) reptile, and (3) whole number.

CONCEPTUALIZATION OBJECTIVE   An intellectual-level cognitive objective requiring students to use inductive reasoning either to: (1) distinguish examples of a particular concept from nonexamples of that concept or (2) discover why a particular relationship exists.

CONSTRUCT VALIDITY OF A MEASUREMENT   How well the behavioral constructs covered by a measurement match those specified in the stated objectives.

CONTENT OF A LEARNING OBJECTIVE   The specific subject matter with which students deal when achieving the learning objective.

CONTENT RELEVANCE OF A MEASUREMENT   How well the content covered by the measurement matches the content of the stated objectives.

CORRECTION FOR GUESSING   Any one of several methods for scoring a multiple-choice test that is designed to discourage students from selecting responses by random guessing.

COST-EFFECTIVENESS OF A MEASUREMENT   The degree to which the measurement is both satisfactorily valid and usable.

CRITERION-REFERENCED METHOD FOR SETTING CUTOFF SCORES   Any one of a number of processes by which standards for cutoff scores (1) are set before the administration of a test and (2) involve *no* comparisons between the scores of different test-takers.

CUTOFF SCORE FOR A MEASUREMENT   A number within the range of all the measurement's possible scores that is used as a standard for interpreting students' scores. (E.g., the standard for "goal achievement" on a 35-point test is set at 25. Thus, students scoring significantly above the cutoff score of 25 are judged to have achieved the goal, whereas scores significantly below 25 indicate failure to achieve the goal.).

DERIVED SCORE   A test score resulting from an arithmetic manipulation of a raw score and other data (e.g., the test average or the maximum number of points on the test).

DICHOTOMOUSLY SCORED ITEM   A test item to which responses are scored either right or wrong (i.e., +1 or 0 with no partial credit possible).

EASY ITEM   A test item to which more than 75 percent of the students taking the test respond correctly.

ESSAY ITEM   A test item that requires the student to write a literary composition of at least one paragraph but normally not more than several pages.

EVALUATION   A value judgment.

FORMATIVE EVALUATION   A judgment about student achievement that influences a teacher's lesson plans but does *not* influence reports of student success.

GLOBALLY SCORED ITEM   A weighted test item with a scoring key requiring the scorer (e.g., a teacher) to *rate* features of students' responses on a scale.

GRADE EQUIVALENT SCORE   A derived score associated with a given raw score that equals the estimated grade level of students in the norm group who averaged the given raw score.

GRADING A TEST   A summative evaluation process in which a teacher converts test scores to indicators (e.g., A, B, C, D, or F) of students' levels of achievement.

HARD ITEM   A test item to which fewer than 25 percent of the students taking the test respond correctly.

INTELLECTUAL-LEVEL OBJECTIVE   A cognitive objective requiring students to use *reasoning* to make judgments relative to its content.

INTERNAL CONSISTENCY OF A MEASUREMENT   The degree to which the different items of the measurement yield similar, noncontradicting results.

INTERSCORER RELIABILITY OF A MEASUREMENT The degree to which the measurement scores are not influenced by who scores the items.

INTERVIEW ITEM A test item that is administered to one student at a time so that: (1) a sequence of questions or directives is orally (sometimes complemented by visual aids) presented to the student; (2) the student orally responds to each question or directive as it is presented, usually with the opportunity to elaborate; (3) subsequent questions or directives may be influenced by responses the student makes to prior questions or directives; and (4) the scoring key is such that the interviewer (a) takes notes or marks a scorer's form as the student completes each response (either during the interview or from listening to a recording) and (b) compiles the scores or results from the item after the interview.

INTRASCORER RELIABILITY OF A MEASUREMENT The degree to which the teacher (or whoever is scoring the measurement) consistently follows the item scoring keys so that the measurement results are not influenced by when the measurement is scored.

ITEM ANALYSIS Any one of a number of methods for obtaining data used to evaluate the quality of individual items of a measurement.

ITEM FORMAT The way a test item is categorized (e.g., essay, multiple choice, or performance observation) according to the mode in which it presents a task and gives students a means for responding.

ITEM POOL A collection of test items, all designed to be relevant to the same learning objective.

KNOWLEDGE-LEVEL OBJECTIVE An objective requiring students to *remember* some specified content (e.g., a fact or process).

KNOWLEDGE-OF-A-PROCESS OBJECTIVE A knowledge-level cognitive objective requiring students to remember a sequence of steps in a procedure.

LEARNING GOAL A broad statement of what a teacher intends for students to gain from a particular learning unit.

LEARNING OBJECTIVE One of a group of statements specifying the contents and behavioral constructs that comprise a learning goal.

LIKERT SCALE A type of multiple-choice format in which the item's stem is a statement and the alternatives are choices (e.g., "strongly agree," "mildly agree," "mildly disagree," and "strongly disagree") designed to reflect the students' degree of agreement with the statement.

LINEAR INTERVIEW SEQUENCE Plan for presenting tasks in an interview item so that the student's responses to one question or directive do not influence subsequent questions or directives.

MATCHING ITEM A multiple-choice item that presents students with two lists and the task of associating each entry of one list with an entry from the second list.

MEASUREMENT The process by which facts or data are gathered through empirical observations.

MODERATE ITEM A test item to which between 25 percent and 75 percent of the students taking the test respond correctly.

MULTIPLE-ANSWER MULTIPLE-CHOICE ITEM A multiple-choice item that requires students to determine whether or not *each* of its alternatives is true or false.

MULTIPLE-CHOICE ITEM A test item that requires students to select a response from a given list of alternatives.

NCE (NORMAL CURVE EQUIVALENT) SCORES Derived scores on a scale of equally occurring intervals that are fabricated from percentiles and range from 1 through 99 with an average of 50 and a standard deviation of 21.06.

NORM GROUP FOR A STANDARDIZED TEST   The sample of students whose scores are used to assess the reliability of the standardized test and establish the test's norms, to which the scores of subsequent test-takers are compared.

NORM-REFERENCED METHOD FOR SETTING CUTOFF SCORES   Any one of a number of processes by which standards for cutoff scores are based on the test performance of a group of students.

ORAL DISCOURSE ITEM   A test item that requires the student to give a talk or speech that is more complex than a simple recitation.

PERCENTILE   A derived score indicating the percentage of norm group scores that are lower than the raw score.

PERFORMANCE-OBSERVATION ITEM   A test item in which the scorer (e.g., a teacher), observing students as they respond to the task, scores the students' methods rather than the end results or products.

POWER TEST   A test that all test-takers have ample time to complete so that the speed at which students respond to items does not affect the results.

PRODUCT-RATING ITEM   A test item that directs students to complete a production task and provides a scheme for judging the quality of the results.

PSYCHOLOGICAL NOISE   A characteristic of an example of a concept that is not an attribute of the concept. For example, regarding the concept reptile, the color brown is psychological noise for a particular brown snake (since all reptiles are not brown), whereas the snake's characteristic of having a backbone is an attribute of all reptiles.

PSYCHOMOTOR OBJECTIVE   A learning objective specifying that students are to develop their bodies' capabilities of performing some particular physical task.

RAW SCORE   The sum of the points scored by a student on the items of a measurement.

RELEVANCE OF AN ACHIEVEMENT MEASUREMENT   The degree to which the following two questions can be answered affirmatively: (1) Do the measurement items match the stated objectives? and (2) Is the measurement designed so that emphases are placed on objectives according to their relative importance to goal achievement?

RELIABILITY OF A MEASUREMENT   The degree that the measurement can be depended on to yield consistent, noncontradictory results.

SCALED SCORE   Standardized test scores derived from a specific technique developed by L. L. Thurstone that allows results from different levels of the same subtest to be compared.

SCORING A TEST   The process by which one (e.g., a teacher) uses the test items' scoring keys to (1) quantify each student's response to each item and (2) record each student's test score as the sum of her or his item scores.

SHORT-ANSWER ITEM   A test item that requires the student to respond with a brief expression (usually verbal).

SIMPLE KNOWLEDGE-LEVEL OBJECTIVE   A knowledge-level cognitive objective specifying a content for students to remember that involves no more than a single response to a particular stimulus.

STANDARD DEVIATION   A statistical indicator of the variability within a group of scores derived by the following formula:

$$\sigma = \sqrt{\frac{\Sigma(x - \mu)^2}{N}}$$

where σ is the standard deviation, x is the scores, μ is the average score, and N is the number of scores

STANDARDIZED TEST   A test that has been field-tested for the purpose of collecting data for (1) assessing measurement reliability and (2) establishing normative standards to be used in interpreting scores.

STANDARDIZED TEST NORMS   Statistics (usually the average and standard deviation) computed from the test's norm group scores that are used as a frame of reference for interpreting the scores of test-takers.

STANDARD SCORE   A derived score indicating the number of norm group's standard deviations a raw score falls above the mean.

STANINE SCORE   A derived score of either 1, 2, 3, 4, 5, 6, 7, 8, or 9 that is converted from a raw score based on the average and standard deviation of a norm group according to the following criteria: (1) Raw scores less than 1.75 standard deviations below the average become stanine 1; (2) raw scores between 1.75 and 1.25 standard deviations below the average become 2; (3) raw scores between 1.25 and 0.75 standard deviations below the average become stanine 3; (4) raw scores between 0.75 and 0.25 below the average become stanine 4; (5) raw scores within 0.25 standard deviations of the average become stanine 5; (6) raw scores between 0.25 and 0.75 standard deviations above the average become stanine 6; (7) raw scores between 0.75 and 1.25 standard deviations above the average become stanine 7; (8) raw scores between 1.25 and 1.75 standard deviations above the average become stanine 8; (9) raw scores greater than 1.75 above the average become stanine 9.

STUDENT ACHIEVEMENT   The degree to which students have progressed relative to a specified learning goal.

SUMMATIVE EVALUATION   A judgment about student achievement that affects a report on the level of student success on a completed learning unit.

TABLE OF SPECIFICATIONS   A list of objectives to be measured by a test, each objective weighted according to its relative importance to student achievement of the learning goal.

TEST   A planned measurement.

TEST BLUEPRINT   A test design plan that includes (1) the identity of the learning unit, (2) anticipated administration time, (3) information about scoring, (4) item format specifications, (5) approximate number of items, (6) specifications for item difficulties, (7) approximate number of points, (8) specifications for determining cutoff scores, and (9) an outline of the test.

TEST ITEM   A component of a test that (1) confronts students with a task and (2) provides a means for observing their responses to the task.

TEST-RETEST RELIABILITY OF A MEASUREMENT   Theoretically, the degree of consistency between the two sets of results from the measurement that are obtained through the following procedure: (1) the measurement is administered to a group of students; (2) student achievement of the goal the measurement was supposed to test is kept from fluctuating; and (3) the measurement is readministered to the same group of students.

TIMED TEST   A test that is administered within a strictly limited time period so that the speed at which students respond to items affects the results.

TRUE/FALSE ITEM   A multiple-choice item that requires students to judge a statement as being either true or false.

USABILITY OF A MEASUREMENT   The degree to which the measurement is inexpensive, brief, easy to administer and score, and does not interfere with other activities.

VALIDATION STUDY OF A MEASUREMENT   An effort to assess the relevance and reliability of the measurement and the effectiveness of its items.

VALIDITY   The degree to which a measurement is both relevant and reliable.

VOLUNTARY-MUSCLE-CAPABILITY-LEVEL OBJECTIVE   A psychomotor objective requiring students to use their bodies to perform physical work within certain specified parameters (e.g., time, weight, and distance).

WEIGHTED ITEM   An item that is *not* dichotomously scored.

WILLINGNESS-TO-ACT-LEVEL OBJECTIVE   An affective objective requiring students to choose behaviors consistent with a specified belief.

References

Ashburn, R. R. (1938). An experiment in the essay type question. *Journal of Experimental Education, 7,* 1–3.

Berk, R. A. (1984a). Conducting the item analysis. In R. A. Berk (Ed.), *A guide to criterion-referenced test construction* (pp. 97–142). Baltimore: Johns Hopkins University Press.

——(1984b). Selecting the index of reliability. In R. A. Berk (Ed.), *A guide to criterion-referenced test construction* (pp. 231–265). Baltimore: Johns Hopkins University Press.

——(1986). A consumer's guide to setting performance standards on criterion-referenced tests. *Review of Educational Research, 56,* 137–172.

Bloom, B. S. (Ed.). (1984). *Taxonomy of educational objectives: The classification of educational goals, book I: Cognitive domain.* White Plains, NY: Longman.

Bloom, B. S., Madaus, G. F., & Hastings, J. T. (1981). *Evaluation to improve learning.* New York: McGraw-Hill.

Brennan, R. L. (1984). Estimating the dependability of scores. In R. A. Berk (Ed.), *A guide to criterion-referenced test construction* (pp. 292–334). Baltimore: Johns Hopkins University Press.

Cangelosi, J. S. (1974). Measurement and evaluation: A broader perspective. *NCME Measurement News, 18,* 18–23.

——(1982). *Measurement and evaluation: An inductive approach for teachers.* Dubuque, IA: W. C. Brown.

——(1984). Another answer to the cut-off score question. *Educational Measurement Issues and Practice, 3,* 23–25.

——(1986). *Cooperation in the classroom: Students and teachers together.* Washington, DC: National Education Association.

——(1988). *Classroom management strategies: Gaining and maintaining students' cooperation.* White Plains, NY: Longman.

Chase, C. I. (1978). *Measurement for educational evaluation* (2nd ed.). Reading, MA: Addison-Wesley.

Clark, C. M., & Peterson, P. L. (1986). Teachers' thought processes. In M. C. Wittrock (Ed.), *Handbook of research on teaching* (3rd ed., pp. 255–296). New York: Macmillan.

Duke, C. R., Cangelosi, J. S., & Knight, R. S. (1988, February). The Mellon Project: A collaborative effort. Colloquium presentation at the annual meeting of the American Association of Colleges for Teacher Education, New Orleans.

Ebel, R. L. (1965). *Measuring educational achievement.* Englewood Cliffs, NJ: Prentice-Hall.

——— (1972). *Essentials of educational measurement.* Englewood Cliffs, NJ: Prentice-Hall.

Emmer, E. T., Evertson, C. M., Sanford, J. P., Clements, B. S., & Worsham, M. E. (1984). *Classroom management for secondary teachers.* Englewood Cliffs, NJ: Prentice-Hall.

Evertson, C. M., Emmer, E. T., Clements, B. S., Sanford, J. P., & Worsham, M. E. (1984). *Classroom management for elementary teachers.* Englewood Cliffs, NJ: Prentice-Hall.

Flanders, N. A. (1970). *Analyzing teaching behavior.* Reading, MA: Addison-Wesley.

Frisbie, D. A. (1988). Reliability of scores from teacher-made tests. *Educational Measurement Issues and Practice, 7,* 25–35.

Gaffney, R. F., & Maguire, T. O. (1971). Use of optically scored test answer sheets with young children. *Journal of Educational Measurement, 8,* 103–106.

Gronlund, N. E. (1982). *Constructing Achievement Tests* (3rd ed., p. 72). Englewood Cliffs, NJ: Prentice-Hall.

——— (1985). *Measurement and evaluation in teaching* (5th ed.). New York: Macmillan.

Guilford, J. P. (1959). *Personality.* New York: McGraw-Hill.

Hambleton, R. K. (1984). Validating the test scores. In R. A. Berk (Ed.), *A guide to criterion-referenced test construction* (pp. 199–230). Baltimore: Johns Hopkins University Press.

Hambleton, R. K., & Swaminathan, H. (1985). *Item response theory.* Boston: Kluwer-Nijhoff.

Harrow, A. J. (1972). *A taxonomy of the psychomotor domain: A guide for developing behavioral objectives.* New York: McKay.

Jones, V. F., & Jones, L. S. (1986). *Comprehensive classroom management: Creating positive learning environments* (2nd ed.). Boston: Allyn & Bacon.

Kohlberg, L. (1987). The cognitive-development approach to moral education. In G. Hass (Ed.), *Curriculum planning* (5th ed., pp. 159–172). Boston: Allyn & Bacon.

Krathwohl, D., Bloom, B. S., & Masia, B. (1964). *Taxonomy of educational objectives, the classification of educational goals, handbook 2: Affective domain.* White Plains, NY: Longman.

Kubiszyn, T., & Borich, G. (1987). *Educational testing and measurement: Classroom application and practice* (2nd ed.). Glenview, IL: Scott, Foresman.

Kuder, G. F., & Richardson, M. W. (1937). The theory of estimation of test reliability. *Psychometrika, 2,* 151–160.

Lanier, J. E., & Little, J. W. (1986). Research on teacher education. In M. C. Wittrock (Ed.). *Handbook of Research on Teaching* (3rd ed.) (pp. 527–569). New York: Macmillan.

Likert, R. (1932). A technique for the measurement of attitudes. *Archives of Psychology, 140,* 52.

Livingston, S. A., & Zieky, M. J. (1982). *Passing scores: A manual for setting standards of performance on educational and occupational tests.* Princeton, NJ: Educational Testing Service.

Mehrens, W. A., & Lehmann, I. J. (1984). *Measurement and evaluation in education and psychology* (3rd ed.). New York: Holt, Rinehart, & Winston.

Mitchell, J. V., Jr. (Ed.). (1983). *Tests in Print III.* Lincoln: University of Nebraska Press.

——— (1985). *The ninth mental measurements yearbook.* Lincoln: University of Nebraska Press.

Myers, D. G. (1986). *Psychology.* New York: Worth Publishers.

Nunnally, J. C. (1978). *Psychometric theory* (2nd ed.). New York: McGraw-Hill.

Pulaski, M. A. S. (1980). *Understanding Piaget: An introduction to children's cognitive development* (2nd ed.). New York: Harper & Row.

Sax, G. (1980). *Principles of educational and psychological measurement and evaluation* (2nd ed.). Belmont, CA: Wadsworth.

Shavelson, R. J., & Stern, P. (1981). Research on teachers' pedagogical thoughts, judgments, decisions, and behavior. *Review of Educational Research, 41,* 455–498.

Smith, F., & Adams, S. (1972). *Educational measurement for the classroom teacher* (2nd ed.). New York: Harper & Row.

Stalnaker, J. M. (1936). The problem of the English examination. *Educational Record, 17,* 41.

Stanley, J. C., & Hopkins, K. D. (1972). *Educational and psychological measurement and evaluation.* Englewood Cliffs, NJ: Prentice-Hall.

Stiggins, R. J. (1988). Revitalizing classroom assessment: The highest instructional priority. *Phi Delta Kappan, 69,* 363–368.

Stiggins, R. J., Conklin, N. F., & Bridgeford, N. J. (1986). Classroom assessment: A key to effective education. *Educational Measurement: Issues and Practices, 5,* 5–17.

Yinger, R. (1977). A study of teacher planning: Description and theory using ethnographic and informal process methods. Unpublished doctoral dissertation, Michigan State University, East Lansing.

Index